POLITICS IN THE CREVICES

Urban Design and
the Making of
Property Markets in
Cairo and Istanbul

Sarah El-Kazaz

Duke University Press
Durham and London 2023

POLITICS IN THE CREVICES

© 2023 Duke University Press. All rights reserved
Printed in the United States of America on acid-free paper ∞
Project Editor: Ihsan Taylor | Designed by Aimee C. Harrison
Typeset in Portrait Text and Comma Base by
Westchester Publishing Services

Library of Congress Cataloging-in-Publication Data
Names: El-Kazaz, Sarah, author.
Title: Politics in the crevices : urban design and the making of
property markets in Cairo and Istanbul / Sarah El-Kazaz.
Description: Durham : Duke University Press, 2023. | Includes
bibliographical references and index.
Identifiers: LCCN 2023013153 (print)
LCCN 2023013154 (ebook)
ISBN 9781478025276 (paperback)
ISBN 9781478020493 (hardcover)
ISBN 9781478027386 (ebook)
Subjects: LCSH: City planning—Egypt—Cairo. | Land use, Urban—
Egypt—Cairo. | City planning—Turkey—Istanbul. | Land use, Urban—
Turkey—Istanbul. | BISAC: SOCIAL SCIENCE / Sociology / Urban |
SOCIAL SCIENCE / Ethnic Studies / Middle Eastern Studies
Classification: LCC HT169.E32 C3325 2023 (print) | LCC HT169.E32
(ebook) | DDC 307.1/2160949678—dc23/eng/20230421
LC record available at https://lccn.loc.gov/2023013153
LC ebook record available at https://lccn.loc.gov/2023013154

Cover photograph by the author.

Frontispieces: Topographic/road map of Giza and Cairo, Egypt,
iStock/lasagnaforone. Topographic/road map of Istanbul, Turkey,
iStock/lasagnaforone.

For Ossama Soliman

Contents

Note on Transliteration, ix

Acknowledgments, xi

Introduction, 1

PART I. THE MAKING OF PROPERTY MARKETS

One. Cairo, 21

Two. Istanbul, 65

PART II. REDISTRIBUTIVE MARKETS

Three. Heritage, 107

Four. Community, 148

Five. Visible Publics, 183

Conclusion, 207

Notes, 217

References, 233

Index, 241

Note on Transliteration

For text transliterated from Arabic, I have followed interlocutors' usage of dialect or classical Arabic. For place names, I have removed most articles (Al/El) ahead of names for ease of readability and following current conventions in the English transliteration of these names, keeping articles only when connecting two words within one name (e.g., Darb El-Ahmar).

Acknowledgments

This book has been many years in the making, and I am grateful to countless people who have stood by my side along the way. I owe my largest debt of gratitude to the dwellers of Fener-Balat, Sulukule, and Tarlabaşı neighborhoods in Istanbul and Darb El-Ahmar, Gamaliyya, and Wust El-Balad (downtown) in Cairo. Even though the six neighborhoods were undergoing intense transformations, their dwellers generously dedicated time and energy to helping me decipher the complexity of those transformations. Numerous families opened their homes to me for hours at a time, inviting me into their most intimate crevices so that I would see, smell, hear, feel the intricacies of home restorations, neglect, forced relocation, and everything in between. They offered me tea, shared their food, included me in visits from friends and family, allowed me to record our conversations, and introduced me to their neighbors for further home visits. Others invited me into their workshops, barbershops, stores, and garages and disrupted their workdays to narrate their experiences with neighborhood transformations, in some cases allowing me to shadow them for hours at a time. Moreover, local associations and NGOs allowed me to observe and join in activities they organized.

I am also heavily indebted to the directors, planners, architects, consultants, and staff that worked with the following organizations: the Aga Khan Development Network (in Cairo), the Ismailia Consortium, the Historic Cairo Organization, the NADIM Foundation, the EU rehabilitation program in Fener-Balat, GAP İnşaat's Taksim 360, Fatih municipality, and the Istanbul Municipality Planning and Design Center (IMP). They generously took ample time from their busy schedules to meet with me (sometimes on several iterations), allowed me to record our conversations, gave me tours of the neighborhoods where they worked, introduced me as a trusted researcher to neighborhood dwellers, and created special CDs and USBs of private documentation of their projects for me, with special thanks to the two organizations that gave me access to decades' worth of the projects' archives. I am forever humbled and grateful for my interlocutors' (whom I cannot name) generosity, frankness, patience, and respect for the research without which writing this book would have been impossible.

In the field, I was fortunate to have an unparalleled support network and inspiring intellectual community. In Cairo, I have boundless gratitude for the lifelong friends and family from my home city who stood by me in every possible way during this fieldwork. I am also eternally grateful to the women and men who animated Tahrir Square and the city, with limitless hope and revolutionary politics many months after Mubarak's departure and left an undeniable imprint on the politics animating this book and my life. Special thanks to Reem Saad for including me in the support group she created for PhDs conducting research within the tumult of revolution and the many other ways she helped me set up my research. In Istanbul, I am grateful to Tuna Kuyucu and Murat Yalçıntan for their investment in the project and help with crucial introductions, and to Murat for allowing me to shadow his urban studio class in Derbent. I was beyond fortunate to find fieldwork companions who would become my Istanbul family and lifelong friends. Thank you Avital Livny for connecting me to the group and your friendship. Working alongside the urbanists Danielle Van Dobben-Schoon, Elizabeth Angell, and Timur Hammond was a rare academic experience of intellectual inspiration, honesty, and friendship, where our Istanbul school of urban assemblages was a trusted space for brainstorming, sharing resources, and experiencing the changing city among brilliant scholars. I am grateful to the rest of our group: Hikmet Kocamaner, Joshua Carney, Elizabeth Williams, Vedica Kant, Eric Schoon, Jim Kuras, and Mehraneh Mirzazad for their constant support, lively social world, and finding the best cultural events in the city. Thank you to Özlem Ünsal and Constanze Letsch for sharing resources on neighborhoods that we were researching simultaneously, including important introductions to neighborhood dwellers. I am also grateful to the Istanbul urban activists group for inviting me into the meetings and activities they organized. Finally, a very special thank you to my research associate Cem Bico for the excellent instant translations, your disarming kindness that always put our interviewees at ease, sharing your knowledge and insights on the city's transformations, and for your friendship.

This project has had many institutional homes. The seeds of the project were planted in a class I took with Timothy Mitchell as an MA student at NYU that taught me to see the political in the most unexpected and subtle of sites and spaces. Especially haunting was seeing the spatiality of that politics through Eyal Weizman's work on Palestine. Tim's influence on the work did not stop with that intellectual spark but continued when he agreed to join my PhD dissertation committee even though we were at different institutions. Thank you, Tim, for the intellectual inspiration, generosity of spirit, and continuing support to this day. I completed my PhD in the Department of Politics at Princeton under the supervision of Mark Beissinger, Amaney Jamal, Deborah Yashar, and Timothy Mitchell. Even though this was quite an unconventional project for the department, Mark, Amaney, and Deborah unflinchingly supported it. Thank you for your belief in my work, for pushing me to clarify my arguments and never take any idea/concept for granted, for treating me as a colleague once I had defended, and for your support for my career to this day. At Princeton, I also met Arang Keshavarzian, who would become an invaluable mentor and almost a shadow member of the committee, generously sharing his time and insights for developing the project for many years to come. Likewise, Cyrus Schayegh, Gyan Prakash, Viviana Zelizer, and Max Weiss generously took an interest in my work, welcomed me into their classes, and had an undeniable impact on the work even though I was never officially their student, and Pascal Menoret, Senem Aslan, and Andrew Arsan would become lifelong mentors and friends. Finally, I was lucky to be part of a supportive and intellectually stimulating PhD cohort that would become the bedrock of my time at Princeton.

I have since had two academic homes that have fully embraced my work and created generative and stimulating intellectual environments that have left an undeniable imprint on the book. At Oberlin College, my colleagues and students in the Department of Politics and across the college took a special interest in the work, created spaces for discussing the book's chapters, brought rich intellectual traditions to bear on my analysis, and agitated on my behalf for funding that would eventually host a generous book workshop for the manuscript at a crucial juncture of its development. My deepest gratitude to the external readers and Oberlin colleagues who took the time to read the entirety of the manuscript and provide generative and constructive discussion during the book workshop: Catherine Fennell, Robert Vitalis, Arang Keshavarzian, Amy Mills, Annemarie Sammartino, David Forrest, Charmaine Chua, and Jenny Garcia, with special thanks to Jenny for also helping me record the proceedings. In addition, a number of Oberlin colleagues read and enriched many (if not all) of the book's chapters over the years, including Chris Howell, Sonia Kruks, Marc Blecher, Steve Crowley, and Jade Schiff. Many more fostered the supportive environment that helped nurture the work, including Ben Schiff, Harry Hirsch, Kristina Mani, Wendy Kozol, Wendy Hyman, Ellen Wurtzel, Pablo Mitchell, and Leonard Smith. I am also grateful to my students who daily pushed the boundaries of my thinking but especially students in my courses on the political economy of the Middle East and urbanism in the Global South who, in their brilliant engagement with literatures crucial to my work, helped me see gaps in my theory and slowly find ways to build a stronger framework. Finally, I was part of a cohort of new faculty that became my instant Oberlin family and a source of endless joy, including Ana Diaz Burgos, Sara Verosky, Sergio Gutiérrez Negron, Aaron Goldman, Peter Minosh, Matthew Rarey, Alysia Ramos, Chris Stolarski, Naomi Campa, Remei Capdevila, Jenny Garcia, David Forrest, Charmaine Chua, Chase Hobbs Morgan, Danielle Terrezas-Williams, Chie Sakakibara, Tamika Nunley, Colin and Sarah Dawson, Evan and Ilana Kresch, and Josh Sperling.

Even though I was at the final stage of book revisions when I joined SOAS, my colleagues fostered the intellectual environment and support I needed for the final push, especially crucial during pandemic times, and approved funding for developmental editing of the book. Special thanks to Hagar Kotef, Julia Gallagher, Rafeef Ziadah, Hengameh Ziai, Meera Sabaratnam, Matthew Eagleton-Pierce, Kerem Nisancioglu, and Salwa Ismail for brainstorming, reading, attending my talks, joining writing days, and overall enriching the book and my time at SOAS so far. I am also thankful to my SOAS students who continued to push and inspire me as I crossed the finish line. Outside of my two full-time academic positions, I have also had the generous support of two other institutions as I completed this work. Brandeis University's Crown Center for Middle East Studies awarded me a postdoctoral fellowship that allowed me the time to turn the project into a book ahead of my first teaching job. Special thanks to Eva Bellin and Naghmeh Sohrabi for their support during that year. In addition, the Jackson School of International Studies at the University of Washington sponsored me as a visiting scholar when I spent my sabbatical year in Seattle, giving me access to the school's intellectual life and amenities such as library carrel space. In Seattle I am especially grateful to Reşat Kasaba, Liora Halperin, Joel Migdal, Ellis Goldberg, Sasha Senderovich, Kathy Friedman, and the Turkish Circle for the intellectual engagement and friendship.

Outside of these institutional homes, I am heavily indebted to many mentors and discussants who have generously engaged the work and taken a special interest in my career, including Farha Ghannam, Lisa Wedeen, Jillian Schwedler, Nancy Reynolds, Laleh Khalili, Jeanne Morefield, Daniel Neep, On Barak, Sheila Crane, Diane Singerman, Brian Silverstein, Jessica Barnes, Julia Elyachar, and Arjun Appadurai. I have also had the privilege of being in several writing groups that spanned many years with Megan Brankley-Abbas, David Forrest, Sophia Stamatopoulou-Robbins, Bridget Guarsci, Ana Diaz Burgos, Radha Kumar, and Yanilda Gonzalez. Omar Cheta and Kevin Mazur also read many pieces of the puzzle that eventually became the book manuscript over the years. Thank you all for the careful reading, for pushing the book in crucial ways, for the accountability mechanisms, and for your friendship. I am also grateful to Omar Farahat, Sarah Parkinson, Begüm Adalet, Mehmet Kentel, Esra Bakkalbaşioğlu, William Bamber, Zachary Kagan-Guthrie, Gwyneth McClendon, Noam Lupu, and many others for their thoughtful reading of segments of the book and for their friendship. Finally, I have been fortunate to have the support of many friends from within the trenches of academia who lived the ups and downs of writing this project and showed unwavering excitement for it over the years, including Lamis Abdelaaty, Mai Taha, Hedayat Heikal, Deborah Beim, Erin Lin, Killian Clarke, Gözde Güran, Paul Apostolidis, Michael Becher, Michael Donnelly, Bryn Rosenfeld, Norah Fahim, Loubna El Amine, Rania Salem, Mouannes Hojairi, Gökçe Baykal, and Randa Tawil. Outside of the academic trenches I have had many friends cheer me on and keep me sane throughout this journey, with special thanks to Ola El-Shawarby, Dina Hashish, Samer El-Baghdady, Sherif Kinawy, Melanie Santos, Rahul Bose, Amy and Steffen Meyer, Hend Abdel Ghany, Ahmed El-Oraby, Dina El-Ghandour, Heba Rabei, Federico and Laura Espriu, Claurelle Schoepke, and Alen Rakipović for the special interest they took in the book and my career over the years. I am also grateful to Deirdre O'Dwyer, who, as developmental editor, immaculately massaged and smoothed out the book's prose. At Duke, a very special thank you to my editor Elizabeth Ault who wholeheartedly believed in the project, then brilliantly shepherded the manuscript through the press's review process and beyond. I am also grateful to the anonymous reviewers who wrote meticulous and constructive reviews that helped me produce a stronger book, and to Benjamin Kossak for his help with production.

As an itinerant academic, I wrote this book in many places, and I want to thank the many libraries and coffee shops that gave me the space and comfort to write outside of my home institutions, including libraries such as Columbia University libraries, NYU libraries, the British Library, University of Washington libraries, the ANAMED library of Koç University; and coffee shops such as Small World in Princeton, Slow Train and the Local in Oberlin, Milstead and Bauhaus in Seattle, and Footnote in London. The book has been written with generous funding support from the Princeton Institute for International and Regional Studies, Princeton's Mamdouha S. Bobst Center for Peace and Justice, the Eisenhower Institute in Gettysburg College, the Lewis Fund of the Department of Politics at Oberlin College, and the SOAS Department of Politics. Excerpts from the book were presented at a number of forums outside my home institutions whose participants enriched the work, including Swarthmore College, NYU's Hagop Kevorkian Center, Ohio State University, Stanford University, the University of Southern California, and annual conferences of the Middle East Studies Association, the American Political Science Association, the American Association of Geographers, the Project on Middle East Political Science, and the Social Science History Association. Moreover, portions of chapter 4 appeared as an article in *Comparative Studies in Society and History* in 2018, and comments from peer reviewers enriched both the article and the larger book project.

Finally, I am deeply grateful to my family for their unwavering support throughout. My extended family has always let me know that they are proud of the work I do. My in-laws Zeinab Selim and Ali Soliman, both academics, have shown a deep appreciation for my work, an understanding for the life choices we have made, and supported me during fieldwork with important introductions. Mona and Amre Soliman and their families have always made me feel like a cherished member of the family and cheered me on. Growing up with my siblings Mohamed, Ibrahim, and Sana El-Kazaz was a wild adventure that I feel very lucky to have lived, and they have always since made sure I know that they are proud of the paths I have taken. My parents' unconditional love gave me the belief and strength to pursue my dreams. Hadia El Helou's incisive sensibility of the people around her nurtured in me an ethnographic sensibility crucial to the making of this book, and Hussein El-Kazaz's keenness to engage with me in deep philosophical debates from a young age gave me the thirst to think through the debates that animate this book and my passion for intellectual life. In the midst of writing this book, Yara Soliman made a most welcome entrance into our lives, and I am beyond grateful for the joy she brings me every single day. Ossama Soliman has lived the entirety of this book's journey as my partner and has been its biggest champion, eagerly brainstorming, reading, and pushing me to clarify my arguments even when it would have been easier to let the holes slide. Thank you for the love, the fun, and unwavering faith in our dreams, even when I sometimes lost sight of them.

Introduction

HAGA SAMIA and her ailing mother have lived in an apartment in Historic Cairo that borders a seventy-four-acre garbage dump for decades. The apartment occupies the top floor of a three-story Mamluk-style building in Darb El-Ahmar neighborhood, and for years Haga Samia's family could see the heaps of rubbish from the living room windows, its putrid smells wafting over every time wind gusted in from the east. The building had also been unmaintained for decades, and when an earthquake shook Cairo to its core in 1992, its structure started to fracture.[1] After living with the fear of impending collapse for half a decade, the family's fortunes took a decided turn in the late 1990s. A developmental organization based in the Hague, the Aga Khan Foundation, had taken an interest in this corner of Cairo, embarking on two urban projects in Darb El-Ahmar that would wholly transform how Haga Samia experienced her home. Initially in 1995, the foundation embarked on a project that would excavate the garbage dump and transform it into one of central Cairo's largest green spaces, Azhar Park. Then in 1997, the foundation initiated a home restoration program that would eventually restore 120 buildings in Darb El-Ahmar. Haga Samia's home was selected for the pilot phase of the program and offered a grant that would cover 90 percent of the costs of restoring the building from the inside out. When I visited Haga Samia in her restored home in 2011, she took me up to the building's rooftop (see chapter 4) to show me with joy and pride the view of the park that had replaced the garbage dump (figure I.1). We then turned to see, from the west side of the building, a breathtaking view of Historic Cairo's many minarets (figure I.2).

During that visit, Haga Samia and I spent hours discussing every detail of the restorations. When the discussion turned to plumbing, the joy on Haga Samia's face dissipated. Working hard not to seem ungrateful, she explained that the plumbing system that the Aga Khan team had installed was more difficult to use than the original. Whereas each apartment had its own water supply before the restorations, the foundation's engineers installed a shared water pump in the building. Haga Samia now had to negotiate with her neighbors about when she would be able to pump water up to her apartment, because only one apartment could use it at a time.[2] The pumping system struck me as strange too, and I filed it away, along with other oddities, as intriguing designs that I would ask the engineers about. At that point, though, I assumed that there would be a straightforward technical logic to explain them.

When I did ask the foundation's engineers about the odd designs, their explanations were anything but technical. They were decidedly *political*. Samy, an urban planner on the foundation's team, explained the shared water pumps as follows:

> Our purpose was that you learn to coordinate with your neighbors. So, for example when we installed water pumps we would find that, in a building with six residents, each of the residents wants to install their own water pump. We would refuse such requests because if they can't resolve issues around using a water pump, then there is no sense in them restoring the house altogether. In other words, they have to talk to each other.[3]

Pumping water up building pipes wasn't the only work expected of the water pump the foundation had installed in Haga Samia's building. Working quietly from within the invisible crevices of building walls, water pumps were expected to engineer collaborative "community," as neighbors were forced to discuss sharing the water being pumped up to their floors. The Aga Khan team was designing the intricate features of restored homes to perform the work of societal engineering.[4] Samy then placed that sociopolitical work within a larger vision, saying, "The idea behind the project wasn't that we fix Darb El-Ahmar. Darb El-Ahmar has more than 5,500 residential buildings and we fixed little over 100 of those. It's a drop in the ocean … housing [rehabilitation] was a *tool* towards something bigger. It was a step towards ensuring the existing community didn't leave." The foundation was working to reverse the displacement of Cairo's most vulnerable populations from the city's core districts as the deregulation of property markets worked with several other forces (see chapter 1) to push them out of Cairo's core. Engineering collaborative community through the careful design of housing restorations would strengthen the bonds residents had with their neighborhood and how *valuable* they saw their property, producing a counterweight to the highly capitalized forces pushing them out of the center. The foundation was intervening in the workings of Historic Cairo's real estate markets.

As my research progressed, I realized that Samy and his team at the Aga Khan Foundation weren't the only ones turning to unorthodox methods to fight for affordable housing in the city. Through a multisited ethnography in Istanbul and Cairo of six neighborhoods undergoing large-scale urban transformation projects, I found a battle for housing raging in both cities. A variety of state and nonstate actors were fighting to secure affordable housing on the one hand and to corner real estate markets for a luxury clientele on the other. This battle was not raging in traditional political arenas, however. Rather than agitate for familiar redistributive policies like housing subsidies, exclusive land grants, or rent controls, urban protagonists were relying on the subtle, quiet machinations of urban planning and design to redistribute and restrict access to the city's housing.

In Istanbul, a group of urban activists turned to the heritage industry to secure affordable housing along the Golden Horn by reframing private residences into globally valued heritage (chapter 3). Meanwhile, the Turkish state appropriated a grassroots environmental movement seeking protections for the city against natural disasters, especially earthquakes, in an attempt to devalue affordable housing in the city's center—claiming it was prone to collapse and a hazard to the city—and ultimately transfer that property to developers (chapter 2). Back in Cairo, a corporate developer worked to corner downtown's real estate market not through corruption but by mobilizing building aesthetics, a topography of hidden alleyways, and the "Egyptianization" of commercial culture to render property "exclusive," secure, and valuable to luxury clientele (chapter 4). Time and again, urban protagonists were deploying the careful design of the urban built-environment to do the work of restricting and redistributing access to housing. In particular, careful urban design was expected to transform how property was *valued* in a neighborhood so as to favor particular groups over others on "freely" traded real estate markets, fostering what I conceptualize as "particularistic value." In a neoliberalizing Cairo and Istanbul, the battle for housing had shifted away from familiar extra-market political machinations to processes that operate from *within* "the market" as a practice and logic. This book asks: What happens when the battle over protections for vulnerable populations shifts from pushing back and contesting the boundaries of the market to finding ways of

Figure I.1. Eastern view from Haga Samia's rooftop. Source: author, November 2011.

operating within it? How do we come to understand and locate the workings of *the political* when battles over the distribution of a city's resources operate from within the logics of the market?

Redistributive Markets

When scholars study redistributive politics, they usually follow the fate of familiar redistributive policies like progressive taxation, food and housing subsidies, and labor laws.[5] In recent decades, struggles around these policies have been decided in favor of reversing redistributive measures. Welfare states and redistributive machinery have been systematically dismantled as economies around the globe have been reordered around the neoliberal tenet that free markets—not states (or political contests)—are the best arbiters of the distribution of a society's resources. In the face of dismantled welfare

Figure I.2. Western view from Haga Samia's rooftop. Source: author, November 2011.

states, most scholars have concluded that redistribution is on the wane in neoliberalizing economies.

In particular, scholarship rooted in critical political economy has read the dismantling of the welfare state as a natural extension to the class project underlying the neoliberal shift. Such scholarship has rejected the notion that neoliberalism was simply another "fix" for the economy that took hold as the technocratic pendulum swung against state involvement in the economy in the 1970s and 1980s, when many of the economies that had embarked on postcolonial, state-led development programs across the Global South plunged into heavy debt. Following several field-shaping accounts (e.g., Harvey 2005; Mirowski and Plehwe 2009; Slobodian 2018) that mapped out the political projects underlying the making of neoliberal ideology and its adoption worldwide, they read the neoliberal shift as fueled by a global corporate-capitalist class in crisis, especially as it could no longer rely on direct colonialism to buttress capitalist accumulation. While astute in reading neoliberalism as borne out of a corporate-capitalist project, most critical scholars were too quick to conclude that these class foundations had successfully permeated the inner workings of neoliberalism to unequivocally enable capital "accumulation by dispossession" (à la Harvey 2005). For this scholarship, a triumphant corporate-capitalist class project had seamlessly translated into neoliberal machinery that foreclosed the space for class-based redistributive struggles and politics *within* that system. By extension, class-based struggles and resistance were mostly read as located on the margins *outside* neoliberal machinations and its market rationales. In this book, I build upon the incisive mapping of the neoimperial and corporate-capitalist class projects entwined with the making of the neoliberal shift but take a step back to question whether these political projects seamlessly translated into the workings of neoliberal machinery to eradicate class-based redistributive politics within the system. What happens if we shift our gaze and open up our search for redistributive politics beyond familiar politicized sites? What do we learn about the workings of neoliberal market rationales and where we *locate* the political in a neoliberal order when we suspend assumptions about the foreclosure of class-based redistributive politics?

To tackle these questions, I situate the book around the workings of property and real estate markets in neoliberalizing Istanbul and Cairo. Property markets are particularly revealing sites for studying redistributive politics, since access to housing has long been central to redistributive struggles in cities. Public housing projects, rent controls, the formalization of informal housing, and similar policies have a long history as state-led redistributive efforts. Likewise, the accumulation of capital through land grants, urban development, and real estate speculation have been studied as core sites for neoliberal accumulation. The struggle over housing is thus historically one of the main sites through which redistribution has been negotiated and today carries special import as simultaneously one of the key sites of capital accumulation.

Istanbul and Cairo are then particularly productive sites for studying how struggles over property unfold in neoliberalizing cities in the Global South.[6] Being two of the largest metropolitan centers in the Middle East and globally, they experienced exponential rural-urban migration that mirrored many metropolises around the Global South post–World War II, creating unprecedented pressures on the cities' urban fabrics and infrastructures, and setting the stage for protracted battles over housing. The two cities are uniquely positioned to reveal how these housing struggles then interact with historically, culturally, and ecologically layered urban terrains (see chapters 1 and 2). The richness of the historical layers and cultural processes of meaning-making that animate Istanbul and Cairo are almost unparalleled, being two of the world's longest-standing active urban centers. Ecologically, they sit on formidable waterways (the Nile River and Bosporus Strait), have varied ecologies, and have long histories with natural disasters (most recently the 1992 earthquake in Cairo and the 1999 earthquake in Istanbul) that have significantly shaped the trajectories of their built environments and housing landscapes. Finally, the two cities experienced rapid neoliberalization and aggressive structural adjustment programs from the 1970s onward, after both economies plunged into heavy debt in the wake of intense state-led industrializing programs. Studying how struggles over property, and redistribution more largely, unfold with neoliberalization within such richly layered urban terrains provides a unique space for asking how neoliberal market-making and political struggles may intersect with historical, environmental, and cultural spheres.

In opening up my inquiry to sites beyond the legal-politico infrastructures traditionally associated with redistributive politics within the richly layered terrains of Cairo and Istanbul, I uncovered a battle raging over housing in both cities. Neoliberalization had not eroded redistributive politics but rather *displaced* that struggle away from traditional political arenas and onto the subtle yet careful design of the urban built-environment. As Istanbul and Cairo neoliberalized, urban coalitions continued to invest considerable resources into restricting and redistributing access to housing in support of both affordable housing and intensified capital accumulation, all the while diverting effort away from traditional political strategies like lobbying legislators or electoral campaigns (although such efforts didn't disappear entirely). When confronted with the dismantling of familiar redistributive sites, urban coalitions got creative and worked with the now dominant market rationales to realize their redistributive agendas.[7] They worked to redistribute access to housing by manipulating the "market value" of property in ways that secured affordable housing or cornered real estate for intensified profit.

Markets are fundamentally circuits for the exchange of commodities. Commodities are only exchangeable if their *value* is calculable and recognizable on those circuits.[8] As an incisive body of literature has shown, the value of any given commodity is not a naturally occurring fact simply discoverable on the open market (e.g., Elyachar 2005; Çalışkan and Callon 2010; Searle 2016). Competing actors dedicate considerable *work* to defining how the value of a potential commodity—like homes—gets calculated on the open market.[9] When our protagonists designed urban built-environments that would engineer "community," preserve heritage, protect against disaster, or evoke cultural movements, they were investing considerable work into shifting how particular groups came to *value* their neighborhood's urban fabric. Engineering a wholesale shift in how that urban fabric is valued would transform its legibility and calculability as exchangeable real estate in favor of some groups over others. In other words, they were mobilizing a carefully designed urban built-environment to produce what I term here *particularistic value* through which they intervene in the workings of real estate markets. The battle for housing in Cairo and Istanbul was unfolding from within the rationales of market dynamics as a struggle over how the value of homes was being defined, claimed, and experienced. Market rationales were not impervious to class politics after all.

When our protagonists deployed "community," heritage, and disaster prevention to perform redistributive work, the technical and logistical decisions experts were making about the design of the city's built environment became layered with the responsibility to carry out redistribution. Time and again in the coming chapters, experts will expect the city's built environment to perform work similar to the sociopolitical work Samy expected of water pumps as they churned away in building shafts. Sociopolitical expectations riddled the design of clotheslines, electrical wiring, rooftops, store signage, balconies, bathrooms, façade paint colors, and many of the most private and intimate crevices of people's homes. The dismantling of traditional, redistributive political forums has come to burden the city's most intimate and private crevices with the weight of redistributive politics.[10]

Redistributive work and the class-based politics that fuel it did not disappear with neoliberalism. While a corporate-capitalist class project may have fueled a systemic neoliberal shift (and I trace how those corporate-capitalist efforts transformed property markets in Cairo and Istanbul in chapters 1 and 2), its agenda had not successfully captured the workings of neoliberal machinery and the market rationales they valorize. Market logics are, in practice, malleable enough to be reappropriated by a variety of political agendas rather than just "accumulation by dispossession." The fact that markets don't organically or automatically commodify "goods" and assign them agreed-upon values opens up the space for a variety of actors to compete over defining that value in ways that engineer *particularistic value* to skew markets for the benefit of some groups over others. Class-based redistributive politics are still manifesting within a neoliberal order, but they have been *displaced* from traditional political forums onto the city's most private and intimate crevices. Some of the city's most pressing class politics are materializing as battles over the design of clotheslines, water pumps, and balconies rather than being fought through political party campaigns or contentious town halls.

A *Displaced* Neoliberal Politics

At the heart of this book's project is a reimagining of where the political is *located* within a neoliberal order. Neoliberalism has long been defined as an order that operates through depoliticizing the political. As scholars accepted the foreclosure of spaces for the contestation of class-based politics within a neoliberal order, they came to equate neoliberalization with *depoliticization* (e.g., Rose 1996; Ong 2006; Brown 2015). The political battle for housing continues to rage in Istanbul and Cairo from *within* the logics of the market. Reclaiming the redistributive politics that this book describes as unfolding subtly and quietly through the machinations of urban design demonstrates that "the infiltration of market-driven truths and calculations into the domain of politics" (Ong 2006, 4), or what Çalışkan and Callon (2010) dub "marketization," does not necessarily depoliticize class-based struggles. What we are witnessing instead is a *displacement* of the political onto the contested design of the most private and intimate crevices of the city as that careful design is deployed to manipulate markets.

Displacing political struggles away from overt politicized arenas and channeling them into market dynamics carries several implications for how they manifest in the city. First, displacement works toward depoliticizing not only class-based redistributive struggles but other urban political struggles as well. When our protagonists sought to shift how a neighborhood's urban fabric was valued on the open market, they turned to a variety of urban design-cultural-environmental practices like heritage preservation, disaster prevention, and engineering community. Each of these practices, as will become clear over the course of the book, is embedded in its own political histories and struggles. Most obviously, for example, heritage preservation is steeped in identity politics and nation-building projects. To subtly mobilize practices like heritage preservation or engineered community to manipulate markets, however, urban coalitions needed to *extricate* those practices from the politics in which they were embedded. A politicized heritage project would loudly distract from a subtle redistributive agenda and, in particular, complicate how the value of housing as heritage would be calculated and recognized on the open market. For decades, several forces had come together to shift awareness away from treating heritage as *monumental* sites that individually commemorate particular histories over others and toward seeing heritage as *environmental* landscapes valued in their totality regardless of the histories they may commemorate (see chapter 3). Such a shift toward an environmental view of heritage slowly extricated heritage preservation from identity politics.

As they sought to safeguard affordable housing, urban activists in Istanbul were far more likely to succeed in deploying heritage to claim value for the neighborhood when heritage was seen as an environmental landscape valued as a totality—including private homes—extricated from identity politics rather than as a set of contested, monumental sites. The activists latched onto another long-term process of depoliticization to subtly empower their own political project, and in doing so they perpetuated a technical understanding of heritage as apolitical, environmental landscapes. In short, what we see is a double performance of depoliticization around the redistributive struggle itself, on the one hand, and the political struggles underlying the urban-cultural-environmental practices deployed to enact it on the other.

In spite of the double performance of depoliticization, political struggles don't actually disappear. They seep into the city's built environment, burdening the city's intimate, invisible, and private crevices with the weighty political projects neoliberalism presumed to efface. These political burdens create innumerable contradictions in the city. The book's chapters illuminate the ways in which the sociopolitical work expected of carefully designed features of homes, such as Haga Samia's plumbing, have compromised the functionality and convenience residents were accustomed to. As those contradictions manifested, they often laid bare the layering of political work onto the design of everyday spaces, and as urban protagonists—whether residents, planners, or activists—challenged those contradictions, they repeatedly *re*animated the politics so many actors were working to obfuscate. Time and again, urban protagonists *repoliticized* the depoliticized, either to pragmatically achieve their own agendas or to politically expose the hypocrisies of channeling the political through depoliticized market rationales, and they did so through the same burdened crevices of the city.

When urban protagonists repoliticized the class, racial, and/or religious projects that were being displaced and obfuscated through the machinations of the market, they did so not through direct political contests but through technical contestations of the design of electrical wiring, balconies, rooftops, and title deeds. While tracing these subtle micropractices of repoliticization recuperates the political and locates it in the intimate, the private, and the invisible crevices of the city, it also unmasks the dangers of such displacement to political life. When political struggles become insidiously channeled into market rationales and obscured, the overt political spaces through which these struggles were once negotiated close up. Having nowhere to go, that politics doesn't disappear. Instead, it manifests and festers within intimate spaces and sites that are much more difficult to negotiate and recuperate as a polity. As the book develops, I explore how the displacement of the political onto the city's intimate and private crevices under a neoliberal order leaves us with a political climate that fosters suspicion and a fracturing polity.

Method and Research Design

To uncover how struggles around housing have been negotiated under neoliberalism, I designed my research as a multisited ethnography in six neighborhoods within central Istanbul and Cairo. Interested in seeing whether and how those struggles unfolded when stakes were at their highest, I focused on neighborhoods that were undergoing large-scale urban transformation projects in the 1990s and 2000s led by actors with varying relations to market dynamics. Each of the selected neighborhoods was being transformed by at least one of the following: (a) a nonprofit agency, (b) a corporate developer, and (c) a state agency. To capture how housing struggles intersected with urban dynamics around heritage, commercial centers, and transit hubs and to limit my analysis to legal regimes around formalized property, I focused on formal neighborhoods in the city's center: Fener-Balat, Tarlabaşı, and Sulukule in Istanbul and Darb El-Ahmar, Wust El-Balad (aka downtown Cairo), and Gamaliyya in Cairo (see maps I.1 and I.2 for the neighborhoods within each city).

Multisited Ethnography vs. Comparative Studies

While I study Istanbul and Cairo and the six neighborhoods side by side, this is a multisited ethnography rather than a strict comparative study. Following market-making practices across the two cities and within the six neighborhoods opened up a multitude of ways for seeing how these practices and their contestation were unfolding in and traveling across neoliberalizing cities. Through a malleable approach to multisited studies, I read dynamics within the six neighborhoods both *together* as building blocks that would allow me to dig deeper into the inner workings of market-making and in *juxtaposition* to one another in a way that allowed me to see each of the sites better through the lens of other sites. For example, as chapters 1 and 2 demonstrate, reading transforming property regimes in Istanbul and Cairo side by side enabled me to see the violence of the 1996 rent control laws in Egypt in ways I could not have seen by focusing on Cairo alone and without juxtaposing it to the violence unfolding in Istanbul; illuminating how dynamics at the core of neoliberal market-making travel and manifest across different geographies. A rigid case-by-case comparison would have shifted the focus away from the mechanics of neoliberal market-making and onto how contextual factors such as varying institutional legacies, regime types, or actors' incentives shape "actually existing neoliberalism" (Brenner and Theodore 2002). While an important endeavor, such a focus on comparing contextual factors is not the core project of this book.

Embarking on a malleable, multisited ethnography shapes not only the nature of the analysis but also how the book is written and structured. I organized the book around the techniques that actors deploy to perform the work of redistribution in both cities, such as heritage preservation and engineered community, rather than comparisons across any typology of the neighborhoods. Privileging those techniques meant that some neighborhoods and protagonists came to occupy more space in the book than others as the intricacies of their transformations offered more insight into unexpected facets of the neoliberal turn. I privileged digging deeper into those illuminating encounters over symmetry in how the six neighborhoods were presented.

Environmentally-Attuned Ethnography

To open up the sites where redistributive work is performed in the city, and especially privileging a spatial lens to the city, I embarked on an ethnographic project that took seriously the relational interactions between humans and their environments in the making of the political. I follow Navaro-Yashin's (2012) insight "that the environment exerts a force on human beings in its own right, or that there is something in space, in material objects, or in the environment that exceeds or goes further and beyond the human imagination, but that produces an affect that may be experienced by human beings, all the same" (18).

To capture that relationality, I bring together three methodological lineages in urban ethnography. The first has long cultivated an inspiring sensibility to the *tactics* that urban dwellers deploy to exercise power in the city (e.g., De Certeau 1984; Lefebvre 1991; Singerman 1995; Bayat 1997; Ghannam 2002; Ismail 2006; Simone 2008; Menoret 2014).[11] *Assemblage* urbanism (e.g., Bennett 2001, 2004, 2005; Mitchell 2002, ch. 1; McFarlane 2011) then emphasizes the political agency of the non-human that exerts the force that goes "beyond the human imagination" that Navaro-Yashin described, but also the power that the *contingent* coming together of the human-non-human exerts. In Bennett's (2005) eloquent words:

> Some actants have sufficient coherence to appear as entities; others, because of their great volatility, fast pace of evolution, or minuteness of scale, are best conceived as forces. Moreover, while individual entities and singular forces each exercise agentic capacities, isn't there also an agency proper to the groupings they form? This is the agency of assemblages: the distinctive efficacy of a working whole made up, variously, of somatic, technological, cultural, and atmospheric elements. (446–47)[12]

Finally, Brennan (2004) and Navaro-Yashin (2012) layer an *affective* sensibility upon the study of human-environment relations to capture the psychological experiences and processes of meaning-making that infuse that relationality. Like Navaro-Yashin, I embark on an ethnography attuned to human-environment relationality as an *analytical* approach rather than "a project in ethical self-formation" (Navaro-Yashin 2012, 20), even if that ethical undertone never really leaves environmentally-attuned inquiry.

To that end, I conducted a year of intensive ethnographic fieldwork (spending about six months each in Istanbul and Cairo) from 2011 to 2012, followed by short trips since. The fieldwork involved conducting over two hundred (mostly recorded) open-ended interviews with urban planners, architects, property owners, CEOs, tenants, bureaucrats, and people working in the six neighborhoods under study. I also then conducted participant observation by spending hundreds of hours in everyday spaces such as residential homes, barbershops, furniture workshops, and women's nongovernmental organization (NGO) spaces. I observed meetings held by urban activists, neighborhood associations, municipality housing-lottery ceremonies; I shadowed university urban-planning field classes; and I built a neighborhood garden with urban activists in Istanbul. Finally, I collected hundreds of documents from the private archives of each of the six projects that included maps, architectural and urban-design plans, societal surveys, investor presentations, real estate advertising, court documents, and so on. I conducted this fieldwork in Arabic, Turkish, and English, depending on the language my interlocutors preferred. Being a nonnative speaker of Turkish, though, I had the privilege of working with my research associate Cem Bico during my first few months in Istanbul while I got a firmer footing in conducting that ethnography alone, especially to access women-only spaces in the city. Beyond the linguistic support, working with Cem and thinking through our daily encounters in the city with his keen sensibility to the urban dynamics unfolding in Istanbul infinitely enriched the ethnography. It made me see just how enriching collaborative ethnographies can be. In writing up the ethnography, I anonymized all my interlocutors except for a corporate CEO who is a public figure in the media. To ensure that my interlocutors were difficult to identify, I presented the same interlocutor as two different people twice in the book, when they divulged particularly sensitive information. All other protagonists are represented as I encountered them during my fieldwork. The pseudonyms also included naming conventions that denote respect as expected by more elderly interlocutors during our conversations: in Turkish—Hanım (f.)/Bey (m.); in Egyptian Arabic—Hag (m.)/Haga (f.) or Umm (f.)/Abu (m.).

The Chapters

Looking ahead, the book's five chapters are organized into two thematic parts. In part I, the first two chapters trace the *making of property markets* in Cairo and Istanbul. They trace how transforming ecological, geopolitical, affective, and sensorial lived experiences of the city throughout the twentieth century and into the twenty-first transformed how urban dwellers valued property in central districts of both cities over time. Chapter 1 focuses on Cairo and shows how changing water ecologies, colonial-capitalism and its infrastructural tentacles, the geopolitics of World War II, affective experiences of the 1952 Cairo fire, changing logics behind rent control, the 1992 earthquake as a (mis)managed disaster, and the city's sensorial experiences with industrialization and automobile-based infrastructure transformed how different groups came to relate to and value property in the city's historic core and downtown. These spatial-affective-material transformations shaped how different groups valued the city's central property over time and opened up new ways for seeing the vulnerabilities, opportunities, and violence experienced with the partial reversal of rent controls in Cairo in 1996, setting the stage for the urban interventions I present in the rest of the book.

Chapter 2 moves to Istanbul and traces how the geopolitics of Ottoman defeat in World War I, affective experiences of the city as a space of melancholy or *hüzün*, antiminority violence and exodus, industrialization and its sensorial experiences, holistic infrastructural programs that reoriented the city from an imperial center into a regional-industrial hub and then a global hub, and electioneering dynamics produced a property-owning class in areas of the city's center that was largely working class and looked quite different from the property owners encountered in Cairo. Appreciating how differently property came to be valued in Cairo and Istanbul helps explain why the Turkish ruling regime resorted to overtly violent expropriation as it transferred property to corporate developers in central Istanbul compared to the Egyptian government as it embarked on the same project. The final section of the chapter turns to the contemporary moment to demonstrate *how* the Turkish regime mobilized notions of urban crisis and disaster risk to depoliticize long-brewing political conflicts and justify violent expropriation, with a focus on state-led projects in Sulukule and Tarlabaşı. Both chapters ultimately argue for seeing the making of *class* itself through the spatial-material-affective transformations that shape how different groups come to attribute value and meaning to property and the city within which they dwell.

Part 2, in turn, traces how *redistributive markets* are manifesting in Istanbul and Cairo. Each chapter is organized around one domain of practices through which property comes to be valued and traces how redistributive politics erupt around how that value is defined, experienced, and claimed. Chapter 3 stays in Istanbul to unpack how *heritage* preservation is being deployed as a pro-poor redistributive practice. It focuses on an alliance that formed between urban activists and the heritage machinery of the United Nations Educational, Scientific and Cultural Organization (UNESCO) and the European Union (EU) that was aimed at safeguarding both affordable housing and heritage in Fener-Balat. I trace how mobilizing heritage as a modality for securing affordable housing relied on the depoliticization of heritage preservation and the identity and nationalist politics in which it was embroiled through its transformation from a *monumental* to an *environmental* practice that valorizes heritage landscapes as depoliticized totalities. The chapter is anchored around the practices through which a variety of stakeholders repoliticize the class-based and identity-based conflicts masked by the EU's intervention, as the contradictions of channeling redistribution through heritage gradually manifest in practice. Finally, it ends by moving outside Fener-Balat to other historical neighborhoods in Istanbul to see how the valorization of heritage as a mediator of social justice agendas works to disrupt and remake power dynamics in the city.

Chapter 4 moves back to Cairo to trace the mobilization of "community" as a redistributive practice. The chapter focuses on the Ismailia Consortium's project in Wust El-Balad and the Aga Khan Foundation's project in Darb El-Ahmar to show how actors are mobilizing a particularistic understanding of "community" to corner real estate markets for luxury clientele, on one end, and secure affordable housing on the other. The chapter unpacks how intricate urban design as well as urban cultural and commercial movements are mobilized to engineer "community" in each neighborhood and the politics of treating a slippery and layered notion like "community" as an identifiable object of intervention.

Chapter 5 then interrogates the contested design of *visible public spaces* as a lens into how competing redistributive practices redraw public/private boundaries in both Cairo and Istanbul, with a focus on the changing accessibility of shared spaces and their servicing. There are many ways in which the design of shared spaces is entangled in redistributive agendas, but in this chapter I focus on two: tourism and communal belonging. The chapter first investigates the complicated relationship tourism has with a redistributive agenda and negotiating the value of property in the city. It then travels to the contested design of parks, streets and alleys, balconies and windows, sewage infrastructures, and gardens to expose how the same redistributive agendas navigate competing tactics for resources in the city and in so doing shape the accessibility and servicing of the city.

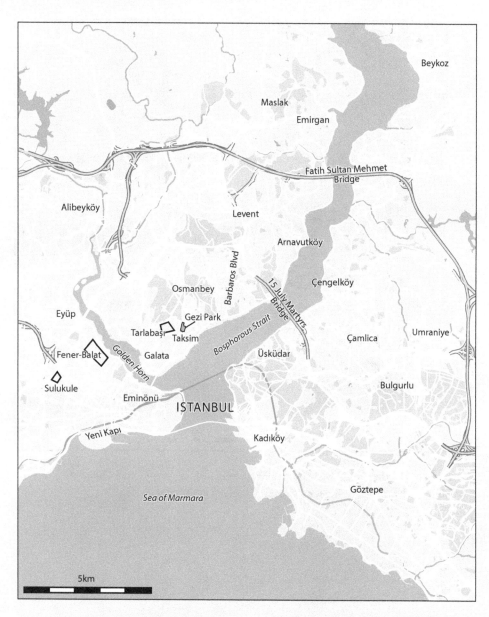

Map I.1. The three neighborhoods within a larger map of Istanbul's European and Asian sides. Source: Google Maps, August 2022.

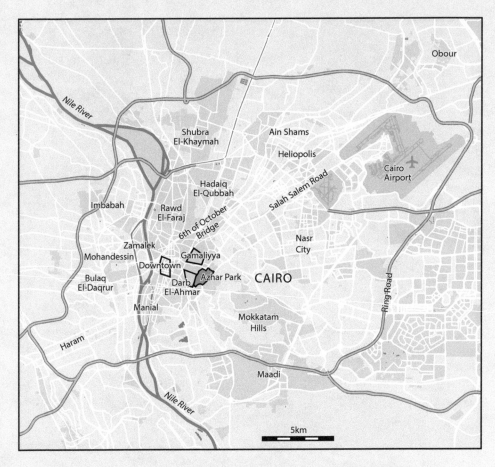

Map I.2. The three neighborhoods within a larger map of metropolitan Cairo bordered by the main ring road. Source: Google Maps, August 2022.

PART I

The Making of Property Markets

Cairo 1

IN THE YEAR 2000, Umm Mustafa and her family paid a monthly rent of 9 Egyptian pounds (E£) (approximately one dollar and forty-five cents) for the one-bedroom, rent-controlled apartment where they had lived for over thirty years in the neighborhood of Darb El-Ahmar in Historic Cairo.[1] Umm Mustafa's landlords had, for decades, earned almost nothing from the five tenants who occupied the building. They left the building unmaintained, and its structures gradually decayed from the inside out. After the 1992 earthquake, the building's structural beams visibly cracked, and Umm Mustafa and her neighbors experienced the same fear as Haga Samia and many others around the neighborhood experienced, that the building would collapse over their heads. Appealing to their landlords proved fruitless. In fact, tenants living throughout the neighborhood told me again and again that landlords *wanted* their buildings to collapse. According to Egypt's rent control laws, building collapse was one of the exceptional circumstances under which inheritable rent control contracts could be annulled.[2]

In 1996, Cairo's property regime witnessed a landmark transformation. The Egyptian government decided to start a process that would reverse rent control laws that had been in place since 1947. This process was gradual, however. As a first step, the 1996 laws eliminated all rent control restrictions for any property first rented after the law's adoption—what came to be known as *el 'eigar el gedeed* (the new rental system)—but kept in place rent control restrictions for property rented before the adoption of the law, or *el 'eigar el qadeem* (old rental system). Thus, tenants such as Umm Mustafa still had rent control contracts, but the opportunity costs of those contracts for their landlords had skyrocketed overnight.

Unfortunately for Umm Mustafa, her landlords reacted to these changes with desperation. When, in the early 2000s, the Aga Khan Foundation's subsidiary, Aga Khan Trust for Culture (AKTC), offered Umm Mustafa and her neighbors a grant to reconstruct their earthquake-damaged building as part of a larger home rehabilitation program in the neighborhood, the building owners informally agreed not to report the AKTC's work as building collapse. Right as the building was demolished, however, one of Umm Mustafa's landlords appeared at the construction site and declared that he would bring a municipality representative the next day to declare the building collapsed, nullifying the tenants' rent control contracts. Building owners did want their buildings to collapse after all. Luckily for Umm Mustafa, the AKTC responded immediately. They managed to bring together the resources necessary to reconstruct the building's core structures through the night and demonstrate that it had not been demolished the next morning when the municipality arrived. Umm Mustafa had survived her landlords' legal maneuvers. Her case was not the exception, however. In Darb El-Ahmar alone, the AKTC dealt with numerous such disputes, eight of which went to court and on at least two occasions members of their team spent a night in jail on account of similar disputes with building owners.[3]

The landlord's tricky maneuvers were hardly the behaviors of a triumphant property owner. When the 1996 law had passed, 42 percent of formal housing in Cairo was rented under old rent control laws (Sims 2010, 146). The law was either hailed as a triumph for Cairo's property owners that would "liberate" the city's captive real estate or protested as a dispossessive law that would eventually rob low-income tenants of their housing and shelter in the city. Both positions read the law as another episode in an age-old battle between property owners and tenants. The maneuverings that Umm Mustafa, her landlords, and the AKTC all found themselves enacting in a post-1996 environment suggest a more layered reading of Cairo's transforming property regime than a two-way battle between landlords and tenants. All three of those actors felt insecure in a post-1996 environment but were also taking chances on the risky possibilities they saw opening up within the cracks of Cairo's transforming property regime.

The Egyptian government's reversal of long-standing rent control laws in 1996 coincided with the rise of a new capitalist class within the ranks of the country's ruling coalition that was heavily concentrated in the construction industry and real estate development. The law allowed that class to rent out its newly built developments, mostly on Cairo's suburban periphery, at market prices without rent control restrictions. Restricting the reversal of rent control to *el'eigar el gedeed* or post-1996 rentals, however, was meant to maintain the stasis that kept low-income housing subsidized at property owners' rather than the state's expense. The vulnerabilities and possibilities that Umm Mustafa, her landlords, and the AKTC were acting on with regard to a building covered under the supposed stasis of *el'eigar el qadeem* tells us that the balance long maintained through rent control had been fundamentally shaken in the post-1996 environment.

Like any other legal transformation, the 1996 law was not a surgical instrument that would only manipulate a specified, calculated relationship but instead was intervening in a dynamic environment that, in the 1990s, was seeing transformation on multiple fronts. The law was intervening in a city reeling from the destruction wrought by the 1992 earthquake, which attracted the attention of a global heritage industry to the ailing, built environment of the city's historical core and an economy newly open to international development aid that followed the machinery of structural adjustment. These transformations, and the laws, destruction, funding, and experts that came with them, produced new possibilities and vulnerabilities for existing owners, tenants, new developers, and champions of low-income housing in the city. It is only possible to understand the dispossessive violence of these vulnerabilities and the possibilities of those opportunities by unearthing the layered histories of spatial-material transformation through which Cairo's property terrain had been experienced and lived in modern times. Unpacking those layers traces how Cairenes had come to materially and emotionally value property in various geographies across the city as the transformations of the 1990s and 2000s set in motion processes of property market-making and unmaking.

To interrogate these layered histories, the chapter focuses on a number of processes and epochs that have been formative in the making of property terrains in Cairo's central neighborhoods: (1) the environmental transformation of Cairo's watery terrain; (2) Egypt's experience with a colonial entanglement of capitalist dispossession and cosmopolitan life; (3) the geopolitics, populism, and logistics through which rent control became a lived reality in Cairo as it faced the earthquake's destruction; and (4) the industrial dynamism and automobile-based infrastructures through which the city center's sensorial experience has transformed over recent decades. The chapter does not make claims to an exhaustive or comprehensive presentation of the city's modern history but rather weaves together how these spatial, material, and affective experiences shaped the emotional and material relationships Cairenes came to foster with their homes and properties. In doing so, it complicates our understanding of notions such as value, decay, rootedness, and affordable housing.

In unpacking Cairo's layered histories, I also trace the class formations that are born through the lived experience of shifting property landscapes and the many spatial-material-affective processes that come together in shaping those landscapes. These classes are not given formations simply *represented* through the distribution of property in the city. Seeing these class formations as dynamically produced through changing property landscapes, rather than reading these breaks as age-old battles between the city's wealthy and poor, informs the more subtle and nonlinear class dynamics and dispossessive politics underlying a change in a country's property regime, such as the 1996 law.

Environment: Water Ecologies and the Unleashing of a "Modern" Cairo

At the dawn of the nineteenth century, Cairo sat within an intricate terrain of canals and lakes that defined its boundaries and seasonal rhythms. The bulk of the city's two hundred sixty thousand inhabitants lived within a "main complex [that] comprised a little less than five square miles of land in the form of an irregular rectangle, roughly three miles long and a mile and a half wide" (Abu-Lughod 1971, 57). Outside that core complex sat two suburban port outposts that connected the city to European (Bulaq) and African (Misr El-Qadimah) trade on the Nile. The core complex had grown organically from the medieval gated city that the Fatimids and then the Ayyubids had built up northeast of the Nile River between the tenth and thirteenth centuries. Within the medieval gated city sat the bulk of palaces and mosques for which Cairo came to be known as "the city of a thousand minarets"; synagogues and churches likewise lined its medieval Jewish and Christian quarters. By 1800, Cairo's core complex extended organically north and east of the city's Fatimid gates to fill a five-mile rectangle (Abu-Lughod 1971, 56–58). The boundaries of this enclosed rectangle were not accidental. Cairenes had carefully negotiated that lived space to maintain their need to stay close enough to the Nile to access its water while avoiding the destructive force of its floods. In lieu of direct access to the river, Cairenes relied on an intricate network of canals and lakes that reached deep into the city's urban fabric.

Running through the heart of the core complex was the Khalij, a canal dug during pharaonic times. Over time, it came to be the artery of Cairo's water network and the eastern boundary of the medieval Fatimid city. Since Fatimid times, the city's organic growth had spread to fill an area approximately as wide as the city to the west of the Khalij. Every year Cairenes celebrated the opening of the Khalij's dike to release the Nile's floodwaters with ritualized pomp. The water flowed into canal tributaries and standing ponds, deep into the dense urban fabric of the gated city. Outside the medieval gates—and still within the city's five-mile core—several large lakes, including Azbakiyya, Ratli, and Fil, stored Nile floodwaters. Because flooding was seasonal, the flowing water would be replaced with welcome gardens, unwelcome stagnant waters, and filthy landfills during the off-season. All in all, by the early nineteenth century, Cairo's terrain was textured by over four thousand seasonal lakes and ponds (Fahmy 2018, 161–62), with an intricate canal system likened to that of Venice (Abu-Lughod 1971, 141). Although often imagined as dry and dusty, Cairo was in fact built around a wet, marshy terrain swaying in its rhythms to the ebbs and flows of seasonal floodwaters.

The gradual but definitive drying up of this terrain in the nineteenth century would set Cairo up for rapid transformation into an unrecognizable city by the turn of the twentieth century, with far-reaching consequences for how property in the core city is being valued today. Highly notable was a mid-1800s public health campaign that joined forces with infrastructural innovations to deal the city's water network a concerted blow. Public hygienists, who subscribed to the miasmatic school of medicine and believed that foul-smelling bad air or "miasmas" spread disease, propagated the belief that the fumes of the city's stagnant waters and temporary landfills were behind its frequent epidemics and unusually high death rate.[4] The miasmatists gained ground within official circles as innovations in water delivery and damming and drainage techniques opened up unprecedented possibilities for infrastructures that could replace Cairo's medieval canal network. Among those infrastructures, an elaborate water delivery system was underway in Cairo that by 1882 had laid out about one hundred fifty thousand meters of piping that connected Cairenes to about 10.8 million cubic meters of water a year (Fahmy 2018, 162). As drainage techniques made more and more of the land around the Nile habitable, the strip of land Cairenes put between them and the Nile narrowed significantly. Finally, once a new dam and reservoir built on Egypt's southern tip in Aswan in 1902 had controlled the Nile's flooding, its banks could be fortified and settled.

The combined forces of the hygienists and engineers gradually tamed the city's terrain by draining up to 3,909 lakes in the 1860s and 1870s, reclaiming its floodplains and the islands floating within the Nile, filling in the Khalij and canal system by 1897, and ultimately wrenching the city from the clutches of the river's menacing floods with the construction of the first Aswan dam. The possibilities for Cairo's expansion beyond its five-square-mile core seemed limitless overnight (actually a grinding half century), after having seen almost no change for over four centuries. Cairo's liberation from its environmental shackles spelled both promise and doom for the city's dwellers. While it opened up new opportunities for expansion, the drying up of the city's water terrain left Cairenes bereft of the seasonal rhythms and celebrations around which they had organized their lives and abruptly robbed the core complex's real estate of its primacy, as the area was decentered from the expanding city's social, political, and economic circuits.

Water Ecologies and the Remaking of Historic Cairo

Sitting within that five-square-mile core were two of the three Cairene neighborhoods I study in this book: Darb El-Ahmar and Gamaliyya. In 1800, the building that Umm Mustafa now calls home sat inside the eastern edge of the gated Fatimid city in Darb El-Ahmar, likely as a three-story, single-family wooden home with a protruding window decorated in latticework (*mashrabiyya*) on a narrow alley that could be reached from the main thoroughfare only by entering through several iron gates locked up by residents at night. On the thoroughfare were workshops and markets where the neighborhood's crafts makers produced and sold all things related to "dress and toilet." On the opposite end of the neighborhood stood Bab Zuweila (a Fatimid gate), with Gamaliyya neighborhood poised gracefully on the other side of it. Gamaliyya's crafts workshops specialized in textiles and copper products, but the neighborhood was also known for having the highest concentration of Fatimid palaces and mosques on its main thoroughfare—Muʿiz Street, named after the city's first Fatimid ruler. While both neighborhoods were inhabited mostly by Muslim Egyptians, they were adjacent to Jewish and Greek quarters within the Fatimid gates and Coptic neighborhoods right outside the northeastern boundaries of the city. Its location within the core complex and within the city's historical Fatimid gates meant Gamaliyya, and to a lesser extent Darb El-Ahmar, were among the city's most distinguished neighborhoods, housing some of its wealthiest families well into the nineteenth century.

As the city's marshy terrain dried up, the expansions that robbed the two neighborhoods of their primacy started with a planned revival, or "modernization," project directly west of the city's boundaries. Khedive Ismail (one of the descendants of Mehmed Ali, who established control, and eventually dynastic rule, over Egypt in 1805) and his minister of public works Ali Mubarak, planned the development of the newly reclaimed floodplains to the west in the mid-1860s. Inspired by the model Baron Hausmann implemented in Paris, they designed the western neighborhoods of Isma'iliyya and Tawfiqiyya around a series of wide boulevards that radiated out of roundabout squares (*maydan*). They installed Cairo's new water delivery system and built Cairo's first permanent iron swing bridge across the Nile.[5] The Khedive's planned neighborhoods remained sparsely built and suburban in feel until the turn of the twentieth century. During that time, the optimism that the cotton boom had built for Egypt's economy waned, as the Khedive's grandiose projects plunged the country into debt. In 1882, the British took control of Egypt. Eventually, faith in the economy's health started to rebound with the turn of the century, and the city's westward expansion saw renewed interest with several real estate developments sprouting outside the core city.

Wealthy families that had inhabited imposing homes within the city, political and military attachés of the British Empire, and Egyptian and foreign migrants seeking new economic opportunities were attracted to these new developments for their ample space as well as their rapidly materializing commercial centers and infrastructures. Indeed, the state and its private partners concentrated infrastructural work outside the core city, eschewing the difficulty of infiltrating its layered and dense urban fabric and following the needs of the city's relocated elite. The commercial centers that developed in the newly expanding city cornered luxury markets in particular, robbing the historical core of a lot of the prestige that commerce had brought the area—if not the dynamism that continued to vibrate through the area's markets—as it continued to be central to nonluxury commerce.

Nevertheless, infrastructural work did not entirely bypass the core city. Water infrastructures slowly but surely reached deep within it, and two major roadways were constructed through its heart. First, Muski Street tore through the city's core to connect its eastern and western edges. It was designed during Mehmed Ali's reign in the 1830s and completed through much violent demolition as part of Ali Mubarak's public works program in the

1860s. Similarly, in the 1920s, Azhar Boulevard was constructed to run parallel to Muski Street, connecting the Azhar Mosque and University complex to the core's western edge (Reynolds 2012, 29). Azhar Boulevard would become quite significant to the fates of Gamaliyya and Darb El-Ahmar, for it was constructed close to Bab Zuweila and created a new physical barrier of speeding cars between the two neighborhoods. Over time, the division concentrated more of the area's lucrative commerce in Gamaliyya while Darb El-Ahmar sank deeper into economic destitution.[6] With these interventions, the city's core did not escape the infrastructural machine that had transformed Cairo into a motorized metro area with a complex underground water, gas, and sewerage network, even if it was gradually marginalized from it.

Movement in the City: Exodus and Rootedness

While the attractiveness of the new expansions cost neighborhoods like Darb El-Ahmar and Gamaliyya their primacy, they did not leave the core a ghost town. In fact, rather than receding, the population of the core complex surged during the interwar period along with the rest of the city. By the end of World War II, Cairo had witnessed a demographic revolution. Between 1897 and 1947, the city's population had increased by more than threefold, from six hundred thousand to over 2 million inhabitants. During the same period, the core city's population had doubled, from about three hundred twenty thousand to about six hundred seventy thousand. With its population doubling, the already saturated core city became even denser and less attractive to the wealthy. As Abu-Lughod documents, "many of the 'important families' removed themselves to the new sections of the city, [and permitted] the conversion of their former homes into subdivided and densely packed tenements" (Abu-Lughod 1971, 172–73).

Most of the buildings I visited during my fieldwork in both Gamaliyya and Darb El-Ahmar were formerly single-family homes that had been divided into multiple apartments or room units. Some of these buildings were owned by a family that had lived in the neighborhood for a long time and had subdivided the building among inheritors into decently sized apartments. A survey of Darb El-Ahmar showed, however, that in 2003, 13 percent of residents were still living as single-family owners of their buildings and 19 percent were partial owners of the divided buildings in which they lived. The majority of the neighborhood's residents, 68 percent to be exact, on the other hand, were—like Umm Mustafa—living in their homes as long-term tenants

(Van der Tas 2004). While some of the rented buildings had been subdivided into decent-sized one- and two-bedroom apartments with private kitchens and bathrooms, a larger proportion of these narrow homes were so densely packed that each floor was divided into two to three rooms inhabited by entire families who then shared one bathroom. Umm Mustafa's family was one of the lucky ones, having their own private living area, kitchen, and bathroom within their one-bedroom apartment.

A stark example of these subdivided homes materialized in Gamaliyya in Beit El-Kharazaty, a large courtyard house built by a wealthy Russian merchant in 1881 (Abdelmonem 2015, 171). It had been gradually subdivided over the twentieth century, and by the time it was restored—as part of a heritage preservation project in 1996—twenty-five families were living in the building as long-term tenants on rent control contracts. One of my interlocutors, Umm Hassan, lived with her family in a room with a private bathroom on the first floor of Beit El-Kharazaty.[7] She had been born and raised there, as had her father, whose family had migrated to Cairo from the village of Tonnah (in the then-agricultural countryside beyond Shubra). Theirs was one of the earliest families to rent an apartment in the building. The apartment was then subdivided between the father and his siblings as they had their own families, and he luckily had a private bathroom within his family's room. When Beit El-Kharazaty was restored in 1996, the twenty-five families living there were relocated to a mass housing block about twenty kilometers from Gamaliyya, on Cairo's outskirts, and provided with stand-alone apartments that doubled if not tripled their living space. As Umm Hassan related her father's story to me, she suddenly choked up as she said, "He lived in Beit El-Kharazaty for eighty-six years. When he left, he died."[8] Umm Hassan's father died three months after leaving Beit El-Kharazaty. He had been so rooted in Gamaliyya that the only way his daughter could make sense of his death was as sheer grief from the separation. To her, moving her father away from his Gamaliyya home had literally killed him. The rootedness with which Umm Hassan's father experienced his life in Gamaliyya was mirrored in the way many of my interlocutors experienced their city. In fact, 86 percent of the respondents to the Darb El-Ahmar survey indicated that they "want[ed] to continue living in the area" (Van der Tas 2004). The overwhelming ethos that residents who continue to be classified and seen as "rural migrants" into the city's center (often decades after their families had settled there) expressed about their neighborhoods and homes was that of rootedness rather than restless temporariness.

A striking example of that rootedness manifested through the story of "Mohamed Lipton" in Wust El-Balad and the bonds he had cultivated with the neighborhood's ecology, and especially its trees. I learned about Mohamed Lipton through the Model Citizens project curated by Dutch artists Elke Uitentuis and Wouter Osterholt during their residency at the Townhouse Gallery in Wust El-Balad. Uitentuis and Osterholt set out to document how urban dwellers in the Antikhana alley of Wust El-Balad experienced their neighborhood and imagined its future. Among the artifacts they created was an audio of "collective memory" that curated narration of how the neighborhood's dwellers remembered the history of its landmarks. Mohamed Lipton's coffee shop was one of those landmarks, and it is narrated that in the 1960s he converted a shop formerly owned by a Greek man into a coffee shop with outside seating.[9] He came to be known as "Mohamed Lipton" because "when he came here, Lipton Tea had just been released into the market." Moreover, Mohamed Lipton was described by one of the narrators not as a Cairene but as a migrant from Upper Egypt, saying that "Haj Mohamed ... wore a *galabeyya* [ankle-length shirt-gown worn by men, most associated with rural living], not shirt and trousers. He wore a *galabeyya* because he was from Upper Egypt."[10] His sartorial choices earned him the everlasting label of a migrant from Upper Egypt, no matter how long his coffee shop had been integral to the neighborhood.

What is striking about how the coffee shop's history is narrated is that although a lot is remembered about the social relationships that people fostered with Mohamed Lipton or through the coffee shop, most of the narrations fixated on the coffee shop's trees and the bonds between its owner and those trees. When Mohamed Lipton opened the coffee shop, he planted "a grape tree (*'enaba*) for the shade ... [as] an ornamental plant for posterity."[11] One of the narrators remembered them as follows: "Trees, trees, trees, the whole place was full of trees.... It was shading the whole street. They called it the *tak'eeba*. People used to come and sit at night on hot days, like these days, under the *tak'eeba*. Aah, and one could drink tea and smoke shisha and sit in the breeze. Beautiful!"[12] The dweller had to describe the trees with this detail because by the time the Dutch artists were documenting the neighborhood's memories, the trees were no longer standing in Antikhana. Intriguingly, several of the dwellers believed that the trees had died in grief over Mohamed Lipton's death. One dweller described the grief that struck the trees and the neighborhood as follows:

> The most difficult moment I experienced in my life was in this coffee shop. It was the moment the *Me'allem* [Lipton] died.... We were preparing the tobacco coal for the shisha ... [and] it looked like something was wrong

with his heart.... We took him to the [hospital]. They told us that he'd been dead for five minutes. We were totally devastated. I hadn't seen it coming. There was a *tak'eeba* with two trees that the *Me'allem* had planted with his bare hands. I tell you, we buried him at 11:00 a.m., and by 1:00 p.m. the *tak'eeba* was falling apart. The *tak'eeba*, the whole thing was falling down in front of us. You didn't see the *tak'eeba*, the way it looked, like it was made entirely of grapes. There were three main grape branches. One branch was huge. All of them falling at once?! Both of his two trees, I mean the ones he planted himself. These two trees falling on their own like that?! With all their roots coming out and not simply cut down? I swear with the roots coming out! It was proof that even things were mourning his death.[13]

Others believed the trees had been cut down by state authorities because they were unauthorized additions to the palace, which was designated as protected heritage, or by people who had a dispute with the coffee shop owner.[14] Regardless of the veracity of the story connecting the trees' fate with Mohamed Lipton's, the narration of his death through the dramatic collapse of the trees firmly roots (literally through the allegory of the trees' roots) Lipton within the neighborhood's ecology and life cycle. Not only were the neighborhood's residents mourning his loss but the city itself was so attached to him that its things—the trees he had planted—died with him.

As the drying up and reclamation of Cairo's watery terrain led to the city's rapid expansion and left the core complex far less attractive to its wealthier families, unexpected opportunities opened up for the city's new arrivals. Granted they were moving into densely packed buildings with overburdened infrastructures, but rural migrants were gaining immediate access to the economic dynamism and social networks that already colored life in the core city. With these opportunities, migrants put down roots that would bind them to neighborhoods like Gamaliyya and Darb El-Ahmar with such force that separation from them could lead to the unbearable grief that purportedly killed Umm Hassan's father. As the numerical value of property within the core city plummeted for its owners along with the environmental transformation of Cairo's complex water terrain, it opened up new possibilities for migrants as they joined its central social and economic circuits and formed unquantifiable bonds with their neighborhoods' dwellers, buildings, animals, trees, and ecologies. The very particular way in which Cairo's topography had transformed as its relationship with the Nile and its tributaries shifted had paved the way for the asymmetrical and nonlinear ways in which different stakeholders came to experience *value* in the city. This asymmetrical experience of value would then strike at the heart of the redistributive struggles over the contours of the "market" explored throughout this book. The transformation of environmental terrains is foundational to how struggles over property and its value manifest in the city.

Entangled Colonialism: The Entangled History of Colonial Capitalism and Cosmopolitanism

On January 26, 1952, rioters set 217 buildings ablaze in Wust El-Balad (aka downtown Cairo), the third Cairene neighborhood I study in this book, in what came to be known as the "Cairo Fire." Protesters had initially assembled outside the royal palace in ʿAbdeen to demonstrate against the violent attack of British forces on Egyptian auxiliary police officers in the canal town of Ismailia the day before. Splitting off from the protests, groups of rioters descended on the streets adjacent to the palace in Wust El-Balad to start 217 separate fires over a span of seven hours that left scores of people dead, hundreds injured, and thousands unemployed. The rioters initially targeted casinos, cinemas, and other establishments that could be considered "morally questionable" as well as bastions of British colonial power such as Barclay's Bank, the British Council, and the Turf Club, an all-British men's club. The attacks then changed course and targeted a wide array of commercial shops, ranging from Wust El-Balad's multistory department stores to car showrooms to specialty boutiques. In the span of seven hours, Wust El-Balad had gone up in flames (Reynolds 2012, 183–89) (see a map of the fire in figure 1.1).

Retrospectively, the Cairo Fire has often been read as Cairo's last stand against Britain's colonial grasp on Egypt, but the fire was actually received with mixed emotions among Egyptians at the time. Some unequivocally celebrated it as an anti-colonial victory, but others were so distraught that they mourned it as an act of self-immolation. Among those who mourned the fire were notable writers, often hailed as nationalist icons, including Naguib Mahfouz and Yusuf Idris, who represented the fire as an act of "suicide" in their writings.[15] The emotions that accompanied the fire mirrored the complicated relationship that Egypt's nationalist project had with how British colonialism manifested in the country, and especially with how entangled its tentacles were with what was understood as "Egyptian" capital. The reactions to the fire foreshadowed the many anxieties that Egypt's postindependence regime would grapple with as they worked to disentangle "colonial" from

Figure 1.1. Map of the Cairo Fire's targets as documented by *al-Musawwar* magazine. Source: "Downtown," *Cairo Observer Print Publication*, March 2015, https://cairobserver.com/print#.XywnPihKhPY.

"local" capital in their effort to decolonize the country and its economy. The specific ways through which colonialism entangled "foreign" and Egyptian capital, setting the stage for the ways in which colonial and class politics became enmeshed in the postindependence period and the sweeping nationalization policies of the 1960s, left a lasting imprint on how property came to be valued and lived in the city.

"Foreign" Capital in Cairo

In the 1860s, with the cotton boom and the opening of the Suez Canal in 1869, a new wave of migrants flocked to Egypt from across Ottoman and European (mostly Italian) ports. The migrants were of all creeds and backgrounds, but the linguistic versatility of non-Muslim migrants with a command of both European languages and Arabic (or Ottoman) gave them special advantage in mediating trade between European buyers and Egyptian suppliers. The linguistic advantage became doubly important when Egypt started signing capitulation agreements with European trading partners that gave their "subjects" special legal status, allowing them to adjudicate their disputes according to their own legal norms (rather than Islamic law) within the newly created Mixed Courts. With the capitulations in place, both newly migrant and long-settled minorities sought out legal affiliation with signatories in order to get the same immunities and advantages, increasingly blurring the lines between "foreign" and local minorities.

The arrival of British colonialism in 1882 further complicated how "foreignness" was understood and practiced in the country. Egypt was never a settler colony, so colonialism was not accompanied in Egypt by a sudden influx of settlers directly and violently dispossessing them of their land. Instead, Egyptians experienced colonialism through the dispossessive capitalist machine it ushered into the country. British colonialism brought with it an unprecedented influx of European capital attracted to the opportunities created by embedding Egypt within British colonial trade, finance, and industrial circuits. As big capital from across the Western world flooded Egyptian markets, the colonial government gave it *exclusive* access to some of the country's most lucrative revenue generators. For example, the British granted monopolistic contracts for the building and operation of almost all of the country's infrastructures to "foreign" companies. In Cairo, the French Cairo Water Company built and controlled Cairo's first piped and filtered water network (Ismail 2017, 147–55), the Belgian Empain company built and operated all of the city's tramways (Abu-Lughod 1971, ch. 9) and its first coal-powered electricity generators (Barak 2013, 152–55), the American Bell company built and controlled its telephone lines (Barak 2013, 205), and the list goes on. Alongside capital arriving from abroad, the British also granted these concessions to minorities long settled in Egypt who had been straddling the local-foreign divide since the institution of capitulations. Among them were the Jewish Suarès group, who were granted a concession to build the railway network in the southern districts of Cairo, and the Greek Salvagos group, who were given similar concessions in Alexandria (Vitalis 1995, 33–36).

These colonially bestowed privileges compounded as capitalists linked one monopolistic venture to another. Relevant to the city, capitalists made millions connecting infrastructure networks with urban real estate development. The Belgian Empain group, for example, was granted seventy thousand acres of desert to the north of Cairo to develop into the suburb of Heliopolis that they turned into real estate gold as they connected the suburb to Cairo's center on their tramway network (Barak 2013, 155). Similarly, the Suarès group and their British partners developed the neighborhood of Maʿadi to the south of Cairo's core and connected it to the city through the light rail network they built (Vitalis 1995, 34–36). More generally, private foreign-local capital left an unmistakable imprint on the city and its future planning through their dominance in the real estate market. Alongside Heliopolis and Maʿadi, a foreign syndicate bought the large tract of land on the Nile that was once Ibrahim Pasha's palace and converted it into the Garden City neighborhood modeled on the British planner Ebenezer Howard's "garden city model," and the British Baehler Society developed land north of the royal palace on the Jazirah (that would become Zamalek) into residential real estate in the 1910s and 1920s (Abu-Lughod 1971, 142).

In time, capitalists transforming the city shifted to include more and more Muslim-majority and minority Egyptians. During the interwar period, and especially after the 1919 revolution gained Egyptians nominal/partial independence from the British, more of Egypt's Muslim landed elite were being incorporated into its industrializing capitalist class. As Vitalis (1995) shows in great detail, two things were common to this rising cadre of Egyptian minority and Muslim capitalists. First, they were all heavily involved with and reliant on foreign capital in building their business empires. Even Talaʿat Harb, who was hailed as a nationalist industrial hero because he founded Bank Misr to specifically foster the "Egyptianization" of industry in 1920, had risen to prominence through partnering with foreign capital before and after founding Bank Misr. Second, Egyptian capitalists were organized into oligarchic multisectoral, familial groups that sprawled horizontally into every imaginable economic sector in ways that mirrored foreign capital. As Vitalis describes it, "The most powerful constituents of the nascent industrial lobby in Egypt were simultaneously the country's richest bankers, largest exporters of cotton, main investors and directors in numerous foreign-backed ventures and, through the extensive network of interlocking transport, irrigation, and land-development companies, some of the largest landowners as well" (Vitalis 1995, 40–41). Thus, even as they organized and pushed for Egyptianization decrees meant to legislate protectionist policies that would further entrench the advantages of local capital in Egypt's economy, they maintained significant partnerships with foreign capital and mirrored its oligopolistic organization. As colonialism fostered a monopolistic economic environment, it had deeply entangled class and colonial politics as wealth became heavily concentrated in the hands of a limited number of oligopolistic landed industrialist capitalists, some of whom were at the forefront of nationalist politics of anticolonialism while intricately entangled with foreign circuits of capital.

Wust El-Balad and Entangled Capital

Nowhere was the complicated nature of Cairo's colonial entanglements more discernible than in the built environment of Wust El-Balad (aka downtown Cairo). At the turn of the century, many foreign and local companies, especially in the financial and services sectors, deployed Cairo's built environment to project political and economic prowess. Companies such as Kodak, Bank Misr, Shell Oil, Trans World Airlines (TWA), and many other banks and insurance companies set up their headquarters in Cairo, and mostly around Wust El-Balad. After the British had concentrated their built political and cultural footprint in and around Wust El-Balad, including the British embassy, colonially privileged private capital followed suit. The villas once built by Egypt's (mostly royal) elite around Ismailiyya's wide boulevards transformed into imposing seven- to eight-story art deco concrete buildings for company headquarters.

The architects, designing the buildings that came to be known as ʿemarat Wust El-Balad, were pushed to compete in how innovatively they could combine art deco with Arabic/Islamic/Egyptian motifs to imply a space bridging those worlds and projecting prowess across them.[16] As these iconic ʿemarat took over downtown's skyline, the neighborhood became notably distinct from the historic core. Alongside unique art deco styles, the buildings were made of concrete rather than wood, rose to seven and eight stories rather than two or three, were three to four times as wide as the larger buildings in the core, and used both Latin and Arabic script on their signage.

The neighborhood also came to be the epicenter of cultural and commercial venues associated with European influence. In the interwar period, cinemas, casinos and nightclubs serving alcohol, cafés serving non-Egyptian pastries and drinks, and large European-style department stores started appearing for the first time in Cairo in Wust El-Balad. Like company headquarters, these commercial and entertainment venues left an enduring imprint on the city's landscape as some of the venues were almost monumental in their architectural grandiosity. For example, the largest of Wust El-Balad's cinemas, among them Rivoli and Metro Cinema, had large screening halls with balconies that could seat up to two thousand people in front some of the largest screens in the world. Department stores, including Cicurel and Sednaoui, operated in large art deco buildings that spanned entire blocks (sometimes two) and up to four or five stories, with large window displays that rivaled Paris in elaborateness.

While the imposing art deco architectural edifice projected foreignness on a number of registers, Egyptians' experiences of the space fluidly crossed imagined boundaries between the foreign and the local. Signage and ads placed Egyptian commerce side by side with its foreign counterparts. Many of the films screened in Wust El-Balad's cinemas were Egyptian and in Arabic. European-style cafés like Groppi or Café Riche regularly hosted anti-colonial organizing. Moreover, as Reynolds's intricate study of the neighborhood's commerce describes, goods displayed in department stores' windows were produced both in Egypt and abroad and tailored to meet the specific consumption needs of Egyptians. She incisively shows that different groups of people (along lines of gender, ethnicity, or class) navigated the department stores and adorned themselves with the goods they bought in accordance to norms developed by Egyptians, crafting their own relationship to "modern" consumption rather than simply mimicking the West. The circuits of capital fueling these department stores were not only deeply embedded within Egyptian and Ottoman circuits of capital but also *spatially* connected to Cairo's historic core (Reynolds 2012, ch. 2).

For example, the owners of Cicurel descended from a Sephardic Jew who came to Cairo from Izmir (in Ottoman Anatolia) in the mid-1880s. He had worked first as an assistant in a haberdashery in Muski, right outside the historic city gates, and then bought the business, which grew into the Cicurel retail empire. In the 1920s, Cicurel moved downtown to open one of Egypt's first and largest department stores. After their father's death, the Cicurel brothers, who had Egyptian citizenship, held important positions in a number of institutions dedicated to Egyptianizing the economy and were founding members of Bank Misr (Reynolds 2012, 57–59). The fluidity of people's mobility, circuits of capital, and geographic connection within the city challenges any dichotomous readings of Wust El-Balad and pushes us to appreciate the complexity of meaning-making that fluid entanglements produced.[17] It was through this fluidity, and the processes of affective meaning-making around it, that nationalist figures such as Naguib Mahfouz came to read the Cairo Fire as "suicide" rather than as an anti-colonial victory.

Class and Cosmopolitan Entanglements in the Post-Colony

Egypt's experience with colonial violence, mainly through the workings of a dispossessive capitalist machine rather than a settler-colonial occupation, layered Cairo's colonial entanglements with class dynamics that continued to shape the city long after British withdrawal. In the immediate sense, it shaped how the Free Officers—the officers who led the bloodless coup of 1952 that put an end to the monarchy and the last vestiges of British colonial rule in the country under the leadership of Gamal Abdel Nasser (who would rule Egypt from 1954)—would wage their battle for postcolonial economic independence. The rise of an oligopolistic local/"Egyptian" capitalist class intricately connected to foreign capital out of the ashes of colonial capitalism pushed the Free Officers to wage that battle on two fronts: externally, against dependency on foreign (especially Western) economic circuits, and internally, against the structural inequities inherent to an economy run by an oligopolistic-capitalist class. As they waged those battles, the Free Officers were initially confronted with the dangers of unshackling Egypt from its dependencies on Western economic circuits without relying on the country's robust local capitalist class. Nasser thus spent the first five to six years of postcolonial rule experimenting with ways to gradually dismantle the oligopolistic nature of that class without an outright attack on local capitalists. Ultimately, Nasser's regime came to the conclusion that short of a complete and uncompromising dismantling of the oligarchic-capitalist class, the country's economy would never overcome the structural inequities it propagated.

Building upon their experimentation with nationalizing some foreign capital in the aftermath of the Suez Crisis in 1956, Nasser's government embarked on a complete nationalization of the private sector in 1961 and 1963, as all medium to large private enterprises were sequestered and transferred to state control. The state had launched an all-out assault on local Egyptian capital as it sought to rid itself of the violence of colonial capitalism. Within the city, the nationalization campaign transformed the state into a major property owner in the city's center. In Wust El-Balad especially, scores of buildings that had once been corporate headquarters or were owned by large development companies were seized as part of these companies' nationalizations and transferred to state ownership. Almost overnight, the state had become the owner of over one hundred of the iconic *'emarat Wust El-Balad*. Rather than resell its holdings, the state decided to rent out most of its property in the city center to government officials and new migrants into the city through rent-controlled contracts—over 75 percent of these units are still under rent control in 2020—changing the neighborhood's demographics remarkably in the span of a decade.[18] State-owned, rent-controlled property in Wust El-Balad was left unmaintained for decades and became ailing, debilitated buildings by the 1990s, with significant ramifications for property markets in the neighborhood as the 1996 laws came into effect.

The affective processes of meaning-making that entangled Cairo's colonial experiences of cosmopolitanism and class politics had a long afterlife. Much ink has been spilled about the politics of nostalgia for colonial-era architecture and "cosmopolitanism" in Cairo, but I want to focus here on the classed and political economic dimension of that nostalgia.[19] The entanglement of class and colonial politics in Cairenes' political imaginary is crucial in understanding the *timing* of that nostalgia and *how* it manifested itself in the city. The rising nostalgia for colonial-era cosmopolitanism coincided with an embrace of market economics as a corrective to what are seen as Nasser's socialist blunders. For that class, Nasser was seen to be throwing out the baby with the bathwater as he attacked the country's capitalist class with a blunt, all-encompassing nationalization campaign. In turn, the revival of the entrepreneurial spirit that Egyptian capitalists had embodied in the 1930s and 1940s, through the workings of a free market, would need to go hand in hand with a revival of "good" and "local" cosmopolitanism.

In this book, the marriage of market economics and Egyptian cosmopolitanism is expressed most vividly by Karim Shafei, CEO of the private developer Ismailia Consortium, in his vision for reviving Wust El-Balad. Shafei sees the consortium's plan for reviving Wust El-Balad growing out of a movement to "Egyptianize Egypt" that embraces a very particular homegrown cosmopolitanism that reflects the intimacies and fluidities with which local and foreign were entangled in the first half of the twentieth century (see chapter 4 for more detail). He makes a point to distinguish that cosmopolitanism from globalizing cosmopolitanism (and especially American globalization) and its Big Capital that mirrored the dispossessive and extractive colonial Big Capital. Instead, all of his examples of how local cosmopolitanism is embedded within a project of Egyptianization refer to the "good" non-colonial foreigners and long-settled minorities of Egypt who were crucial to the Egyptian capitalist circuits and spirits that Nasser had crushed with his blunt attack on the country's capitalist class.

Shafei was not alone in expressing class dynamics and understandings of property value through a fine-tuned articulation of Cairo's cosmopolitanism. Although Cairo's cosmopolitan past rarely came up explicitly during my conversations with Cairenes throughout my fieldwork, its specter often made an elusive appearance during my conversations with Wust El-Balad's dwellers about the neighborhood's heyday. What was striking was that they almost always referred to that cosmopolitanism through a reference to particular individuals and their nationalities or non-Arabic names, but never through blanket statements about a "cosmopolitan era." They were specific about the mixture of peoples they associated with a thriving Cairo lest I confused all foreigners as members of that celebrated mixture.

I encountered this dynamic during my conversation with ʿAmm Ayman, a tailor who was born and raised in Wust El-Balad. We spoke at his store, attached to the back of one of the iconic cinemas that was nationalized by the state and continues to be owned by the state's holding company in 2020. After the 1996 rent control law came into effect, the state's holding company carved out new storefronts from the empty passageway behind the cinema and started renting them out through non-rent-controlled contracts. After paying a number of bribes, ʿAmm Ayman was able to secure a storefront at a 10 percent yearly increase in rent. The specter of cosmopolitan Cairo quietly slipped into his description of better days in Wust El-Balad's past:

> Cairo was not this [city of] *hamagiyya* [or chaos]. There used to be respect for people but now there is no respect for people. . . . Even the supermarkets, that they used to call *baqal* [or grocer]. That *baqal* would be *younany* [Arabic word for "Greek"] or *greeggy* [Latinized version], and he would treat people well. Things used to be clean; not like today. I mean, today if you walk here along Qasr El-Nil street or this whole area, there isn't a single public restroom except underground in the Tahrir metro station. A long time ago there used to be public restrooms all over. On Champion Street there was a public restroom. In Tahrir Square there was a public restroom, and so on.[20]

ʿAmm Ayman seamlessly slipped the Greek grocers into his account of a clean Wust El-Balad where people treated one another with respect and the city hadn't descended into chaos (or *hamagiyya*, with its socioeconomic connotations). When he layered recollections of a cosmopolitan past with those of the neighborhood's heyday, and the classed connotations of descriptors like "respect(able)" and "*hamagiyya*," he did not just mention "foreigners" or a "cosmopolitan Cairo" in a general sense; he was instead specific about the Greeks being welcome members of that imaginary, both as the long-settled *younany* minorities and the foreign *greeggy* migrants, and not just any non-Egyptians.

In a similar vein, the dwellers of Antikhane zone within Wust El-Balad who shared their memories with the Model Citizens project used very specific language in describing the mixture of neighborhood inhabitants in the interwar period. One of the residents whose family had lived in Antikhane for a number of generations described his building's residents:

This building had a mixture of nationalities living in it. There were Greek, there were Armenians, there were Italians, there were Jews. Of course, with the passage of time some people traveled and others emigrated. I lived and still live on the top floor. There was a Greek family living across the hall from us, and on the third floor there was another Greek family, and a family that was half Levantine and half Jewish.[21]

Another respondent recorded that "on the second floor there lived a doctor, Dr. Barakat. He was [*deep pause for effect*] the King's doctor."[22] And yet another remembered that "the top floor was owned by Madame Maris. It's where the library [of the Townhouse Gallery] is now. The apartment was her father's, Gamil Helal.... They own the restaurant Estoril, at the end of the passageway."[23] In all three of these accounts, the respondents relied on various markers to signal that the building, and by extension the neighborhood, had once been home to the city's privileged classes and of high market value. For the first (still current) resident it was via reference to the mixture of very specific nationalities that lived in the building; for the second it was by association with a doctor so distinguished that he tended to the king himself; and for the third it was through reference to the Coptic owners (from the names) of Estoril, a Cairene establishment for decades and one of the few restaurants still serving alcohol in the area.[24] As they reclaimed value for the neighborhood and their property through intricate allusions to a cosmopolitan past, Karim Shafei, ʿAmm Ayman, and Antikhane's dwellers were threading the needle of Cairo's delicate class-cosmopolitan entanglements that Nasser's blunt policies had compromised. They did so right as Nasser's legacies were being openly challenged through an aggressive embrace of market economics.

Rent Control and Its Afterlives: Geopolitics, Populism, Earthquake, and Living Decay

The rent control laws of 1947 codified a 1941 emergency decree by the Egyptian state that froze tenants' rental rates as a temporary wartime measure. The laws would not be relaxed until 1996, when the first legislation was enacted to gradually reverse rent control. In this section, I interrogate the logics that came together to entrench rent control in Cairo, with a focus on the Allied Forces' geopolitical strategy during World War II and the postindependence state's populism. I then turn to how the institutionalization of rent control over a half century interacted with norms around inheritance and the striking of the 1992 earthquake to shape how tenants of rent-controlled apartments in Cairo's central neighborhoods experienced daily life in their (mostly decaying) homes and how owners came to value that property over time.

World War II and the Geopolitics of Rent Control

As the world erupted into all-out war in 1939, Egypt was still politically confined within the orbit of British influence, even if that control had been loosening. With the advent of World War II, the British tightened their grip to ensure that the Allied Forces' interests were not disrupted as the battlefront moved to North Africa. As Vitalis and Heydemann (2000) have shown, the British strove to both fulfill their military needs in North Africa and to appease local populations to ensure that the war effort did not cause local revolts or, worse, bring outright support of Axis campaigns in the region. By 1941, the main problem that the British were facing was "a shortage of shipping" (Vitalis and Heydemann 2000, 116). Colonized Middle Eastern economies had become heavily dependent on exports for their economic survival, with Egypt reliant on cotton exports and on imports for most of its basic foodstuffs and manufactured goods. Because of this reliance on trade, Middle Eastern economies "require[ed] almost 100 percent of shipping capacity in the region" (116) to survive. By 1941, shipping capacity in the Mediterranean had shrunk considerably as the coastline was compromised following the Vichy occupation of France and Italy's Axis membership. Moreover, German submarine attacks made movement in the sea that much more treacherous. As shipping capacity shrunk, the British gave their military shipping needs, connecting Allied North African forces with soldiers and supplies from Britain and the United States, primacy over the civilian trade needs of Middle Eastern economies. To offset the looming economic crises of cutting off that trade, the British enacted an aggressive campaign of state interventionism in the economy in Egypt and other colonial strongholds in the region.

The British, in conjunction with local authorities, deployed a plethora of institutions and policies that were meant to increase the local supply of foodstuffs and manufactured goods to both supply the war effort and decrease Middle Eastern economies' reliance on imports. Creating the Middle East Supply Center, based in Cairo under the command of the British shipping ministry, they subsidized a variety of industrial plants to produce essential wartime goods and instituted a variety of tariffs to protect those fledgling uncompetitive industries. They also instituted agricultural monopsonies to ensure the state was the only buyer from farmers, controlling which crops were grown and pushing agricultural production away from cotton and toward needed foodstuffs. Additionally, they enacted programs around pricing and currency in an effort to control wartime inflation. In spite of these efforts, economies across the Middle East experienced rampant inflation during the war, and authorities had to intervene heavily through redistributive measures. Vitalis and Heydemann argue that the British often delegated decision-making on such measures to local authorities, which produced a lot of variation in how they were implemented. In Egypt, the authorities' overriding approach was to minimize direct taxation that would be seen as a clear and targetable burden on its population (especially its organized oligarchic-capitalist-landowning class) and instead decree a variety of indirect redistributive measures. In lieu of direct taxes, they built more industrial plants to boost employment in urban centers, increased customs duties, and deployed strict price fixing and rationing to ensure food distribution was equitable (Vitalis and Heydemann 2000, 129–31). Among those measures, the Egyptian authorities introduced rent controls in 1941.

Rent control was the indirect redistributive measure par excellence. It ensured that people's security in their housing would not be affected by wartime inflation, and instead placed that burden on homeowners (a disorganized group from across the socioeconomic spectrum) through incremental and seemingly temporary measures rather than a direct and targetable tax hike on the organized and power-wielding oligarchic-capitalist class. In addition to the general vulnerabilities produced through inflation, the war also directly affected the real estate market by heavily limiting the supply of new construction and increasing demand for it. Workers flocking to cities to work in wartime factories found an ever-shrinking supply of housing as building materials and construction laborers were diverted away from real estate construction and toward the war effort. It was in reaction to both general inflation and rental hikes produced by the heavy demand that the state then decreed emergency rent controls in 1941 (McCall 1988, 158).

When the war ended, many wartime factories closed down, leaving their newly migrant workers suddenly unemployed (Vitalis and Heydemann 2000, 131). Moreover, shortages in construction supplies kept available housing far below demand in Cairo. With rent controls garnering little collective backlash from the disorganized urban landlord class, the state went on to institutionalize rather than dismantle rent controls as a convenient redistributive measure. Although most of the state-interventionist decrees introduced by the Middle East Supply Center were reversed with the end of the war, in 1947 the Egyptian Parliament codified rent control measures that froze rents to their 1941 rates for all tenancy contracts signed before 1944 (McCall 1988, 158).

Although often attributed to the socialist agenda that Nasser would adopt after independence, rent control saw its origins in Egypt with the machinations of World War II. The Allied Forces' geopolitical need to offset shipping shortages had set in motion a series of policy experiments that would transform Egypt's political and property terrain for decades. Vitalis and Heydemann argue that tracing the origins of state-interventionist decrees back to the Allied efforts to manage the Egyptian economy (even if some of these measures were put on hold for a decade or so before they were revived again) illustrates how that experimentation had "helped consolidate notions of the economy as a legitimate object of regulation, and of the state as the necessary agent of economic coordination and management... [and] valorized the belief that a 'national' economy could be directed to achieve distributive justice" (133). Experimentation with rent control in particular laid bare the weakness of the landlord class that lacked the organization, tools, or prescience to battle the creeping institutionalization of rent controls that would slowly eat away at the revenue they extracted from property.

Rent controls then became one of the most convenient redistributive measures Egyptian authorities could turn to time and again to solidify their rule in the coming fifty years. Geopolitical calculation by outside powers during World War II would leave an unmistakable imprint on Cairo's property regime, with a lasting impact on the physical materiality of the city's property terrain and the class formations that developed in the city over time. This transformed the relationship between tenants and owners from one mediated by "market forces" to one shaped by political prowess, ensuring that tenants and landlords would have increasingly divergent experiences of the value of property they owned or inhabited over time. Thus, geopolitical wartime strategies forged politicized class formations along the lines of property ownership and tenancy (rather than, say, occupational group) into Cairo's socioeconomic landscape.

Populism and Its Exceptions

After the Free Officers rose to power in 1952, they refrained from adopting heavily state-interventionist or "socialist" policies in most arenas during their first decade in power, even though they would eventually adopt a lot of the policies experimented with during World War II. Rent controls and land reforms were the exception to that strategy. Experimentation with rent controls during the war had unequivocally demonstrated its efficacy as a redistributive measure and institutionalized its legal precedent in a way that made it too obvious and convenient to ignore as the Free Officers worked to build their popular base. As they came to power, they immediately expanded urban rent control to *all* rental contracts, abrogating the exemption that the 1947 law made for contracts signed after 1944. Moreover, the legislation not only froze all rents but decreased them by 15 percent (McCall 1988, 158). Eventually, when Nasser and his regime adopted their sweeping program of socialist reforms, they further institutionalized rent control through six successive laws. By 1969, rental rates were frozen (even in the face of inflation), and tenants were given the right to inherit rent control contracts without limits on the inheritance of subsequent generations. Further, landlords were forbidden to pay tenants compensation for their rental contracts or "key money" to incentivize them to vacate their units (El Araby 2003, 438–41).

Interestingly, rather than retrenching, the rent control machine only solidified into place with the end of Nasser's socialist era and the rise of Nasser's successor Anwar El-Sadat (henceforth Sadat) in 1970. Although Sadat adopted an economic platform, known as "open-door policies" or *Infitah*, meant to overhaul Nasser's state-interventionist economic model and revert to the dynamics of free-market economics, he chose not to reverse the rent control regime.[25] Significantly, immediately after the January 1977 bread riots that erupted in protest of the removal of government subsidies on daily staples such as flour (Ghannam 2002, 37), Sadat's government further entrenched rent controls. In 1977, the government enacted a law that fixed rental rates at 7 percent of original construction costs and gave the renters not only the right to inherit rental contracts but also to sublet units under specific circumstances. In 1981, the law was further modified to protect tenants from eviction, even if the original contract had expired, except in the very narrow cases of (a) the building's collapse, (b) nonpayment of owed rent within fifteen days, (c) the vacancy of the unit, or (d) improper use strictly defined (El Araby 2003, 441).

Rent control was proving a convenient populist redistributive measure for Egypt's rulers, even as they liberalized other economic arenas. In the words of David Sims (2010), the country's successive rulers saw that "the surest way to commit political suicide [was] to champion the removal of rent controls" (147). Even so, Sadat's regime started to introduce exceptions that slowly carved a space for allies to garner revenues from real estate. A 1981 law "[exempted] all luxury units from rent control, in specified zones" (El Araby 2003, 441) in order to allow Sadat to exempt on a case-by-case basis the real estate developers who were among his main political allies. Sadat had set forth precedents for the eventual institutionalization of exceptions that his successor Mubarak would put into place in 1996.

Lived Realities of Rent Control and the Dissipating Wealth of Cairo's Propertied Classes

When, in 2008, Karim Shafei, CEO of Ismailia Consortium, put out feelers to start buying buildings in Wust El-Balad, he received forty offers of sale in the span of a week.[26] A lot of the offers came from the owners of the ornate art deco *'emarat Wust El-Balad* built in the interwar period. In spite of how coveted these buildings once were, their owners were rushing to sell them to the first buyer who came along. A majority of the units within *'emarat Wust El-Balad* were rent-controlled units that were being rented at negligible rates. For example, within the twenty buildings that Ismailia Consortium did eventually buy from private owners, six hundred units were rented under old rent control contracts. According to Shafei, units that could be rented for E£3,000 on the open rental market were being rented out for as low as E£7 a month.[27] Maintaining the buildings had become more costly than the rents owners collected. Thus, many buildings fell into a state of severe disrepair, as had Umm Mustafa's building in Darb El-Ahmar. Because buildings in Wust El-Balad were on the whole structurally strong, they were not as structurally compromised by the 1992 earthquake as Umm Mustafa's building, but their amenities, including elevators, electricity, and water/sewage infrastructures, had been severely incapacitated over time. Thus, even if the buildings were evacuated immediately of all rent control tenants, significant capital would still be required to repair and refurbish these massive and severely debilitated buildings so that they would actually attract the kind of clientele Karim Shafei imagined would pay E£3,000 on an open market. *'Emarat Wust El-Balad* had lost much of their intrinsic value as the actual physical fabric of the buildings had deteriorated over the years.

In addition, time may have stood still for rental rates, but it was very much in motion as the inheritors of a property exponentially increased from one generation to the next. This was especially true for large buildings in Wust El-Balad. According to Karim Shafei, most of the buildings his company encountered were built by families in the early twentieth century and currently owned by their inheritors. Because of the application of Islamic laws of inheritance, "today most of the buildings [in Wust El-Balad] are owned by multiple inheritors ranging from, say, ten up to buildings where [the Consortium] negotiated with one hundred inheritors."[28] Such owners were usually scattered too. For example, "One of them is eighty-five years old and has hearing problems, and another is seventeen and living in Germany, and others are living in Assiut [in Upper Egypt] and so on, [and] can't manage the building properly."[29] Although inheritance over multiple generations will always create complicated networks of property ownership that span a wide spectrum of personalities and geographical locations, so long as the property is generating revenue or expanding, inheritors have an incentive to carefully manage the network and equitably divide the revenue. When the inheritors aren't receiving returns and perhaps get accosted by tenants for maintenance requests if they are visibly organized and accessible, there is little reason to manage the web of inheritors or the building they share. Hereditary practices had worked in tandem with the lived experience of rent control to produce a terrain of property that was valued very differently from how the city's property owners had once valued it.

Disaster: The 1992 Earthquake and Its *Mis*management

On October 12, 1992, Cairo was shaken to its core by an earthquake that registered 5.8 on the Richter scale at its epicenter, thirty-five kilometers south of the city. The earthquake was deemed unusually destructive for its magnitude: 545 people were killed and about 50,000 were displaced around Cairo (Robinson 2013, 171). The earthquake's force combined with landlords' neglect and the state's *mis*management to entrench decay and precarity into Cairene tenants' daily experience of their rent-controlled homes.

Whereas the reinforced foundational structures of *'emarat Wust El-Balad* remained mostly intact in the wake of the earthquake, the damage to the historical core's urban fabric was severe. The narrow three- to four-story buildings in Gamaliyya and Darb El-Ahmar, still reliant on wood and stone rather than steel and concrete in their structures, were already heavily strained by neglect and lack of maintenance over the last half century. Thus, in 1992, their strained foundations collapsed or became so severely damaged that inhabiting these buildings became nothing short of life threatening. I entered several homes in both Gamaliyya and Darb El-Ahmar where ceilings were caved in so visibly they could have been arched at 30 and 45 degrees. Other buildings had severe water damage from pipes that burst either during or soon after the earthquake. Neither the pipes nor damaged ceilings that I saw had been fixed in nearly two decades (see figures 1.2 and 1.3 for visuals of

Figure 1.2. A partially collapsed building that is still inhabited in Darb El-Ahmar. Source: author, November 2011.

Figure 1.3. A collapsed building in Darb El-Ahmar. Source: author, November 2011.

the exteriors of the damaged buildings). Yet most tenants continued living in their hazardous and in some cases partially collapsed homes to keep their rights to rent control contracts. And as seen with Umm Mustafa's building and confirmed by many of my interviewees, owners were not simply neglecting to repair and maintain their buildings, they were watching closely in the hope that they would collapse and liberate them from their tenants' rent control contracts.

The state further normalized the practice of awaiting building collapse through its bureaucratic response to the earthquake. In its wake, for example, the state conducted a survey of the condition of buildings in Darb El-Ahmar and produced demolition decrees (*qarar 'ezalah*, sing.) or partial demolition decrees if a house was in grave danger of collapse. According to Rania, a member of the Aga Khan Foundation team, the state produced demolition decrees for 90 percent of buildings in Darb El-Ahmar.[30] Her colleague Mounir noted that the numbers were highly inflated because "the engineer [conducting the survey] couldn't be bothered [to accurately survey the buildings]. The municipality's engineer may have even been an agricultural engineer and not an [architect] and filled out the survey *we khalas* [meaning without actually conducting the survey]."[31] Initially, the idea behind demolition decrees was to ensure that Cairo's residents wouldn't be living in perilous conditions in the aftermath of the earthquake, and the state promised to relocate residents of buildings with hanging demolition decrees to state-provided housing. In actuality, the state did not relocate any of the residents to state-provided housing but by law buildings with demolition decrees were to remain untouched, and residents, owners, or tenants were not allowed to repair them.

The muddled postearthquake survey codified the anticipation of building collapse into an accepted and legally sanctioned norm. Rent control, in conjunction with the state's muddled response to the earthquake, decimated the historic core's urban fabric and the value property owners may have once seen in their buildings. Even as it entrenched the existentially threatening dynamics of awaiting building collapse, in a twist, the earthquake shined a spotlight on the historical core. It would soon attract a sudden influx of attention and international and state funding to the area after decades of neglect. Most of that funding would be motivated by the need to save the heritage of "the city of the thousand minarets" and the infrastructure that serviced its monuments, but some of it would be directed toward the rehabilitation of private homes. Overall, geopolitical war strategies, populist rationales, the lived dynamics of building neglect, inheritance norms, and the *mis*-management of disaster combined to decimate the physical fabric of rent-controlled buildings in Cairo's center. These factors disrupted how the properties were valued while entrenching a divide that placed building owners and tenants within diametrically opposed camps in the city, even as other characteristics (such as occupational group or birthplace) may have, in other contexts, grouped them within the same socioeconomic class.

Industrial and Infrastructural Sensoria: Industry, Cars, and a Contested Sensorium

Early on during my fieldwork, several people told me I should visit a gallery set up by the Aga Khan Foundation in Azhar Park that sells products made in Darb El-Ahmar neighborhood. Once there, I found myself surrounded by colorful hand-stitched textiles, hand-carved wooden boxes and trinkets inlaid with mother of pearl, handblown glasswork, and hand-carved brass and copper trays and lanterns. Everything in the gallery was handmade, individually unique, and small in size. The sounds and activity that these products evoked were the quiet rhythmic sounds of artisans in almost-silent focus as they carefully threaded their needles, worked with fine handheld tools to inlay wood with mother-of-pearl, or made small pounding noises as they carved brass. The images that go along with these products in several of the booklets and reports produced by the foundation about the neighborhood document those same intricate, quiet artisanal activities.

Leafing through the booklet that the foundation created as a gift from the neighborhood to the Aga Khan when he visited Darb El-Ahmar, I found employment in the neighborhood represented through the following images: four images of tentmakers hand-threading textiles; an artisanal stencil-maker; two images of carpenters inlaying wood with mother-of-pearl; a blacksmith using a torch to weld a metal door; two men hand-rolling leather hides into submission; a tile maker polishing marble tile with a small handheld electronic polisher; and two stonemasons carving stone. All of the women and men in the images are doing intricate work with their nimble hands, and some of the images zoom in on that work by just picturing the disembodied fingers of the artisans as they craft wood or stencils. The booklet's images immerse the reader in the same quiet rhythms of the artisanal handicrafts workshops of Darb El-Ahmar.[32]

When I visited the workshops lining the streets of Cairo's historical core in both Darb El-Ahmar and Gamaliyya in person, however, I was often met with the loud noises of machinery rather than the quiet sounds of hand-craftsmanship. At the northern entrance to Darb El-Ahmar, right inside Bab Zuweila, sits the tentmakers' market, or *souq el-khayamiyya*, where artisans tirelessly hand-decorate textiles of all shapes and sizes. Here, the sound of boisterous sociality between tentmakers and their customers followed me through the market. Deeper into the neighborhood, a large furniture industry thrives. Although some of these workshops specialize in intricate wood carving, most of the furniture workshops operate at a greater, mechanized scale and use relatively heavy machines to cut, polish, and design large pieces of wood, textiles, and furniture filling. These furniture workshops produced not only the sounds of industrial saws, drills, hammers, and polishers but also a flurry of shards as wood was sanded down and synthetic and cotton fibers spilled out from plush furniture. The debris mostly stayed within workshops, filling workers' lungs and getting in their eyes; some of it also escaped into the air outside, to be inhaled by Darb El-Ahmar's residents before the carpenters managed to hose down the area with water at the end of their workday.

On the other side of Bab Zuweila and across Azhar Boulevard, Gamaliyya was also replete with industrial workshops. In Gamaliyya, there was some mechanized carpentry, but most of the industrial workshops specialized in metalworks and especially metal turnery, or *tashgheel maʿaden*, using industrial equipment, and especially lathes, to turn an array of heavy metals of all shapes and sizes into new desired shapes. Large, spinning lathes are so loud and forceful that the ground underneath them feels like it's shaking while the machine is spinning. On central Muʿiz Street—the focus of the state's urban transformation project in Gamaliyya—there were barely any such workshops left during my fieldwork. As I walked deeper into the neighborhood's side alleyways, however, I heard and felt the shaking under my feet. I soon learned it was coming from the metalworks machines scattered around the neighborhood as they spun and turned metal day and night.

According to a UNESCO survey of workshops and storehouses in Cairo's historic core in 2008, industrially mechanized workshops are the rule rather than the exception in both Gamaliyya and Darb El-Ahmar. In Darb El-Ahmar, of the 471 carpentry workshops and storefronts, 445 were mechanized carpentry workshops and only about 20 were workshops specializing in hand-craftsmanship. In Gamaliyya, of the 255 workshops and storefronts that specialized in metals, including curating rare gems, making and selling jewelry, hand-carving metals, and selling metal trinkets to tourists, 128 (about half) were workshops that specialized in industrial metal turning, or *tashgheel maʿaden*, and only about 30 worked in hand-carving metals (not counting jewelry makers). These surveys also indicate that other industrial workshops have made Gamaliyya and Darb El-Ahmar their home. For example, in the two neighborhoods there are about twenty-five workshops that specialize in storing and cutting coal for use by restaurants and coffee shops; another thirty shops specialize in storing and producing flammable chemical products; another thirty workshops specialize in marble production and finishing.[33] The sounds, smells, shaking tremors, and industrial debris had, by the late 2000s, become the dominant sensorium through which Cairenes experienced productive energy in Cairo's historic core.

Mapping Cairo's Industrialization in Time and Space

Although Gamaliyya and Darb El-Ahmar have a long history as neighborhoods of craftsmanship, the sensorium experienced with the rise of mechanized industry only emerged as a powerful presence relatively recently. According to a survey conducted in 1986, of the 212 mechanized "manufacturing enterprises" found in Gamaliyya at the time, about 92 percent of that light industry arrived in the neighborhood between 1970 and 1986, with fewer than 10 of those mechanized workshops having been in operation in 1956 (Meyer 1987, 138–39). Before 1970, most of the craftsmanship was indeed specialized in handmade artisanship. The industrial sensorium that enveloped the area by the 2000s was born out of the break-up of large industry and its deperipheralization within Cairo's geography in the 1970s and 1980s.

Industrialized manufacturing had a history that long predated Nasser's rise to power in the 1950s. Significant efforts had been made to "Egyptianize" such industry since the 1930s, but it remained handicapped during colonial times for a variety of reasons, not least of which was competition with high-quality imports. Nasser was bent on reversing that handicap and embarked on an aggressive campaign that initially focused on building up the country's industrial capacity within an open market environment but then moved toward protectionism in the 1960s coincident with the nationalization campaign described earlier. As Egypt embarked on Import-Substitution-Industrialization (ISI) in 1960, Nasser and his administration famously called for industrializing across all sectors, "from the needle to the rocket" (Waterbury 1983, 81). This initial state-led industrialization campaign materialized in Cairo as a mushrooming of six industrial towns on the city's periphery, "most notably the iron and steel complex in Helwan (inaugurated in 1958) [on the southern periphery of Cairo], the cement factories in Helwan and Tura, and a number of textile and heavy industries in Shubra al-Khayma [on the city's then northern periphery]" (Sims 2010, 51–52). Within industrial towns, the state built considerable mass housing for the factories' workers as the state's industrial five-year plan asserted that the "six towns should be developed as satellite industrial towns, self-contained, with all their public facilities. Failing that it is feared that chaos will spread" (El-Shakry 2006, 84).

Building industrial towns on Cairo's peripheries sat within a larger decentering of Cairo as a city from the state's planning apparatus. As El-Shakry (2006) insightfully demonstrates, Egypt's postcolonial regime had shifted the focus of governance away from the capital and its dense center and toward societal engineering within agricultural communities and satellite industrial towns. In the postcolonial moment, "the city becomes the locus of government, while the countryside becomes the object of governance" (75). Rather than being centered within the state's program as an object of governance, central Cairo straddles along as a site of "benign neglect" (75), and neighborhoods like Darb El-Ahmar, Gamaliyya, and Wust El-Balad become blind spots in governmental planning.

"Benign neglect" and decreased servicing of central neighborhoods worked together with the competition that handicraft artisanship had been facing from manufactured goods for some time, pushing residents away from the historical core and toward jobs and subsidized housing materializing in industrial towns. Even if they didn't leave their homes in the core, many of the neighborhoods' artisans and craftsmen (or their offspring) boarded up their workshops and storehouses and found work within factories or a myriad of new bureaucratic jobs that the postcolonial regime was creating in the capital. Spatially, both neighborhoods once had artisan workshops scattered throughout, mostly as the ground floor to residential buildings. Workshops and storehouses were also clustered in both neighborhoods within market areas and, especially in Gamaliyya, in large buildings, called *wekala* (sing.), that often housed storehouses for raw materials, productive artisan workshops, and consumer-facing shops for the same products in the same building, creating coordinated productive and commercial ecosystems within. The pull of artisans away from these workshops resulted in the widespread vacancy of artisanal workshop and commercial space in the 1950s and 1960s.

The end of Egypt's Nasserist era brought unexpected vitality to the boarded workshops. Nasser's experimentation with ISI, among other socialist programs throughout the 1960s, came to an abrupt end upon his death in 1970. Egypt's defeat during the 1967 war with Israel precipitated a crisis of confidence in Nasser's political program due to "a complex product of both internal ideological and class contradictions within the regime's pursuit of socialism, and external political conflicts" (El-Shakry 2006, 86). Galvanized by that crisis, Nasser's successor, Sadat, worked to overhaul Nasser's socialist and protectionist economic program by adopting the Infitah economic platform that reverted to the dynamics of free market economics. Key among those policies was an opening up to foreign trade and investment and a systemic weakening of the state's control over state-managed public enterprise and, by extension, the country's burgeoning industry.

Gradual privatization and a liberalization of wage and employment regulations within state-owned industry soon crushed the promises of full employment that came with state-led industrialization. While most workers employed in state-owned enterprises did not lose their jobs outright, wage liberalization rendered these jobs less secure and attractive than they had been during the past two decades while opportunities outside the public sector became far more lucrative. At the same time, a coordinated oil embargo across Arab countries in protest of Western support of Israel in the 1973 war skyrocketed oil prices, and oil-rich countries experienced an unprecedented boom. A host of lucrative opportunities opened up in the Gulf for migrant labor from across the region, and Egypt experienced a major surge in remittance income in the 1970s and 1980s. Infitah policies also created many new opportunities at home as trade barriers fell and a new commercial class emerged around import-export middlemen, banking, insurance, and other sectors servicing foreign trade. While scholarship often focuses on this new commercial class as the product of Infitah, little attention is given to how the industrial sector developed at the time.

Tracing the history of the smells and noises of workshop activity in the historical core reveals not a story of industrial decline but of a shift in the scale and geographical terrain of the city's industrial sector. In a post-Infitah Cairo, industry moved from large factory towns on the city's periphery into the city's historical center and newly formed informal neighborhoods on its outskirts. Within the core, mechanized industrial workshops, working with light rather than heavy machinery and employing four to ten rather than hundreds of workers, moved into the workshops and storehouses, or *wekalat* (pl.), that had been boarded up throughout the interwar period. By the mid-1980s, they had become a force to be reckoned with. Many workers trained in state-owned factories and in the Gulf moved back to the neighborhoods where they had been raised in the historical core and, in some cases, to the actual workshop spaces owned by their families that had remained idle for decades. According to one study, more than 85 percent of the people operating and working in mechanized workshops had been born there, and at least 60 percent of them continued to live in the historical core (Meyer 1987, 143). I encountered several people that lived such journeys during my fieldwork. For example, the coppersmith Hamed, who had been raised in the Gamaliyya district, received a university education and worked in a chemical factory on the city's periphery during Nasser's reign only to return to Gamaliyya to operate his family's metal workshop in the aftermath of Infitah. Others relied on savings from remittances as labor migrants to build upon family resources or start workshops from scratch in vacant spaces. The stickiness of Cairenes' roots in the city and the unique spatial organization of commercial and workshop spaces—especially through *wekalat*, which allowed coordinated production and distribution—had deperipheralized industry and its vibrant sensorium away from peripheral factory towns and into the city's center.

Industry and the Fallacies of "Informality" Studies

The bursting of industrial vibrancy and its sensorium onto the historical core was never celebrated as an industrial boon for the country as Nasser's industrialization campaign had been. Instead, the mechanized workshops that saturated Gamaliyya and Darb El-Ahmar were quickly subsumed by both academics and practitioners within the larger phenomenon of "informality" that soon became one of the main lenses through which Cairo was understood. Lumped together with informal housing, street vending, rotating savings associations, and many other informal modes of existence in the city, mechanized industry was soon either vilified for the chaos its unregulated existence created or couched as a bare survival mechanism. Even when the development industry that followed structural adjustment into Egypt in the 1990s started framing the informal sector as an invaluable entrepreneurial space, it was framed as sitting on "dead capital" that lost its entrepreneurial potential by working outside the realm of formal circuits of capital and market rationales as well as in the wrong geographies of the city.[34]

Dismissed as mere survival mechanisms burying the country's productive capacities within the vagaries of informality, neither state nor nonstate authoritative actors in Cairo were framing mechanized workshops as sources of material, symbolic, or communal value. Meanwhile, the heritage industry arrived right as mechanized industry was problematized within the city's *crisis* with informality. When the international heritage industry and its funding attracted a lot of attention to the plight of Cairo's historical core in the aftermath of the 1992 earthquake and the Egyptian government followed suit—commissioning the Ministry of Culture's heritage preservation project in Gamaliyya, for example (chapter 5)—the neighborhood's mechanized workshops were presented as bastions of *decay* rather than productive energy. Stripping workshops down to the sensoria they produced, the conservationists and architects working with the state's heritage preservation project singled mechanized workshops out as one of the main sources of the neighborhood's physical deterioration. Moushira, one of the project's directors, linked that sensorium to degeneration in our conversation, saying:

> The sawdust [from carpentry] has bad effects [on the monuments]... because it turns into a very soft powder that clings to and stains the facades [of the monuments] completely. And, when it combines with car exhaust, it absorbs the exhaust and creates a layer of dirt on the [monuments'] stones. [Moreover], the machinery they use like rolling machines [*darfallah*] is heavy machinery that produces intense vibrations that adversely affect the monument's structural soundness. So, we try to distance these activities from the monuments.[35]

Guided solely by the sensoria emanating from workshops, without affording for the possibility that workshops may be valued along other axes, Moushira explained that all mechanized workshops would need to change their activity (*taghyeer el nashat*) as part of the project's plan. She explained her team's general philosophy toward these workshops, saying:

> We have activities such as trading in copper and aluminum. Some stores produce and sell handcrafted products that we protect and keep [in the neighborhood], but others trade in heavy metals in kilos. How is the tourist going to benefit from that?... And there are also the workshops like those specialized in carpentry. How will that benefit the tourist? In no way at all. So we try to negotiate with them to change their activities in ways that would be in closer alignment with the area's touristic atmosphere.[36]

For Moushira and her team, mechanized workshops produced neither the sensoria nor the goods suited for a historical neighborhood with heritage being conserved to attract tourists to the city.[37]

The hegemonic acceptance of "informality" as the main lens through which Cairo's development was to be understood from the 1990s onward presented mechanized workshops as yet another realm of unregulated chaos or, at best, mere survival, burying their potential productivity under layers of opaque informality. With the arrival of a heritage industry working to circumscribe particular sensorial experiences—meant to protect monuments and attract tourism—as the ideal, mechanized workshops that were already shrouded in the opacity of informality were turned into active agents of the neighborhood's decline as a built environment, lived space, and property market. Framing mechanized workshops as agents of decay not only dismissed the possible productive energies of the sector and how it may be valued in a generalized sense, it also masked the specific circuits that directly connected these workshops to Nasser's industrialization program. Many of these workshops' owners and workers had been trained in Nasser's factories and had built the workshops using machine parts from dismantled factories. It hid the politics of celebrating Nasser's industrialization program so valiantly only to turn around and vilify the manufacturing production that it had spurred as industry stubbornly followed workers' roots from peripheral factory towns and back into the city's center.

Car Sensoria: Transport Infrastructures and the Rise of the Construction Industry

Alongside the sounds and smells of industrial workshops, Cairenes' experiences of the city's center followed the trajectory of automobiles in and out of their neighborhoods and the sensoria they evoked. While Cairo had seen a burst in the construction of transit infrastructures (and especially tramways) in the interwar period, the postcolonial state invested little in upgrading or building new transit infrastructures for several decades. As Nasser kept his governmental gaze fixed on rural and industrial planning rather than city governance, transit infrastructures were propelled by sheer inertia as their operators muddled along, allowing them to absorb as much of the city's growing population as possible despite teetering on collapse. With the Infitah, Sadat's regime slowly recentered its gaze on urban governance by putting enterprise ahead of infrastructure. It was not until 1987 that the state invested in a major transit infrastructure, when the north-south underground metro line was finally opened (Sims 2010, 233).

In response to that neglect, two types of vehicles started to fill the transit vacuum of ailing tramways and an underserviced bus system: the microbus and the private car. In the early 1970s, an enterprising industry developed around privately run microbuses that seated eleven to fourteen people, and it quickly developed a shared system of routes that nimbly navigated dense, formal and informal areas of the city inaccessible to large buses. The microbuses' routes and fares involved no state coordination whatsoever. It soon became the fastest-growing mode of shared transit in the city, and by 1998 it accounted for roughly 28 percent of all vehicular trips in greater Cairo and a full half of all public and private shared transport, with 650 known routes (Sims 2010, 230). Similarly, Cairo saw an explosion in the number of private cars traveling its streets. Between 1971 and 1998, the percentage of vehicular trips made by private car (in comparison to all other modes of transit) more than doubled, from 7 percent to 20 percent (Sims 2010, 235), as the city's population was growing exponentially. These trends have continued unabated. With the tramway declining to becoming almost defunct and the metro serving only one geographical axis in the city, most Cairenes are riding buses, microbuses, private taxis, or private cars on the city's overly congested roads.

Rather than investing in an expansion of Cairo's public overground and underground transit infrastructures, the government concentrated their efforts on making more space for cars to travel and on building vehicular bridges, flyovers, and tunnels all over the city. Sadat started this trend modestly by commissioning the 6th of October Bridge and the flyovers connected to it, which took Cairenes over street traffic across a northeast-southwest axis of the formal city. During Hosni Mubarak's reign (Sadat's successor from 1981 to 2011), the government embarked on a frenzy of construction of road networks around Cairo. The frenzy grew visible across Cairo while the government failed to meet Egyptians' expectations on so many other fronts, and Mubarak's regime earned itself the nickname the "government of tunnels and bridges" (*anfaq we kabary*). Among the projects that transformed the city's landscape in the 1980s and into the 2000s were the 26th of July Bridge, connecting Wust El-Balad to the city's western expansions on the Nile and across it; the city's first ring road; and the Azhar Tunnel, dug under Azhar Boulevard, dissecting the historical core to connect the edge of the northeastern formal city to Wust El-Balad.

While the government's focus on road infrastructures rather than an expansion of public transit has often been criticized through the lens of bad governance and a lack of vision, that focus was not incidental or haphazard. The private corporations building these roads and flooding the country's markets with automobiles were a central faction within Mubarak's ruling regime. Throughout the 1980s and 1990s, Mubarak had been courting a number of large-scale capitalists as allies. They became the beneficiaries of the privatization campaigns meant to reverse Nasser's nationalizations, and they regularly "won" government bids for infrastructure projects. Some of them, such as Ezz Steel, a conglomerate owned by businessman Ahmed Ezz, secured monopolistic rights in the market. That capitalist group was heavily concentrated in industries around the construction and real estate development industries as well as car imports. Among those favored conglomerates were the construction conglomerate Arab Contractors (Osman Ahmed Osman and Co.); Ezz Steel; Orascom Construction PLC, in telecom, construction, and tourism; the Bahgat Group, in construction and real estate; the Mansour Group, which became the world's largest distributor of GM cars and the sole distributor of Caterpillar construction vehicles in the Middle East and East/West Africa; Ghabbour Auto; and the Mohamed Mahmoud Sons Group, which includes distribution company MTI.[38] As Timothy Mitchell (2002) describes, "these family-owned enterprise networks typically began as construction companies or import/export agents ... most expanded subsequently into tourism, real estate, food and beverages, and computer and internet services" (282–83). With these conglomerates heavily concentrated in construction as their foundational business and with important players such as the Ghabbour and Mansour groups heavily invested in cars, the regime's economic base was ardently pushing toward vehicle-focused infrastructure. While initially Mubarak balanced between the clout of this business arm and the military within his regime, that balance tipped in favor of the business arm with the rise of Mubarak's son Gamal into a prominent position in the regime as leader of its political party, the National Democratic Party (NDP). With Gamal's political ascendance, many of the same conglomerates took on visible political positions in the party and in ministerial roles throughout the late 2000s. The regime's focus on infrastructural work and facilitating real estate development in far-flung suburban complexes around the city—which would connect to the city through even more extensive roads—was deliberately orchestrated through this business-ruling alliance and not a haphazard product of bad planning.

Cairo's downtown and historical core sat at the epicenter of the regime's frenzied bridge and tunnel building, at least into the mid-2000s, and each of these projects would significantly shift Cairenes' sensorial experiences of car congestion. Two of the projects that left a large imprint on the city center were the 6th of October Bridge inaugurated in 1996[39] and the Azhar Tunnel inaugurated in 2001.[40] Initially the bridge worked (together with existing bridges like the 26th of July flyover) to lighten congestion as traffic moved along the city's west-east axis and across the Nile, but they also concentrated traffic downtown as one of the main flyovers feeding cars onto the bridges landed right onto Tahrir Square. This flyover was also the closest one to the historical core, and much traffic traveled through Azhar and Muski Boulevards to connect to the bridges via Tahrir Square. Throughout the 1990s, both Wust El-Balad and the historical core saw unprecedented congestion as their main boulevards became feeders for the city's largest bridge.

The Azhar Tunnel transformed that dynamic dramatically as it eased traffic going through the historical core from the city's western zones, and Azhar and Muski Boulevards now strictly serviced those traveling to and from the center. While easing congestion, it magnified Wust El-Balad's vehicular woes. Now the traffic diverted into the tunnel came out right in the heart of Wust El-Balad by Opera Square, bringing the honking and exhaust that had plagued the outskirts of Wust El-Balad deep into the neighborhood. The honking, swearing, music, and fumes coming from the cars were not the only additions that came to the neighborhood with the Azhar Tunnel. Alongside the slow-moving vehicles grew a steady contingent of street vendors who made use of their position close to Wust El-Balad's stores (as suppliers) and frustrated drivers (as consumers).

Initially the street vendors and their hawking sounds were flexible and mobile around the vehicles, ready to scatter at the arrival of the police. After the large-scale withdrawal of police forces from Cairo's streets in the aftermath of the 2011 revolution, street vendors set up an entire marketplace around the vehicles traversing Wust El-Balad—on the sidewalks and into the streets themselves. The vendors sold from standing stalls elaborately laden with a large amount of merchandise that transformed into an inflexible physical structure that was no longer vulnerable to the piecemeal policing strategies that had previously constrained vending. It took nothing short of a very visible, concerted, and controversial violent assault on that street vending marketplace to dismantle its hardened physical infrastructure, a full four years after the revolution.[41]

Eventually, it was not a new infrastructural project physically located downtown that transformed the area's experience with congestion but the slow and gradual diversion of a portion of Cairo's traffic away from the center and onto its ring roads. As more and more vehicle-owning upper-class Cairenes moved to the burgeoning suburban development on the city's eastern and western flanks, and multinational corporations and educational infrastructures followed suit, the ring roads connecting those suburbs absorbed a lot of traffic from those upper-middle-class car owners. Vehicle congestion is still a major feature of Wust El-Balad's sensorium, but it is no longer accelerating at the same rate as the city's population and vehicle ownership growth rates.

Meanwhile, in 2008, the state pedestrianized Gamaliyya's arterial Muʿiz Street and all alleyways feeding into it. The many planners I talked to described how pedestrianization was essential to the heritage conservation underway in the neighborhood, giving tourists the space and freedom to explore the neighborhood without competing with vehicles for space within its narrow passageways. More urgently, they argued—as Moushira has—that vehicle exhaust often combines with the residue flying out from workshops to produce a damaging layer of soot on monuments. Yet, not surprisingly, pedestrianization wasn't entirely welcome in the neighborhood. In particular, many a workshop and store owner complained to me that it restricted cargo traffic to the wee hours of the morning, vastly complicating the flexibility of their businesses and daily work rhythms.

To bring it all together, one of Gamaliyya's store owners, Malek, described his own experience of the neighborhood's sensorium and how he saw various factors shaping it:

> Years ago the dust would descend on us here from the Darassa hill, which has since been converted into the Azhar Park. The dust would fall on us and on the Hussein Hospital in large quantities . . . and then, with the number of cars passing through here and the large number of working workshops, there was so much environmental pollution here to the point that there would come times when we couldn't breathe and we would be breathing in dust. So, they would always say keep sprinkling water like our old tradition . . . to keep the dust down and wash our faces. . . . And then of course the situation got milder when a lot of the workshops were closed down and the [Azhar] tunnel that was built decreased a lot of the car exhaust in the area, and the [Azhar] park that was created also decreased the pollution in the area quite a bit.[42]

Through this account, Malek demonstrates a striking awareness of his environment and the many ecologies shaping his everyday sensorial experiences. It also crystallizes the ways in which the complicated politics that went into the closure of workshops, the tunnel's construction, the creation of Azhar Park, and the area's pedestrianization can often be obscured through a *crisis* discourse that collapses Cairo's lived realities and their politics down to a main singular issue—such as pollution—circulated and internalized by Cairenes, not to mention the development and planning agencies daily shaping the fate of the city.

Conclusion

When a new capitalist class concentrated in the construction industry emerged as a power center within Egypt's ruling coalition, it initially used its clout to gain exclusive rights to the many infrastructural projects the state commissioned in Cairo throughout the 1970s and 1980s. By the 1990s, most of those conglomerates had become heavily invested in real estate development, and they pushed for the state to extend the initial exceptions from rent control that Sadat's regime had made for specific developers into a more general rule. Through that push was born the 1996 law that abolished rent control for any rental contracts signed after that date (*el'eigar el gedeed*) while maintaining rent control for already existing contracts. With most of the development benefiting from the 1996 law mushrooming into peripheral suburbs or "desert cities" around Cairo—on land owned by the state (more specifically, the military) and granted to these conglomerates at negligible prices[43]—the formal neighborhoods of central Cairo mostly stayed out of developers' orbits.

While many developers were tied up in "desert cities," the 1996 laws created new dynamics for landlords, tenants, and international donors arriving in Egypt with the heritage and development industries in the city's center. Multiple spatial-material-affective processes, including the lived logistics of a half century of rent control, the sparking and mourning (then and now) of a downtown fire in the wake of entangled colonialism, an earthquake mismanaged, the circuiting of a dismantled industry back to the historical core, and the infrastructural channeling of vehicle traffic into downtown produced an environment lived and/or represented as "decaying" and "collapsing." Sources for that "decay" were politicized to marginalize some actors, such as industrial workshops, and distract from state failings, such as ailing infrastructures or an unmanaged earthquake. Making the decay *visible* through, say, international media attention around the 1992 earthquake also brought Cairo a lot of funding. It especially attracted an international heritage industry to the historical core, such as the AKTC project in Darb El-Ahmar and the state's own project to restore Gamaliyya. Navigating Cairo's spatial-material-affective layers also produced Cairenes' varying experiences with "rootedness" in the city's center. For example, an environmental transformation that enabled the city's explosion outside of the historic core produced a remarkably rooted rather than itinerant rural migrant class. Cairenes' rootedness also then channeled a dismantled industrial project into the city's core.

Intervening in this environment, the 1996 law both complicated and facilitated transformative projects. As related through Umm Mustafa's building, desperate landlords now wanted to claim any restoration work by international donors as collapse to annul the very rental contracts those donors saw as the guarantors of low-income housing. On the other hand, the law ensured that more property owners saw potential sources of rental income in personal homes/workshops previously "not worth" the investment that rehabilitation demanded. By the mid-2000s, the city's highly capitalized developers also started to turn their gaze back to the city's center. Following the effervescence of a cultural scene in central Cairo—with venues such as the Sawy Culture Wheel (Saʾeyet El Sawy), Rawabet Theater, Darb 1718, and Zawya Cinema sprouting in neighborhoods like Wust El-Balad, Zamalek, and the historic core—some developers saw how luxury real estate within the formal, if ailing, zone could be attractive to a younger generation of wealthy residents. Moreover, transformational restoration work was helping dust off the center's "decay," ironically right as some of those projects were working to safeguard low-income housing in the city. As large-scale developers turned to the city's center, they needed access to clusters of property to convert into luxury rentals. One of the more ambitious developers, the Ismailia Consortium, sought out more than twenty-five *ʿemarat Wust El-Balad*, with over one thousand units total. Ambitious as it was, the consortium was able to acquire those buildings without any direct involvement from the state. With the capital they fundraised from the Sawiris family and several Gulf investors, they were able to buy up each and every one of the buildings at a fraction of their likely "market value." They then paid key money to most of the tenants with rent-controlled contracts, who then vacated the buildings. Processes involving Nasser's nationalization campaigns, the logistics of decades of rent control, complicated inheritance networks, the 1992 earthquake, and transport infrastructures that diverted cars, street vendors, and their sensoria downtown came together to drive owners to see their property as material and emotional burdens that they were happy to off-load to the first buyer rather than some of the most iconic and valuable property in Cairo. When the 1996 law reversed rent control, it incentivized heavily capitalized developers to see an opportunity and slowly but surely transfer a lot of property from one class to another.

Unlike the violent expropriation unfolding in Turkey (chapter 2), the transfer of property to Egypt's rising class of developers was not violently forced, nor was it coordinated by the state. It materialized (and continues to do so) gradually, subtly, and in spurts, but that does not deny that a wholesale transfer of property and wealth was enabled in Cairo by the 1996 law. Because the heavy hand of the state is not visibly orchestrating this wholesale transfer, it is easy to write off the property takeover that the Ismailia Consortium pulled off in Wust El-Balad as simply the dynamism of a healthy property market. Reading the 1996 law as intervening into a property terrain shaped by layers of spatial-material transformations and accompanying affective meaning-making exposes violent vulnerabilities that the 1996 law produced and the dispossessions of the propertied and tenant classes it enabled in the specific context of Cairo's city center. The violence of the abstractions manufactured through legal infrastructures, and especially property rights regimes,[44] is eloquently described by Timothy Mitchell (2002):

> The principle of abstraction on which the order of law depends can be generated only as the difference between order and violence, the ideal and the actual, the universal and the exceptional. But the violent, the actual, and the exceptional—all of which the law denounces and excludes, ruptures itself from and supersedes—are never gone. They make possible the rupture, the denunciation, and the order. They are the condition of its possibility. (79)

In unmasking the violence underpinning the work of the "market" that allowed the Ismailia Consortium to buy up so many of Wust El-Balad's jewels and unearthing the layers of Cairo's spatial-material-affective transformation served to unmask the making and unmaking of class in the city. It mapped out how these processes came together to transform what it meant to be Cairo's propertied or tenant classes as a lived and symbolic formation throughout the last half century.

Istanbul 2

KEMAL BEY LIVES IN A NARROW THREE-STORY, one-family brick building built in 1913 in the historical neighborhood of Fener in Istanbul. The building is one street in from the arterial boulevard that separates the neighborhood from the Golden Horn waterway. Kemal Bey and his family "bought" the building from a Greek family in 1973, soon after they moved to Istanbul from a small village in Turkey's Black Sea region.[1] When he first moved to Istanbul, Kemal Bey worked as a teacher and played in an amateur football league before becoming a football coach for local teams in Istanbul. He is now retired and living on a state pension.

The building's façade is adorned with a *cumba* (pronounced jumba), a large, decorated protruding window iconic of Istanbul's older wooden urban fabric. Above the *cumba* sits a small balcony on the third floor overlooking the street, where one or two chairs could fit for street watching. There is room for a small store or office space on the ground floor. Unlike the rest of the building, the ground floor is built in concrete rather than brick. Kemal Bey explained to me that the ground floor had originally been constructed from wood, as were most buildings in that neighborhood, but that the wood was consumed in a fire in 1978 that damaged the ground floor but left the rest of the building untouched. Because he could not afford to rebuild the ground floor in the same expensive wood, he rebuilt it in reinforced concrete. When we went out on the third-floor terrace protruding from the building's back we saw that the home had a stunning view, or *manzara*, of the Golden Horn and the city (figure 2.1).[2] I was dumbfounded by the view. How did a public school teacher who had just migrated from a small village in the Black Sea region come to own a three-story home with such a priceless view and iconic architecture in the heart of the historic city?

I was not alone in asking that question. At the turn of the millennium, Kemal Bey's building got a lot of attention. First, Kemal Bey received several offers from real estate brokers hoping to buy his home. The price was never right, and he barely entertained these offers because the value he placed on being able to sit on his terrace while sipping his tea and taking in the Golden Horn far outweighed any of these offers. Then, in the early 2000s, he was offered, and accepted, a grant by the European Union (EU) to fully restore his building to its original historical design as part of a neighborhood rehabilitation program (see chapter 3).

After enjoying his newly restored home for a few years, in 2009, Kemal Bey found himself in the midst of a panicked neighborhood campaign to protest the state's declaration of Fener and its adjacent neighborhood, Balat, as an urban-renewal zone according to the Renewal and Preservation Law no. 5366 of 2005. According to the law, neighborhoods decreed "renewal zones" in Istanbul's historical center would be "renewed and preserved" wholesale either by a state agency or a public-private partnership. To enable these wholesale renewal projects, the law empowered state authorities to condemn and forcibly vacate private property as an act of *acil kamulaştırma* or "emergency nationalization" when the redevelopment necessitated it. Before Fener-Balat, the state had declared the two other neighborhoods studied in this book, Sulukule and Tarlabaşı, renewal zones, and in both neighborhoods, property had been forcibly "nationalized" by the state. In Tarlabaşı, 41 percent of property owners forcibly lost rights to their private property through emergency nationalization.[3] Eventually, the neighborhood was entirely evacuated of its residents by the summer of 2012 (figure 2.2) and razed to the ground by the summer of 2015 (figure 2.3). Sulukule was similarly vacated and razed to the ground. It was then redeveloped by the state's Mass Housing Authority (TOKİ) in the image of an American-suburban complex with rows of identical, prefabricated three- to four-story apartment buildings by 2012 (figure 2.4). Seeing the fate of the neighborhoods that had come before them, Kemal Bey and his neighbors organized a neighborhood association and fought tooth

Figure 2.1. The view from Kemal Bey's home in Fener, Istanbul. Source: author, May 2012.

Figure 2.2. Evacuated, pillaged, and burned buildings in Tarlabaşı neighborhood in Istanbul after the neighborhood was declared a renewal zone. Source: author, April 2012.

Figure 2.3. Demolished buildings in Tarlabaşı neighborhood.
Source: author, July 2015.

and nail, through media campaigns and legal battles, to overturn the state's declaration of the neighborhood as a renewal zone prone to such forcible expropriation. As Kemal Bey and his neighbors were fighting for their neighborhood and rights to their property, the state intensified its assault on private property rights. In May 2012, the parliament, with majority representation from the Justice and Development Party (Adalet ve Kalkınma Partisi, or AKP), passed the *Afet Yasası* or Disaster Law that allowed state assessors to "emergency nationalize" and redevelop any building deemed unsafe in the event of an earthquake. With that expansion, Istanbul's private property regime was under attack and anyone was susceptible to losing rights to their property.

Property transfers in an age of neoliberalization were far more overtly violent in Istanbul than in Cairo. This chapter seeks to trace the processes that illuminate both *why* the Turkish state resorts to forced expropriation when violence is riskier than in Egypt, in a context where the regime relies almost entirely on elections for its political survival, and *how* the regime builds upon longue-durée transformations in the city to enable and normalize such violence despite the electoral risk. The key to understanding why the state resorts to violence, even though it is politically riskier, lies in comparing how

Figure 2.4. Sulukule neighborhood after demolition of the old neighborhood and construction of new development. Source: author, July 2012.

owners *value* their property in zones of affordable housing in Cairo and Istanbul. Whereas owners of (mostly rent-controlled) affordable housing in Cairo's city center saw their property as captive to their tenants and a financial and emotional burden, the owners of affordable housing in Istanbul's city center aspirationally saw the value of their property as boundless. In Istanbul, rural migrants who became the workforce powering the city's industrialization starting in the 1950s would become the owners—rather than tenants—of much of the city's core urban fabric. They would come to value these buildings both as their homes and their most prized possessions. Moreover, as the city promised a real estate boom with its transformation into a global hub, they saw their property's value limitlessly increasing with that boom. Nothing short of overt violence could pry these buildings away from their owners before they saw their buildings realize their potential as lucrative property in the central districts of a "global" Istanbul. In the first half of the chapter, I outline how rural migrants like Kemal Bey came to own some of the city's most lucrative property and their *manzaras*. As in Cairo, spatial-material-affective transformations in the city shaped the formation of the city's classes and the struggles that manifested among them over time.

The first half of the chapter is thus organized around three historical epochs characterized by major shifts in how Istanbul as a city was positioned vis à vis the country's political-economic center: (1) peripheralization, (2) reorientation into a regional industrial hub, and (3) recentering into a global hub. Within each of those epochs, I explain how spatial-material-affective processes similar to those explored in Cairo produced a terrain of prime real estate owned by rural migrants clustered into neighborhoods organized around their village and kin networks. These similar processes include: the geopolitics of Ottoman defeat in World War I; the affective experience of the city as a space of melancholy (or *hüzün*); anti-minority violence and exodus; industrialization and its sensorial experiences; holistic infrastructural programs that reoriented the city from an imperial center into a regional industrial hub and then again into a global hub; and electioneering dynamics.

The second half of the chapter delves into *how* the AKP's ruling regime builds upon these longue-durée processes to enable the violent transfer of property and normalize those practices as "necessary" for the public good rather than an infringement on citizen rights. I do so by focusing on three case studies as microcosms for seeing how city-wide processes and a politics of "urban crisis" became entwined with neighborhood-specific processes and legal maneuvers to enable dispossession. The three case studies follow the implementation of the Renewal and Preservation Law in Sulukule and Tarlabaşı and the making of the Disaster Law by tracing a struggle over the city's "morality" and its entanglement in expropriation in Sulukule, the vagaries of infrastructural work in Tarlabaşı, and the unnaturalness of fire and earthquake disasters in Istanbul and how they feed into the Disaster Law.

Peripheralization

Geopolitics: A Defeated Empire and Republican Isolationism

Istanbul underwent a dramatic *peripheralization* as it became embroiled in the geopolitical struggles of World War I that would define modern-day Turkey, with long-lasting ramifications for its contemporary urban fabric. Istanbul had been the seat of the Ottoman Empire since 1453. As such, the city had long housed the empire's political and economic elite. Moreover, as a port city, Istanbul had long attracted a foreign merchant class. This merchant class, as in Cairo, became ever more visible in Istanbul's fabric as the Ottoman Empire signed an increasing number of capitulation agreements with

Western powers in the eighteenth and nineteenth centuries that gave some non-Muslim and foreign merchant communities immunity from Ottoman laws, as they claimed status as financial and trade intermediaries. More pronounced than in Cairo, however, by the turn of the twentieth century, foreign and non-Muslim merchant communities had come to constitute the majority of Istanbul's residents (Keyder 1999, 10).

When the Turkish Republic was formed in 1923, its leader Mustafa Kemal Atatürk sought to distance the new Republic from the Ottoman Empire that preceded it. Barely escaping colonial occupation with the empire's demise and defeat in World War I, Atatürk believed that the survival of the nascent Republic depended on dissociating it from both the ideological underpinnings and geopolitical vulnerabilities of the defeated empire. Istanbul was embroiled in both facets of that distancing. As the seat of the empire, Istanbul was seen as an unmistakable symbol of the empire and its doomed Islamic-imperial ideology. Geostrategically, Atatürk now saw Istanbul's geography as a port city with a foreign or non-Muslim merchant class of doubted loyalty and direct access to Western powers as a vulnerability rather than an asset. In that vein, "he stated that Istanbul's occupation [in World War I] showed that the seat of government should be located in a place out of reach of enemy armies" (Gül 2009, 86). Istanbul was seen as a geopolitical Achilles' heel for the nascent Republic, and Atatürk worked to actively peripheralize the city in the Republic's political geography.

One of the first of Atatürk's decrees in founding the Turkish Republic was to create a new capital in the small town of Ankara, with a mere population of twenty-five thousand at the time (Gül 2009, 86), in the geographical center of Anatolia and around five hundred kilometers away from Istanbul. To cement the idea that Istanbul was being peripheralized and replaced as the country's political and economic center, "Atatürk did not visit Istanbul [after his ascent to power in 1923] until 1927, although he had toured the entire Anatolian region and passed through the Bosphorous [that runs through Istanbul] in the preceding years" (Gül 2009, 88). In the span of five years, Istanbul was actively peripheralized from the center of an empire to a marginal outpost of a nascent Anatolian Republic.

The peripheralization of Istanbul had several immediate ramifications on the city's urban fabric. With the movement of the center of government to Ankara, many of the country's political and intellectual elite moved to Ankara from Istanbul, draining it of the clout that surrounded that elite. The peripheralization of Istanbul had an even more dramatic impact on its economic environment. Once in power, Atatürk espoused étatism or state-led economic development as one of the principles of the Republic that favored a Muslim-majority economic elite over the non-Muslim communities that had once dominated Turkey's commercial spheres.[4] The new economic elite was now based in Ankara around the government's center and the state-led industrialization project it promoted and subsidized. Istanbul's coastal and economically strategic location as a port was no longer as important at a time when the state embarked on a fairly insular industrialization campaign. The non-Muslim merchants who had once thrived in Istanbul saw themselves become increasingly marginalized from the country's economy, and many of them left Istanbul in search of more hospitable environments outside Turkey. Moreover, some of Istanbul's non-Muslim communities left because of the population exchanges orchestrated after World War I. Through the Treaty of Lausanne, Atatürk had negotiated population exchanges of most non-Muslim populations that still resided in Turkey after World War I and the horrific violence that befell some of these communities, especially the Armenian Genocide. Istanbul's non-Muslim communities were exempt from these population exchanges, but some of the non-Muslims that did reside in Istanbul had a hard time proving that they were in fact *établis* with proven residence in the city before the war and were forced to leave Istanbul and Turkey as part of the exchanges. As a result, after having been a majority in the city at the turn of the twentieth century, the city's non-Muslim population declined from around four hundred fifty thousand in 1914 to almost half at two hundred forty thousand by 1927. Overall, as the city's Muslim and non-Muslim political and economic elite left the city, Istanbul experienced an unprecedented decrease in its population from 1.2 million people at the turn of the twentieth century to a meager seven hundred thousand by 1927 (Keyder 1999, 10–11).

While Istanbul as a whole was affected by this exodus, two of the three neighborhoods I study in this book, Fener-Balat and Tarlabaşı, were especially affected by this exodus, as they were both home to mostly non-Muslim resident and foreign communities. The Fener and Balat neighborhoods on the Golden Horn (amalgamated into one district by the EU's project) have long histories as home to non-Muslim communities. Balat had been known as one of two districts in the city (alongside Hasköy) where its Jewish community had clustered for centuries. Fener became home to the Greek Orthodox patriarchate after the fall of Constantinople in 1453 and became the city's main district for the Greek community (Eldem, Goffman, and Masters 1999, 152). The elevation of many of the city's non-Muslim and foreign residents into the city's economic elite was reflected in its changing topography, particularly the construction of the Pera district. The Pera district developed adjacent to the financial artery of the city, which developed around contemporary Istiklal Boulevard, with the thickening of financial and trade ties between Ottoman and Western partners. It was constructed to cater to the city's growing non-Muslim elite after its neighboring Galata neighborhood had been oversaturated as their first port of call. With the construction of Pera, many of the city's upwardly mobile non-Muslims moved from the Golden Horn into the Pera district, creating clear socioeconomic demarcations between the newly minted elite of Pera and Galata and the middle-lower-income non-Muslim communities in neighborhoods like Fener and Balat (Eldem, Goffman, and Masters 1999, 204). Squarely within nineteenth-century Pera sits the contemporary Tarlabaşı neighborhood, where the majority of residents have been forcibly evacuated from their homes in the past decade.

As the city witnessed an unprecedented demographic decline, it was also peripheralized within the country's planning agenda, without any formal planning efforts made in the city until after World War II (Gül 2009, ch. 4). Moreover, as it was marginalized from early Republican modernist planning schemes, Istanbul's "wooden fabric" was left to decay as fires consumed older neighborhoods (unpacked further below), and the legendary wooden houses on Istanbul's waterfront that were once the residences of the country's elite were used as coal storehouses (Akcan 2012, 102). Atatürk's geopolitical maneuvering transformed the city's demography, planning initiatives, and care for its built environment in ways that would irreversibly shape the property terrain upon which neoliberal market-making projects are unfolding in contemporary Istanbul.

Affect: Peripheralization and an Irritable Melancholy

Istanbul's peripheralization did not just manifest in materially demographic or physical senses. The affective experience of the city's peripheralization also produced processes of meaning-making that would have long-lasting effects on its contemporary property terrain. A peripheralized Istanbul was beset with an affective experience of *hüzün*, a melancholy that produced an irritability between residents and their built environment that would ultimately shape how property is valued today. As Orhan Pamuk popularized in his 2006 literary work *Istanbul: Memories and the City*, "In the last one hundred fifty years (1850–2000) [as the Ottoman Empire began its decline], I have no doubt that not only has *hüzün* ruled over Istanbul but that it has spread to its surrounding areas" (210). Such *hüzün* is not a solitary melancholy that individuals experience alone, "but the *hüzün* of Istanbul is something the entire city feels together and affirms as one" (95).

Pamuk's description insinuates *hüzün* as a natural by-product of defeat, but such melancholy was actively invested into Istanbul's urban environment as a political movement to protest the country's route to modernization under Atatürk. Esra Akcan (2012) incisively argues that "the official decay of the city produced a literature of *resistant* melancholy among early Republican writers and architects, who portrayed İstanbul as the last remnant of a lost civilization" (102, emphasis added). As Akcan describes, an entire genre of literary writing developed in the 1930s and 1940s that revolved around depicting Istanbul as a city in melancholy that avidly chronicled its decaying and disappearing urban fabric, such as Reşat Ekrem Koçu's *İstanbul Ansiklopedisi* (Encyclopedia of Istanbul) published between 1944 and 1951 (Akcan 2012, 116), as lamentation for a lost civilization as well as Istanbul's marginalization from a modernizing project.

Although one could well argue that the marginalized and decaying city naturally produced an affect of *hüzün*, I agree with Akcan that these literary writers actively invested the city's materiality with a melancholic affect to resist Atatürk's work to erase the country's past en route to modernization. Nonetheless, these writers struggled with the tensions of modernization, both admiring modernization's ideals and harboring anxieties about occupying an "inferior" position vis à vis the West as they pursued it. These sentiments ring out through writings such as Ahmet Hamdi Tanpınar's 1946 novel *Mahur Beste*:

> What you call civilization resembles this old mansion.... Then, there comes a moment when the mansion burns down.... Now you can try to make something out of this trash as much as you like, you can love our old songs and our old world, live attached to it as you like, but once the magical breath has vanished, what can possibly come out of this wasteland? The whole of İstanbul ... seemed to her to share the fate of this orphan whose secret was just disclosed. The Orient was dead [*Şark ölmüştü*]. (Akcan 2012, 103)

It's the mansion and its materiality that best captures the tensions of modernization for Tanpınar. Similarly, the Bosporus (the strait connecting the Sea of Marmara and the Black Sea) was instilled with that affect when Abdülhak Şinasi Hisar wrote,

> The Bosphorous has an effective and melancholic beauty like a full moon.... I cannot believe this past has been wasted.... The Bosphorous is the most beautiful part of the unmatched İstanbul, and yet, like all subtle and gracious things, it has a sad beauty [*mahsun bir güzellik*]. (Akcan 2012, 114)

As a melancholic Istanbul was deployed to politically resist Atatürk's route to modernization, it also became a material landscape through which that movement grappled with the complicated relationship it had with modernization.

The peripheralization of the city from central economic and political networks certainly decreased Istanbul's attractiveness to many of its property owners, but I argue that an affective experience of the city's materiality as a melancholic space produced a subjective experience of loss and peripheralization in everyday life in ways that go beyond a simple rational calculation of interests. Melancholy evokes an "irritability" exerted by the environment on its inhabitants, such as that incisively described by Yael Navaro-Yashin (2012) in her study of postwar Northern Cyprus. There, she describes the postwar phantoms Northern Cypriots lived with as they occupied homes abandoned by Greek Cypriots during the war and the hauntings they produced. She argues that these residents experienced "irritability as a disresonating feeling produced by environments that harbor phantoms" (20). The loss of civilization and the political struggle around modernization as a project to erase that past may not evoke the same phantoms as the Cypriot War, but the civilizational struggles and phantoms evoked by an environment permeated with melancholy produces a similar *dis*resonating irritability between Istanbul's inhabitants and their environment. Such irritability takes on a life of its own in shaping how attractive the city is to its inhabitants or to potential migrants who may have considered moving to Istanbul in a changing Turkey, ultimately shaping the dynamics of the city's property markets beyond simple rational calculation. The exodus that befell Istanbul during the first two decades of the Turkish Republic should be studied not only as a product of the political economies of peripheralization and population exchanges but also the political movements associated with the irritable affective experience of *hüzün*. Affective meaning-making worked in tandem with "harder" political-economic realities to produce a city materially and emotionally abandoned in the interwar period. Exodus and abandonment would leave an unmistakable imprint on how the city's urban fabric would be transformed after World War II and on the class politics undergirding the contemporary struggle over its property.

Regionalization: From Imperial Center to Regional Hub

Industry, Infrastructure, and Their Smells

After its initial peripheralization, Istanbul was reincorporated into the country's economic circuits in the 1950s, but rather than reoccupying its position as the country's central political and economic hub, it was reoriented into a regional industrial hub. Istanbul's trajectory took a decided turn when Adnan Menderes came to power as head of the Demokrat Partisi (Democrat Party, DP) in 1950, with the first change of the ruling party since the inception of the Turkish Republic. The party placed the redevelopment of Istanbul at the center of its electoral campaign and launched a massive infrastructural program in the city once Menderes was elected.

By the 1950s, Turkey's modernization was committed to deepening state access into the Anatolian hinterland and producing strong regional centers of production that focused on an internal market instead of producing, as in Ottoman times, one economic center as the country's outlet to global markets.[5] Thus, the DP's project to redevelop Istanbul in the 1950s brought the city back from its marginalization but did so by positioning Istanbul as one of several regional centers and industrial hubs, with transport linkages to its immediate regional hinterland rather than global markets. Menderes's projects brought industry and automobile traffic to the heart of Istanbul. The DP invested in an extensive highway system that tore right through the city's historical center to connect Istanbul to its rural backyard. The importance of the city's port and waterways were meanwhile significantly downplayed, and, remarkably, Menderes chose to transform the Golden Horn's waterfront into the city's primary industrial zone (Gül 2002, 138). Overnight, Fener-Balat— the neighborhood where Kemal Bey owns a waterfront home—was transformed from a residential and artisanal neighborhood into an industrial one.

With industry and highways came a new sensory experience. As Fener-Balat's residents remembered their neighborhood's past in conversations with me, they regularly evoked its *smells* to describe its changes. Indeed, Istanbul's residents seemed to experience the political through their city's smells. As I rolled grape leaves with six women from Fener-Balat in the kitchen of a women's association, Emine Hanım opened up the conversation about the neighborhood's past by exclaiming, "In the past the Haliç [or Golden Horn] was so smelly! God bless the Prime Minister [Erdoğan] for cleaning it." In instant agreement, the rest of the women nodded their heads and made disgusted faces to signify just how smelly the Golden Horn had been during its industrial epoch. Sema Hanım interjected that it was Bedrettin Dalan, when he was mayor of Istanbul in the 1980s, who had cleaned up the Golden Horn and its smelly fumes—not Erdoğan during his reign as mayor in 1994. From there a heated debate erupted about which leader was responsible for what the women saw as the single most important development in their neighborhood's recent history. They wanted to make sure I would give credit where it was due in my research.[6]

The smells of the Golden Horn accosted me again as I was sitting in a barbershop discussing the neighborhood's past with the owner, Koray, and two of his customers. As we talked about how local services had changed over time, Koray started talking about improvements in garbage collection and then went into a long diatribe about the Golden Horn: "Twenty years back, we couldn't sit on the Haliç. We couldn't stand the smell. Now we go fishing there and can eat the fish. I'm not talking politically, but it was Tayyip Erdoğan who cleaned it up. . . . When we were young there was a park on the *sahil* [or waterfront], but the smell was so bad we put clothespins on our noses to play." The rant ended with a resounding laugh as everyone in the shop remembered the clothespins.[7] The putrid Golden Horn continued to be a common conversation piece wherever I went in Fener-Balat, as did the debates around attributing its cleaning up to Erdoğan or Dalan, with people subtly and not so subtly hinting about whether they believed the Islamist predecessors of Erdoğan's Justice and Development Party (AKP) or the center-right Republicans behind Dalan's ascent to power had salvaged the city.

With the changing smells of the city came factories on the waterfront that blocked the view, or *manzara*, that Kemal Bey boasts today. When he moved into his house in 1973, rather than greenery on the banks of the Golden Horn, his view of the waterway and the city beyond would have looked onto large factories with pollutant-spewing chimneys. The residential experience of the neighborhood and its walkability was also assaulted by the sudden appearance of long-distance trucks and fast-moving cars on the highways that Menderes built in the heart of the historic district. There is no doubt that pragmatic questions of access and connectivity drove a lot of the planning decisions that brought industry and highway networks to the city's center, but I also want to suggest here that the irritability that came with the resistant melancholy pervading Istanbul's urban fabric in the interwar period shaped what came to be seen as an invaluable *manzara* (view) in the city. The dark cloud that came to be associated with Istanbul rendered its once picturesque waterways less treasured than during the city's imperial heyday, or as they would again become with the city's relaunch as a "global city," enabling the transformation of the banks of the Golden Horn into an industrial zone. The city's transforming landscape was intertwined with both the imperatives of large-scale infrastructural transformation and the irritable affect through which it was experienced and lived.

Exodus, Electioneering, and the Making of a Newly Migrant Propertied Class in Istanbul

While changing sensory experience rendered the city less attractive to its elite, waves of anti-minority violence put the final nail in the coffin of Istanbul's diverse makeup in the 1950s. Non-Muslims had already been leaving Istanbul since the inception of the Republic, either voluntarily or due to forced population exchanges, but the exemption of Istanbul from population exchanges had meant that a good proportion of the city's non-Muslim communities had remained into the mid-twentieth century. The fate of these communities started to change with World War II, when the state levied a minority tax that mostly targeted the city's Jewish population but soon extended to its Greek and Armenian populations.[8] Then, with the eruption of disputes in Cyprus and other confounding factors, in 1955, Istanbul witnessed one of its most violent episodes: anti-Greek and minority riots, known as the *Olaylar*, shook the city to its core as the bodies and properties of non-Muslim residents (or those resembling them) were targeted with unprecedented violence on September 6 and 7 that year.[9] Finally, Greek residents who remained in the city after the riots were forcibly deported from Istanbul in response to the breakout of the war in Cyprus in 1964 (Keyder 1999, 11). By the 1980s, Istanbul's "Greek population had dwindled to less than two thousand, Armenians to fifty thousand, and Jews to twenty-five thousand" (11). As they were leaving Istanbul, some non-Muslim residents managed to sell their centrally located properties, mostly at negligible prices, to new migrants. For the most part, however, property owned by non-Muslims in neighborhoods like Fener-Balat and Tarlabaşı were vacated in a hurry, then nationalized and became "de facto assimilated into the same category as public land" (145). Thus, a large proportion of Istanbul's central neighborhoods became vacant state-owned property by the mid-1960s.

As minority communities fled the city, the repositioning of Istanbul as a regional industrial hub attracted a new demographic of rural migrants seeking employment in the city. Even though rural-urban migration was a common phenomenon in countries embarking on protectionist industrialization around the developing world, Istanbul's migrant population was uniquely positioned to become the city's new property-owning class rather than tenants or slum dwellers, as in Cairo. That divergence comes from the confluence of peripheralization, of non-Muslim communities' exodus and electioneering in Istanbul that set its trajectory apart from Cairo. As rural migrants brought heavy demand for affordable housing in the city's central neighborhoods, the earliest migrants bought property from fleeing minorities. For the most part, however, migrants occupied vacant housing in the center of the city and received rights to it retroactively through electioneering campaigns. With the advent of multiparty elections, politicians vying for electoral support promised and delivered ownership rights in return for votes as part of particularistic deals (Keyder 1999, 147). Thus, rural working-class migrants quickly became one of the city's most dominant property-owning groups as non-Muslim populations and an Ottoman-era elite fled the city and multiparty elections brought in aggressive electioneering campaigns that legalized the occupation of vacated buildings.

This new property-owning class created zones of affordable housing in the city, facilitated through kin and village networks. Migrants depended on kin and fellow villagers who had already relocated to Istanbul to secure job opportunities and housing upon their arrival. Those who were early migrants often rented housing that they had occupied upon arrival to members of their family or village at artificially low prices. Early migrants also rented housing to nonkin working-class migrants, but because most demand was coming from the working class, rental rates remained quite low in central Istanbul (Kuyucu and Ünsal 2010, 1487). Istanbul's neighborhoods had become divided into enclaves dominated by migrants from different regions and villages of Turkey. For example, Fener-Balat became dominated (although not exclusively) by migrants from the Black Sea region, while Tarlabaşı first saw a wave of migrants from the Black Sea and the eastern regions of the country (not necessarily Kurds) in the postwar era followed by, in the 1980s and 1990s, a wave of Kurdish migrants fleeing state violence. As the city's property-owning class transformed, Istanbul's demography shifted toward a heavily working-class population living in village-based enclaves that mapped Istanbul onto the country's new regionalized geography.

Affect, Class, and Identity Politics on the Eve of Globalization

In the 1980s, Istanbul would be thrust onto the global scene by its mayors, and I pause here for a discussion of how class and identity politics intersected in shaping the political terrain leading up to that globalizing moment and the expropriative politics it would entail (see below). Istanbul's postimperial trajectory has often been told as a linear story of neglect and decline that beset the city with the inception of the Republic, until it was saved from oblivion in the 1980s with the city's revitalization as an internationally prominent hub. That narrative—aside from being inaccurate since it misses the many transformations that shaped the city in the interim, and especially the DP's sweeping intervention—reflects and perpetuates a class politics that would empower the expropriation of private property in the mid-2000s, even if not intentionally. Statements propagating this narrative claim that "in the years from 1914 to 1923 [Istanbul] passed from being an imperial metropolis to something less than even a national capital inside the Turkish Republic of Mustafa Kemal [Atatürk].... Now once again, after 70 years—albeit a brief moment in the 3,000 year span of its history—Istanbul seems set to resume its role as cultural bridgehead and international metropolis" (Robins and Aksoy 1995, 223). Another declares: "As a consequence of a number of successive trajectories, related to both the world conjuncture and various developments within the Turkish context at the time, the privileged position of nineteenth-century Istanbul started to decline in the early twentieth century.... The year 1980 marked a turning point" (Bezmez 2008, 818-19). This narrative not only sidelines the interventions of the 1950s and 1960s, but it more importantly misses or *dis*misses the centrality of its working-class populations to the city's vitality, property markets, and future trajectories.

Scholars have not been the only culprits in propagating this narrative. Orhan Pamuk's framing of the city through *hüzün* narrated melancholy as the dominant ethos defining the city well into the 2000s. Engin Işın (2010) convincingly critiques Pamuk by arguing that the gaze that produces such a reading of the city is an elitist one. Pamuk sees the city as melancholic because he does not recognize what he terms the *şehrin keyfi* (enjoyment of the city) that its working-class "outsiders," as opposed to "native" *Istanbullus*, bring to the city as vitality to be embraced or celebrated. In particular, Işın contrasts the two gazes by saying,

> While Pamuk laments the disappearance of a specific Ottoman diversity in the city, he fails to observe, let alone rejoice, in the appearance of another,

creative and energetic diversity created by its [rural migrant] outsiders and strangers. It is not then only the scenes of pleasure—people having their tea, grilling fresh-caught fish from the sea, simply strolling, playing cards, taking a coffee break, or catching a glimpse of many views of the Bosphorous—but the acts of enjoyment by its strangers taking various risks that define *şehrin keyfi*. (42)

In asserting another gaze on the city, Işın then argues that the choice not to see the "outsider's" vitality is shaped by one's socioeconomic position and one's class-based lens. To bring the point home, Işın ends by asking, "Is Pamuk's longing for the city expressed in *hüzün* not about Ottoman Istanbul but the contemporary Istanbul that his social group—self-defined *Istanbullus*—mourns?" (46). Işın's incisive critique of Pamuk relates to a larger point about the ways in which a narrative that leaves out the revitalization of Istanbul in the 1950s and 1960s and the centrality of its propertied working class to that vitality is implicated in a class-based discourse that almost erases the claims that this working class makes to the city and its property and emboldens their contemporary violent dispossession.

The class politics that manifested in Istanbul as it underwent violent transformation did not just pit an old/new economic elite against the city's working classes, however. Intraclass politics plagued the working classes, even as the city's new property regime threatened their foothold in the city. Grappling with a complicated and divisive terrain of identity and class politics on the eve of expropriation, they mobilized the city's sensory landscape to navigate that politics and stake competing claims to the city's property terrain. Strikingly, in Tarlabaşı, rural migrants turned to *sartorial aesthetics* to make claims on the city when stakes were at their highest.

Since Tarlabaşı is part of the Pera district, it was once home to a mostly non-Muslim commercial class. As I interviewed dwellers who lived through the violent expropriation campaign that began in the mid-2000s, they repeatedly described how they saw people *dress* in the neighborhood over time to recover the neighborhood's *value*. Burak Bey, who owns a metal workshop that his father acquired through extended family members in 1950, recalled how "in old times you couldn't go to Pera without a cravat [or necktie]." Similarly, Murat Bey, who owns a bakery that was established in 1886 by Greeks, and that his family bought when they moved to Istanbul from the Black Sea region, related: "In the 1960s . . . Beyoğlu was aristocratic; you couldn't enter it without a cravat." And again the cravat appears when Semih Bey, who runs a grocery that his family has been operating in the neighborhood for thirty

Istanbul   81

years, narrated to me: "When I first came here, this street was for those with cravats." Finally, Erbay Bey went so far as to suggest that Tarlabaşı should undergo a heritage preservation project where people wear historical clothes, including the white gloves, canes, and cravats once worn in the neighborhood. Erbay Bey's family is from Rize in the Black Sea region, and they moved to the neighborhood forty-eight years ago to open a *meyhane* (restaurant serving alcoholic beverages). When the demography of the neighborhood changed into a Muslim-majority one, they stopped serving alcohol and transitioned their business into a restaurant specializing in *köfte* (Turkish meatballs).[10]

What set these men apart from other residents I met was that they were all early migrants to Tarlabaşı and almost exclusively non-Kurds from the Black Sea region. They worked hard to distinguish themselves from later, mostly Kurdish migrants, and they turned to the cravat for that distinction. Amy Mills insightfully argues that early rural migrants to Istanbul recover their linkages to minority identities as a way to claim being the city's true inhabitants who once lived its cosmopolitan past and preceded the mostly Kurdish migrants they suggest ruined their city. Mills analyzes this politics through early Black Sea migrants' revival of the Greek history of the Kuzguncuk neighborhood, along with their discursive exclusion of Kurdish migrants (Mills 2010, ch. 5). Although some of my interlocutors did invoke their past Greek and Armenian neighbors and the relations they had with non-Muslim communities around the neighborhood before the exodus, as Mills describes, many more turned to the cravat and other sartorial and visual aesthetics to describe the demographic shift they witnessed in the neighborhood since immigrating in the 1950s. The materiality of the cravat provides an even more powerful modality for navigating the politics of the city's demographic shifts than the direct reference to non-Muslim residents that Mills discusses. The sanitized materiality of the cravat allows early migrants to claim elite, cosmopolitan pasts that distinguish them from Kurdish migrants without having to grapple with the violence that drove non-Muslim communities out of the city and gave them access to real estate that was far beyond their means. Setting themselves apart as the ones who *saw* the cravats during the neighborhood's heyday, they then blamed succeeding migrants for bringing "village ways" to the neighborhood and precipitating its demise. Early migrants were mobilizing the sanitized materiality of the cravat to cleanse the anti-minority violence that gave them access to the city while simultaneously claiming distinction from later Kurdish migrants.

Rather than evoke a politics of ethnic demarcation for its own sake, the cravat allowed early migrants to recuperate the neighborhood's *value* in the city while making exclusive claims to that value. My interlocutors often invoked the cravat and other aesthetic markers of a cosmopolitan elite in discussing the neighborhood's future, and not just as nostalgia for a bygone past. A case in point is Erbay Bey's aforementioned vision for a heritage preservation project featuring people dressed in the luxurious clothes of the past. Such dress could demarcate Tarlabaşı as a neighborhood that has always been central to the city's commercial arteries and a home for its elite, with the current debilitation an aberrant blip rather than the norm. Importantly, as inhabitants who once witnessed the neighborhood's heyday, they lay exclusive claim to the potential value the neighborhood might someday generate for the city. They claim special status as the ideal caretakers of the futuristic neighborhood at the exclusion of later migrants whom they claim precipitated the neighborhood's demise. Tarlabaşı's early migrants were making the very case for excluding particular groups from rights to ownership that others were making to strip them of their own claims to property in the city's central districts. The violent expropriation of property did not appear out of thin air. Rather, complicated and divisive class and identity politics gradually but surely laid the groundwork for the launch of a predatory attack on the city's property terrain.

Globalization

Infrastructures of a "Global City"

As Istanbul's new working- and middle-class property owners settled into their homes and newfound place in the city's political nexus, Istanbul underwent yet another major infrastructural transformation. Reorienting the city again, this project abandoned the regionalization initiated by Menderes and the DP and worked to reconfigure Istanbul as the country's gateway to global markets. In its initial phase, this infrastructural program aimed to center Istanbul as a gateway to global trade and financial and touristic networks in the aftermath of the "failure" of protectionist industrialization or Import-Substitution-Industrialization (ISI). By the 2000s, that program had transformed from one that saw Istanbul as a space for facilitating global flows of capital and people to one that treated the city's landscape itself and its real estate as central to the country's economic engine.

When the bloody 1980 military coup ended Turkey's experiment with ISI and launched market-liberalizing reforms,[11] the city's new mayor, Bedrettin Dalan, embarked on a path to revitalize Istanbul as the country's economic and cultural (if not political) hub. He planned for it to join the ranks of a rising set of "global cities" (Sassen 2001), and the key to launching Istanbul as such was infrastructure. Dalan and his team invested in transportation networks and public transit to open up the city's center to the financial industry and tourism and to connect the city to other global centers through its waterways and airways. Like Menderes, Dalan saw infrastructure liberating Istanbul from the constraints that were holding it back. Rather than investing in industrialization and highways that would connect to the regional hinterland, however, Dalan and his team actively deindustrialized the city and invested in infrastructure to connect the city to global markets. Notable among their infrastructural works was the conversion of the Golden Horn into a cultural epicenter, the pedestrianization of Istiklal Boulevard to create a commercial center, and the creation of arterial Tarlabaşı Boulevard to join the two (Keyder 1999, 16–17).

Many of these projects entailed violence in their execution; for example, three hundred buildings were demolished to create Tarlabaşı Boulevard (Bartu 1999). Likewise, numerous factories and residential buildings were forcibly condemned on the Golden Horn (Bezmez 2008). This violence remained limited in scope, however, and was meant to facilitate infrastructure designed to attract global flows of capital and people to Istanbul. It did not entail a concerted assault on private property such as that codified into law in the mid-2000s. At this early stage, real estate development was still important to the economy insofar as it enabled a stream of capital and people to the country without yet being central to the country's economic engine.

When the center-right governments that had brought Dalan to power were replaced by the Islamically oriented Welfare Party that installed Recep Tayyip Erdoğan as Istanbul's mayor in 1994, the new government doubled down on Dalan's strategy and invested heavily in infrastructure and public service provision. As seen with the debates that erupted around which government had cleaned up the Golden Horn and its smells, the mid-1980s to the late 1990s are remembered as an era of infrastructural and public works projects. Indeed, people often assigned responsibility or credit for these projects depending on their political affiliations. Overall, however, deep into the 1990s, successive regimes saw the city as a center for global trade and tourism but not for aggressive real estate development. That would change with the turn of the millennium. Thus, the deindustrialization and infrastructural projects initiated by Dalan and carried forth by the Welfare Party simultaneously stripped rural migrant property owners of their livelihood, costing them factory jobs in particular, while elevating their property values. As the city reoriented into the country's gateway to global markets, owners came to see the value of their property as limitless. It was upon this class, beset by both vulnerability and aspiration, that the dispossession fueled by a rising corporate-developer class descended in the mid-2000s.

A Rising Corporate-Capitalist Class and Neoliberalizing Property Markets

The shift that transformed Istanbul from being seen as facilitating global flows to a terrain that would be predatorily excavated for revenue-generating real estate was precipitated by the rise of a corporate-capitalist class heavily concentrated in construction and property development in the mid-2000s. The history of this class is entwined with the evolution of the industrialists behind the rise of Turkey's Anatolian Tigers. The Anatolian Tigers are a group of cities in Turkey's Anatolian center that relaunched it onto the world economy in the 1990s, after the paralyzing debt the country had accrued in the 1970s. The Anatolian Tigers' industrialists were the main beneficiaries of the export-led growth incentives that the state adopted in the 1980s as it worked to liberalize the economy after the bloody coup that dramatically ended the country's experiment with ISI. They were initially concentrated in furniture manufacturing, textiles, and adjacent industries.[12] For the most part, they are also known to share a commitment to Islamic values that contrasts sharply with the secular tendencies of Turkey's old economic elite.[13] This rising economic elite became the main economic base for several Islamically oriented political parties in the 1990s, culminating in the AKP that has been in power since 2002. Initially, in the mid-1990s, the industries in which the Anatolian Tigers' corporate classes were heavily invested (like textiles) expanded aggressively, and urban centers such as Istanbul were seen as trade and financial centers meant to *service* those thriving industries but not replace them. Around the early 2000s, this corporate class's relationship to urban centers shifted dramatically. With decreasing marginal returns on the industries that had fueled the Anatolian Tigers' initial economic ascendance, the industrialists turned to the construction industry as their new engine of capital accumulation, manifesting as real estate development and infrastructure work. Conglomerates that had once focused on textiles and furniture now expanded into construction.[14] Initially, they aggressively developed Istanbul's undeveloped outskirts but soon turned to the city's developed center as prime real estate that would garner far more lucrative returns. As the main economic base of the ruling AKP, the Anatolian Tigers' industrialists put pressure on the state to gain access to lucrative property in the city's center.

While the eventual makeup of this corporate-capitalist class resembles that of the corporate class that pushed the state to adopt policies like the reversal of rent control in Cairo, they were distinct in important ways. First, they are a corporate-capitalist class that has a far wider and diversified base than the narrow and easily identifiable oligarchic class in Egypt. Thus, when they turned to construction and real estate development, the demands they were making on the city were far more diverse than those made by the narrow oligarchy in Cairo, and the rewards were expected to be distributed along a far more sprawling network of interests. As the Networks of Dispossession project and others have shown, the nature of that network was still oligarchic, with wealth (and urban development bids) concentrated among a handful of dominant conglomerates.[15] There was far more scope, however, for a variety of actors who had accumulated wealth through export-led industry to be involved within that structure, albeit a somewhat oligarchic one, and to make demands on the city. The state's efforts to fulfill these demands thus needed to be far more encompassing to include that wide-ranging corporate-capitalist class in comparison to the narrow and tailored legal maneuvers and patronage that the Egyptian state could rely on to satisfy its corporate-capitalist elite.

Second, the corporate-capitalist class that arose from Anatolia's hinterlands was, for the most part, also united around an ideological political project: the re-Islamization of the public sphere. Their allegiances manifested in their organization within chambers of commerce that identified along ideological lines (the new MÜSIAD and TUKSON chambers organized along religious lines as opposed to the older secularized chamber, TÜSIAD) and in their support of Islamically oriented political parties.[16] Their alignment around an ideological political project meant that their pursuit of capital was often entwined with projects operating on other axes (with appeal to a wide grassroots audience) that could obscure the dispossessive nature of that accumulation, even when blatant. In contrast, the corporate-capitalist class that dominated Egypt's ruling regime[17] had not aligned itself so clearly around an ideological project with the capacity to obscure capitalist accumulation.

Violent Expropriation and the Politics of "Urban Crisis"

The violent assault on property rights in Istanbul first manifested through the criminalization of informal housing through law no. 5237 in 2004. Until then, there was a tacit agreement between the government and its citizens that informal housing would be tolerated in big cities like Istanbul. In fact, informal housing is known as *gecekondu*, literally "night housing," because the tacit agreement was that housing built overnight would be left alone by municipalities. Moreover, a lot of *gecekondus* retroactively received legal deeds through the electioneering campaigns described earlier. The 2004 law criminalized *gecekondu* construction for the first time in Turkey's modern history and rendered it punishable by five years in prison (Kuyucu and Ünsal 2010, 1484). One of the main modes through which migrants had settled Turkey's cities was now under direct attack, and several state-led development projects started targeting *gecekondu* neighborhoods, such as Başıbüyük in the district of Maltepe, as early as 2005.[18]

Property expropriation then targeted affordable housing in the city through the Renewal and Preservation Law of 2005, which rendered housing such as Kemal Bey's vulnerable to violent expropriation. The progression from decreeing neighborhoods renewal zones to demolition and reconstruction was not a linear one, however. Legal battles mired that progression in both Sulukule and Tarlabaşı neighborhoods. In Sulukule, after the neighborhood was razed to the ground and reconstructed into American-style, prefabricated suburban housing, the courts issued an *iptal karar*, a decision that revoked official approval of the Sulukule project on the grounds that it was harmful to the people. The decision came only two weeks after the first group of homeowners were offered new homes in the neighborhood.[19] The *iptal karar* was seen as a symbolic victory for activism around Sulukule, but it did not change the reality of the neighborhood's forever-altered physical landscape or property ownership rights.

In Tarlabaşı, the courts intervened at varying points during the battle over the neighborhood. First, legal battles stalled the nationalization of property in the neighborhood from 2008 to late 2011, and even though the property was eventually condemned, forcibly vacated, and razed to the ground, the reconstruction has stalled regularly and the project remains largely incomplete (as of 2019) due to a variety of legal battles, including *iptal karar* decrees.[20] In Fener-Balat, the state's attempt to implement a similar plan was stymied at its inception and never took off by an *iptal karar*.[21] While others have studied the fascinating politics to the nonlinear temporalities produced through legal battles, I focus here on how they illuminate the battles erupting within states (as nonunitary actors) that complicate private property regimes.[22]

In tandem with the development of a legal infrastructure for violent expropriation, the state's executive arm also transformed to facilitate the transfer of property to the country's corporate-capitalist class. Tracing the history of TOKİ, Turkey's mass-housing authority, is especially instructive in mapping the dramatic transformation of governmentality away from extra-market practices and toward "marketization" with the turn of the millennium. TOKİ was initially created in the 1980s as an agency, operating out of the executive office of the prime minister, designed to provide public housing and absorb the shocks of mass unemployment that came with deindustrialization. The end of the 1990s saw TOKİ's social housing mandate shrink and then get completely defunded with the austerity measures taken in response to the 2001 inflation crisis. In the wake of its defunding, TOKİ was then reborn as a self-funded (profit-driven) developer, still operating from the prime minister's office. With its rebirth, the era of extra-market, redistributive social housing and the makeshift shock-absorbent policies of the 1980s saw their final days. By the mid-2000s, TOKİ was undertaking massive and violent redevelopment. The agency that had collected the most information on the city's vulnerable populations in the name of welfare provision had transformed into one of the main arms of a machine mobilizing that knowledge to target affordable housing for dispossessive property redevelopment.

Ultimately, it became clear that the AKP was deploying its expropriative regime in the constrained spaces of "renewal zones" to pilot its legal infrastructures (such as finding vulnerabilities like the *iptal karar* decisions) and corporatized executive agencies like TOKİ before launching a more concerted assault on property rights in the entirety of the city. When, in 2012, the Turkish parliament passed the Disaster Law that increased the state's power to implement "emergency nationalization" across Istanbul, the prospect of emergency nationalization had expanded beyond circumscribed renewal zones to include property owned by middle-class AKP supporters.

The question then becomes: How could the AKP regime embark on a campaign that would render its own voter base's property vulnerable to expropriation when elections are crucial to the party's hold on power? Analysts initially explained this conundrum by arguing that the AKP was focusing on property owned by minority ethnic and religious communities that were not central to the party's voter base, and in particular the Roma community in Sulukule and the Kurdish community in Tarlabaşı (e.g., Holland 2017). This argument became less tenable, though, as the AKP expanded the purview of its expropriation campaign to nonminority neighborhoods such as Fener-Balat before eventually enacting the all-encompassing Disaster Law.

Rather than focus on short-term electoral strategizing, the rest of this chapter traces how the AKP has entangled the longue-durée spatial-material transformations of the city with specific political struggles and dynamics unfolding within Sulukule, Tarlabaşı, and disaster-prone areas to enable and normalize expropriation.[23]

The Politics of Morality and "Urban Crisis" in Sulukule

Walking into Fatih Municipality's headquarters in Istanbul, one of the first things a visitor sees is a video on auto-play about the municipality's urban transformation project in Sulukule neighborhood. The video plays with light background music and no narration, rotating from one image of Sulukule to the next, starting with images from before the project was implemented and turning to images of the neighborhood after its renewal. Earlier images depict a neighborhood falling apart, with buildings caving under the pressure of water or fire damage, crumbling rooftops, broken windows and doors, interiors with peeling paint and cracked walls, abandoned buildings, and people living among mounds of rubbish and waste. These images come with no annotation except for a blurb that enumerates how many buildings there are within the renewal zone.[24]

The representation of Sulukule through these images evokes a neighborhood in physical *crisis* due to naturally occurring decay in need of physical solutions and "renewal." However, the developments through which Sulukule residents came to live in caving buildings with crumbling rooftops were neither natural nor purely physical. They did not stem from the physical location of the neighborhood on a fault line or floodplain, nor from the ignorance or unwillingness of the Roma community to care for its built environment. It stemmed from a drawn-out political struggle over *public morality*.

Sulukule is known for having long housed a thriving entertainment industry run mostly by Roma. Although its contours may have changed over the years, Sulukule's reputation as an entertainment district dates back to Ottoman times. During the Republican era, this entertainment industry was reorganized into *eğlence evleri* or *devriye evleri*, translatable to "entertainment houses," where guests came for Roma music and dance, especially belly dancing, along with light meals and alcohol (mostly local rakı) (Foggo 2007, 41). The entertainment industry served as the economic and cultural engine of the neighborhood. Those who weren't musicians or entertainers thrived on servicing the neighborhood's visitors as cooks or taxi drivers or by selling handicrafts to the entertainment houses' guests.[25]

That industry would disappear almost overnight when the wrath of the Yedikule district police chief Süleyman Ulusoy, also known as Hortum ("the hose") Süleyman for allegedly beating his victims with a thick rubber hose, descended upon the neighborhood in 1992.[26] Ulusoy especially targeted and terrorized people within the entertainment industry. Although the entertainment houses were not in breach of any laws, Ulusoy's terrorizing campaign closed thirty-seven of the houses, and eventually around three thousand people lost their livelihood in the neighborhood (41). Although Ulusoy's methods may have been peculiar in their style, this campaign was by no means the product of an isolated circumstance or a personal vendetta. It was part of a larger political campaign to protect "public morality" that gained political clout in the early 1990s under the supervision of Istanbul's police chief Saadettin Tantan. Tantan would later leverage his tenure and achievements as police chief to win local elections and become mayor of Fatih Municipality in 1994 as a member of the center-right conservative party ANAP (the Motherland Party).[27] As mayor of Fatih, Tantan continued his campaign and found ways to close down and evacuate the few remaining entertainment houses in Sulukule in 1994.[28] Rather than being demoted or marginalized for his methods or targets, Ulusoy was rewarded for his campaign in Sulukule and transferred to the more prominent position of district chief of police in central Beyoğlu (where Tarlabaşı is located). There, he waged a notorious battle against the city's transgender population and sex workers in the late 1990s. Finally, he joined the AKP and in the early 2000s, he was embraced by the Islamically oriented establishment enough to run for elected office, though unsuccessfully.[29] Ulusoy's campaigns for "public morality," as they were reported in the media (Aydın 2005), were not specific to his persona but were part of a larger political agenda embraced by a rising conservative force in the city.

Sulukule never recovered from the closure of the entertainment industry (Foggo 2007, 42). Throughout the interviews I conducted on the edges of the municipality's project in Sulukule, I heard from residents who had lost their livelihoods and turned to temporary fixes such as street vending. Moreover, the majority of my interlocutors had either been incarcerated themselves or had family members who were incarcerated for petty or drug-related crimes. It is not surprising that poverty would leave a noticeable imprint on the neighborhood's built environment. Without the financial flows coming from the entertainment sector, few residents had the funding to maintain their residences or workspaces and the infrastructure that supported them. The spaces of the entertainment houses were either rented out at minimal charges or left to their ruin, often as animal barns (42). The representation of the neighborhood as suffering from natural, physical decay rather than the consequences of a political assault on its main industry—as in the video playing at Fatih Municipality's headquarters—serves to redraw the contours of the "crisis" and its "solutions" away from a reckoning with the politics of public morality that brought rampant unemployment to the neighborhood and toward dispossessive physical redevelopment.

The violent expropriation that came with categorizing Sulukule as a "renewal zone" was orchestrated by the state's corporatized mass-housing authority TOKİ, discussed above. The redevelopment that replaced the neighborhood's existing architecture with prefabricated apartment buildings relocated 85 percent of Sulukule's residents to TOKİ-built mass housing on the city's outskirts, in the neighborhood of Taşoluk, about thirty kilometers away.[30] Relocated residents were not offered that housing gratuitously, as compensation for the housing "nationalized" in Sulukule, but were expected to buy it from TOKİ through a significant down payment and mortgages that lasted ten to fifteen years. By the time I was conducting my fieldwork in 2012, most families filed bankruptcy and forfeited their TOKİ apartments, returning to find affordable rentals on the outskirts of the redeveloped zones in Sulukule and neighboring Karagümrük neighborhoods. According to Şükrü Pündük, one of the main organizers against Sulukule's redevelopment, of the three hundred families initially relocated to TOKİ housing in Taşoluk, only twenty-seven families had remained in that housing by 2009 (less than a year later).[31] The agency that had collected all of the state's information on low-income housing as a social welfare provider had been unleashed as an unstoppable force for predatorily targeting affordable housing for redevelopment in the city. In a double move, the redevelopment of Sulukule both transferred property from its low-income residents to TOKİ as a for-profit developer and drove these residents into the throes of the "debt economy" where they were burdened by mortgage payments owed to none other than TOKİ itself.

Infrastructures of "Crisis" in Tarlabaşı

Rather than a battle over public morality, the "crisis" that engulfed Tarlabaşı was manufactured through the political-economic project that sought to relaunch Istanbul as a "global city." Tarlabaşı was one of the biggest victims of the infrastructural work that Dalan undertook in the 1980s to open up Istanbul to global flows. It was divided in two when Tarlabaşı Boulevard was built to connect the city's financial center with the old city and the Golden Horn. Not only were three hundred buildings demolished and their residents displaced, drastically disrupting the neighborhood's social and economic life, but the boulevard also cut off the northern half of the neighborhood from the networks it once thrived on. The boulevard was designed as a multilane, high-speed road with almost no pedestrian crossings, and a high iron railing was constructed to stop pedestrians from trying to cross the boulevard from the northern to the southern half of what was once considered one neighborhood. Northern Tarlabaşı was effectively cut off from what remained of its southern half and, importantly, from the newly pedestrianized Istiklal Street that now functioned as the city's financial and cultural heart. It was impossible for residents in Tarlabaşı's northern half to interact with the economic and social resources they once relied on, either because they were displaced from the neighborhood altogether or were now beyond the iron-railed boulevard.

Over time, workshops or services that found themselves on the southern side of the boulevard thrived, staying close to Istiklal and the financial flows and tourists it brought. During my fieldwork, I dreaded having to cross the boulevard and worked hard to arrange my days so that I would need to be on only one side or the other of the iron railing on any given day. Residents regularly told me that the greatest transformation in the neighborhood's history was the boulevard's construction. One of them, Erbay Bey, who owns a shoe repair shop on the southern side, explained that the boulevard was the most momentous development in the neighborhood's history. He felt quite lucky that his shop ended up on the southern side, where his business brought in traffic from Istiklal Street, but he saw his counterparts on the northern side of the iron railing suffering and closing down their businesses one after the other.[32] Not surprisingly, the headquarters of the contractors who were redeveloping Tarlabaşı, Çalık Holding, were located on the southern side of the boulevard, keeping a strategic distance from the northern neighborhood and its residents while keeping a bird's-eye view of the neighborhood (figure 2.2 is taken from the rooftop of the headquarters).

Again, Tarlabaşı's loss of economic livelihood and the consequent physical deterioration of its urban fabric was not a story of natural urban decay or inflows of "ignorant" migrants from Eastern Turkey, as I was told a few times, but was the direct result of a political-economic project to relaunch the city as a global hub. In their drive to attract flows of capital and people into Istanbul, infrastructural projects were designed to favor those flows over existing populations, especially ones not integral to servicing those flows. Eventually, these deliberate political-economic projects and the infrastructural works that came with them created an urban fabric that was represented in the mid-2000s as naturally decaying and only salvageable through wholesale physical transformation. Once Tarlabaşı was categorized as a renewal zone, Çalık Holding—whose CEO was none other than Prime Minister (now President) Erdoğan's son-in-law—"won" the bid to redevelop the neighborhood in partnership with the local municipality. As the webs linking the ruling regime and the corporate-capitalist class wound tighter and tighter, Tarlabaşı's redevelopment evacuated the entirety of the neighborhood and over 41 percent of its residents were forcibly stripped of their property rights in a massive, violent transfer of property to Istanbul's corporate class.[33]

(Un)Natural Disaster: The Fires and Earthquakes of Istanbul

FIRE

The fire that consumed the first story of Kemal Bey's home as it ravaged Fener in 1978 was not an isolated tragedy. Fires had for centuries been regularly consuming Istanbul's urban fabric, which was historically largely wooden in construction. As the city got denser, fires became more of a pressing danger. To track the growing intensity of that threat, Zeynep Çelik (1986) reports that while there are no large fires recorded in the first two centuries of Ottoman rule, 109 fires were reported in the second two centuries, between 1633 and 1839, starting with the massive Cibali fire of 1633. The threat became even more severe as the city's density increased exponentially in the nineteenth century, and 229 extensive fires were recorded[34] between 1853 and 1906 alone (52–53). Çelik notes the fear that the episodic experience of extensive fires struck in Istanbul's residents, captured in the chronicles of a nineteenth-century Italian traveler, Edmondo De Amicis: "The word 'fire' means for the inhabitants of Constantinople 'every misfortune,' and the cry *Yangin Var* is charged with a dread meaning, terrible, fateful, carrying with it dismay—a cry at which the entire city is moved to its depths, and pours forth as at the announcement of a scourge from God" (53). As the severity of a fire's threat and the sense of dread it created intensified in the nineteenth century, it spurred three important developments for Istanbul's urban fabric.

First, the fires precipitated an unprecedented amount of planning and reorganization of the city, providing both the urgency and the means for extensive redesign during the nineteenth century. Several factors came together to spur this replanning, including admiration for Haussman's remaking of Paris (that had also struck the Khedive in Cairo). Controlling the fires pushed the city's government to find ways to decrease density and facilitate the movement of fire brigades into the most inaccessible neighborhoods.

This translated into replanning the city around wider streets and boulevards unobstructed by cul-de-sacs or buildings with obtrusive extensions (such as the *cumba* windows and terraces that could extend far beyond a building's layout). While regularizing the urban fabric around wider and straighter streets in other cities meant highly unpopular demolitions, in Istanbul, the fires demolished the urban fabric that would then be rebuilt along wider and more regularized streets, resulting in far less contestation of the city's remaking. The 1856 Aksaray fire and the massive 1865 Hocapaşa fire were especially instrumental in galvanizing the implementation of grid planning in the city. Because the government followed the fires rather than unrestrained urban plans, however, Istanbul was remade in patches that mapped onto the city's existent topography rather than entirely reimagined through a concerted plan from above. Importantly, the new plans preserved the city's organization around insulated if connected neighborhoods, even if a lot of the cul-de-sacs that had kept alleys within those neighborhoods were replaced by open, connecting streets.[35]

Second, the fires provoked a revolution in the city's building materials and a wholesale transition away from using timber for construction. In the 1850s and 1860s, the government introduced regulations urging and then decreeing that all new construction use *kargir* materials that combined stone and brick for supporting walls and iron and copper for structural beams and roofing. While all new construction was expected to use *kargir* materials, exceptions were made for those who could not afford them, especially in zones that were categorized as "secondary" and with a lighter concentration of valuable sites compared with central zones (Çelik 1986, 52). Later, in 1907, after a two-year debate surrounding its suitability as a building material, reinforced concrete was incorporated into the roster of acceptable *kargir* materials for new construction (76). Because of these regulations, new zones built up after the 1850s such as Pera (and Tarlabaşı within it) were constructed almost entirely using *kargir* materials while older neighborhoods with lower-income populations, including Fener-Balat, remained largely built out of wood. Through my ethnography I saw that in neighborhoods like Fener-Balat, where timber still heavily features as a building material, residents remain psychologically attuned to the dangers of fire, with fear of it permeating daily life in the subtlest of ways, whereas residents of neighborhoods such as Tarlabaşı were less attuned to that fear in their everyday lives.

Third, the threat of fire brought the insurance industry to Istanbul. After the 1865 Hocapaşa fire, and especially the 1870 Beyoğlu fire, several insurance companies that had been developing risk cartographies in Europe saw an opportunity in Istanbul and rushed to fill it. Initially, three British companies arrived and by 1900 there were forty-four insurance companies operating in Turkey. In 1916, they formed a union to share information and regularize pricing, naming it the Association of Foreign Insurance Companies Operating in Turkey (Sabancıoğlu 2003, 89–90). By the turn of the century, insuring real estate had become a major industry in Istanbul, and that industry needed to build cadastral knowledge of the city to operate. Companies needed to know not only where a building they were insuring was located but also its construction materials, whether it sat on a street accessible to the fire brigade, the quality of water supply in the area that would be needed to quell the fire, and so on.

With that impetus, the companies commissioned Istanbul's first all-encompassing mapping project. In 1904, a British company commissioned such maps but limited their reach to areas where the city's foreign population dwelled and worked. After several other smaller mapping campaigns, the most ambitious attempt was commissioned to Jacques Pervititch, who produced a series of extensive maps of most of Istanbul's inhabited areas starting in 1922 and continuing well into the Republican era, with the last map dated to 1945 (90–91). The maps comprised the most comprehensive cadastral survey of the city in its modern era, including details of the materials for each story of a building and annotations related to fire risk. The insurance industry used the maps for decades, until the infrastructural works introduced by the Democrat Party in the 1950s altered the city so significantly as to render some of the information obsolete (91). The maps have continued to be referenced, however, by various state and nonstate agencies, especially for mapping the intricacies within central neighborhoods that were unaffected by large infrastructural projects. I saw the maps used by architects working with the Istanbul Planning Agency in their mapping of several neighborhoods categorized as "historical zones." The threat of fire had produced the impetus not only for large-scale replanning in the second half of the nineteenth century but also an unprecedented mapping campaign that produced some of the most detailed and well-annotated maps of any city in the modern era.

The management of the danger of fire in the city changed dramatically with the peripheralization of Istanbul during the Republican era. As the city was actively marginalized from the country's politico-economic center and left unplanned and unmaintained, rebuilding after fires fell exclusively to private insurance companies, with little involvement from the state. With the exodus of the city's elite, vacant buildings whose owners were no longer paying for insurance were left to rot once scorched by fire. At this early stage, the exodus was limited to higher echelons of the elite, however, and middle-class Muslim and non-Muslim populations remained in the city's central districts, maintaining their mostly insured buildings against fire damage.

The reincorporation of Istanbul into the country's political-economic engine as a regional industrial hub in the 1950s transformed but did not necessarily reverse patterns of decay by fire precipitated in the Republican era. The interest that the DP took in Istanbul as a regional hub translated into extensive infrastructural intervention and the maintenance of public spaces seen as central to industrialization and the transit of goods and people. Within residential spaces, however, the state took a less interventionist approach. As a reminder, the city experienced its most intense episodes of anti-minority violence and dispossession during the 1950s and 1960s. With the exodus of most non-Muslim communities, the state adopted an informal approach to the reoccupation of vacated housing, through which rural migrants such as Kemal Bey would come to live and then retroactively (through electioneering campaigns that delivered housing titles) own housing in the city's center. The transfer of so much of the city center's property to newly migrant populations under legally ambiguous conditions meant that fire damage was dealt with in a relatively ad hoc manner in that epoch. Seeing that they facilitated the absorption of a swelling rural migrant workforce essential to industrialization, the state turned a blind eye to these legal ambiguities and the electioneering opportunities they created for decades. In allowing for such informalization of property rights, the state avoided interventions such as coordinating rebuilding efforts in a neighborhood in the wake of fire, as had been done in Ottoman times. Such interventions would necessitate accurate accounting for the ownership of plots to be rehabilitated, which would open up a lot of thorny disputes around land tenure and declare the state's de facto acceptance of illegal land settlement through its formal servicing and rebuilding.

As the state retreated from coordinating rebuilding efforts, private insurance companies also exited the scene. Insurance requires both the legal property titles and financial comfort that most of the working-class residents of neighborhoods with a wooden fabric, like Fener-Balat, did not have access to, and so most properties remained uninsured. Without state coordination or the capability of private insurance companies on hand, rebuilding efforts after fire damage were dealt with on a case-by-case basis, and rebuilding efforts depended entirely on the financial means of residents. In some cases, the fire damage was constrained enough that residents managed to rebuild on their limited means, often using cheaper materials such as concrete, as

Kemal Bey had done, but in a lot of cases, especially with extensive damage, residents abandoned homes entirely and found housing elsewhere. Such abandonments increased rather than decreased in the 1980s and 1990s, as the deindustrialization of the city, and especially the Golden Horn, left many residents and owners unemployed and destitute in these areas. When I asked about visibly scorched buildings in Fener-Balat, neighborhood residents told me that vacated homes often stood abandoned and rotting for decades (figure 2.5). A history of aggressive industrialization (and deindustrialization), anti-minority violence, and ambiguous legal infrastructures came together to produce the ruined buildings that urban renewal brochures subsequently presented as an aesthetic blight on the city in need of physical removal through neighborhood-level expropriation—without addressing any of the political-economic dynamics that produced that scorched and abandoned terrain.

EARTHQUAKES

On August 17, 1999, an earthquake recording 7.4 on the Richter scale hit northwestern Anatolia along the eastern bounds of the Sea of Marmara, about eighty kilometers outside Istanbul's center. The Marmara Earthquake, as it came to be known, killed around twenty thousand people and left hundreds of thousands homeless. Even though its epicenter was eighty kilometers outside the city, Istanbul suffered a lot of damage in the quake's aftermath, with at least one thousand people dying under the rubble of collapsed buildings within the city's bounds. The earthquake was a wake-up call to a city that had long known it sits within one of the world's most seismically active regions. Istanbul had experienced over thirty destructive earthquakes in its two thousand years of recorded history, and the Marmara Earthquake galvanized fears that the city would soon be hit directly. The memories of that earthquake were relived when consecutive devastating earthquakes shook Turkey in the eastern city of Van in 2011 (Angell 2014, 668) and again outside Gaziantep in 2023. After a period of dormancy, the threat of earthquakes haunted the lives of Istanbul's dwellers once more, prompting fears of unparalleled destruction in a city that had grown exponentially over the last century to over 8.5 million residents in 1999 and 16 million by 2020.[36]

After the Marmara Earthquake, Istanbul's residents didn't sit idly by in paralyzed anticipation of disaster, however. Several sectors of society banded together to demand more action from the government to prepare for the next earthquake. Through expert reports, popular media, and protest slogans it became clear that Istanbul's residents were not treating this earthquake simply

Figure 2.5. Buildings constructed using timber severely damaged by fire and abandoned in Fener-Balat, Istanbul. Source: author, May 2012.

as a "natural disaster." They blamed, at least partially, state negligence for the extent of the damage. In her ethnography, Elizabeth Angell (2014) captures that sentiment at a protest she attended in commemoration of the Marmara Earthquake, where protesters repeated, "Earthquakes don't kill people, buildings do" (669).

The focus on the buildings in this slogan brings together a constellation of dynamics that worked together to intensify the earthquake's destructiveness in Istanbul. First, experts blamed the materials used to construct Istanbul's buildings. In an interesting twist, the transformation away from wood to *kargir* materials, and especially reinforced concrete, was seen to accentuate the city's vulnerability to earthquake damage. On a basic level, wooden buildings are more agile and often closer to the ground. With fewer stories than newer *kargir* buildings, they are less likely to collapse in the event of an earthquake. Even when they do collapse, they are less likely to cause as much death and injury to those who get trapped within them compared with a building made of *kargir* materials, especially reinforced concrete. The concerted effort to save the city from ravaging fires by transforming its building materials in fact circled back to manufacture another set of vulnerabilities (Angell 2014, 670-71).

The discussion of building materials took an even more politicized turn when the contents of the reinforced concrete used over the past four decades or so were questioned. As happened in Cairo in the aftermath of the 1992 earthquake, allegations were made that corrupt officials had allowed construction companies to mix a variety of weaker and cheaper materials into their concrete to maximize profits (Angell 2014, 671). The faulty mixtures had brought Istanbul's buildings crumbling down via an earthquake that hit over eighty kilometers away from the city.

In addition to corrupted concrete mixtures, the state was blamed for a more generalized laxity around enforcing earthquake-related building regulations. The informalization of property rights that had governed how the state dealt with rebuilding the city in the aftermath of fires in affordable housing zones, either occupied by rural migrants or constructed by them as *gecekondus* on the city's periphery, also shaped how it dealt with earthquake regulations. Housing that had ambiguous legal status was left uninspected by the state to avoid wading into thorny legal disputes, and new construction on the informal periphery was left completely unregulated. The impetus to let informalized housing absorb the rural migrant workforce had created yet another set of vulnerabilities for the city and its terrain (Angell 2014, 671).

A diverse movement that brought together engineers, residents (especially in areas affected by the Marmara Earthquake), scientists, urban activists, and many more developed to protest the state's negligence and demand more action in protecting the city. Thirteen years after the Marmara Earthquake, the government responded. In May 2012, the AKP-majority parliament passed the Disaster Law, allowing the state to forcibly condemn and expropriate buildings assessed as "unsafe" in the event of an earthquake through "emergency nationalization." The law was released to much fanfare, with several government officials organizing ceremonious events to mark the law's legislation. During a conference on "urban transformation" that I attended in June 2012 in Eyup neighborhood, then minister of environment and urban planning Erdoğan Bayraktar framed the Disaster Law as realizing the demands of the scientific and expert community to protect the city from its vulnerabilities to earthquake disaster, deploying much of the language that had been circulating in the public sphere by the grassroots movement decrying state negligence.[37] The Disaster Law was framed as an intervention responsive to the movement that had been demanding state action to safeguard the city against earthquakes for over a decade.[38]

The timing of the law's legislation on the heels of the *iptal karar* decrees that nullified urban transformation projects implemented through laws like the Renewal and Preservation Law, and the modalities through which the law was going to be implemented, soon produced much cynicism about the law's main objective. In particular, many questioned why the law had been crafted to allow for wholesale demolition and redevelopment of "disaster-prone zones" and why forced "emergency nationalization" was being deployed to implement earthquake safety regulations rather than softer methods. During our conversations, many experts and urban activists decried that such implementation of the law was primarily designed to service the development industry's needs for wholesale demolition and redevelopment rather than concern for the city's vulnerability to earthquakes.

Moreover, much of the construction planned in lieu of "unsafe," condemned buildings were high-rises that were taller than the condemned buildings, which raised many questions about safety in the event of earthquakes, even if constructed using "safer" materials. In short, experts and activists believed the state was hijacking their movement to enable capital accumulation through large-scale demolition and redevelopment. Regardless of whether the AKP's regime was genuinely invested in safeguarding the city against earthquakes, the way they tackled the threat demonstrated that at the core of their priorities was a project to transfer property to the real estate development industry dominating their elite economic base. The violent transfer of property, again, did not materialize out of nowhere to attack private property rights. Rather, it built on a longue-durée movement that had been slowly but surely working for years to cement in the imaginaries of the city's dwellers the disastrous threat of the next earthquake. The fear of that threat is a powerful force, and through it the state could justify, as "necessary," demolition and dispossession that would otherwise be seen as indefensible infringements on citizen rights. Building on this movement's decade-long organizing is the *work* that goes into the making of neoliberal property relations. Even when neoliberal capital accumulation is at its most overtly violent, it entangles itself within other projects (preferably apolitical expert and scientific ones, such as seismology) to enable and normalize the dispossession undergirding accumulation. It is the work of creating such entanglements that is the key mechanism through which neoliberal market-making becomes depoliticized and elides violence.

Conclusion

The transfer of property in Istanbul's city center from existing property owners to a corporate-developer class allied to the ruling regime proved far more violent in Turkey than in Egypt. Whereas Cairene property owners saw their rent-controlled property as financial, logistical, and emotional burdens, Istanbul's working- and middle-class property owners saw the *value* of their central property as limitless. The price to sell was never right for Istanbul's property owners, who aspirationally saw their property's value skyrocketing with the city's globalization. Nothing short of brute violence would pry that property from its owners and transfer it to regime-aligned developers. The legal trappings of a deregulating law such as the 1996 rent control laws in Egypt that exploited a burdened property-owning class to quietly enable a wholesale transfer of property from one class to another would not work in Istanbul.

Tracing how spatial-material-affective transformations impacted each city's property terrain across chapters 1 and 2 illuminates how property owners in Istanbul and Cairo came to value their property so differently. In this chapter, it's possible to see how the geopolitics and affective experiences of Istanbul's peripheralization; industrialization, anti-minority violence and exodus, and electioneering practices as the city was integrated into regional orbits; and the infrastructural remaking of the city into a "global hub" and the rise of a corporate-developer class all came together to produce an aspirational low- and middle-income property-owning class in the city's center who saw their property's value as limitless. This contrasts markedly from the ways in which Cairo's transformations produced a class of existing property owners who undervalued their property, so that they saw it as a burden rather than an asset, making them willing to sell to the first bidder. Moreover, the divergence between the rootedness of tenants and the alienation of owners from their property in Cairo is not replicated in Istanbul. Instead, tenants in Istanbul closely aligned with owners in how they valued their homes and neighborhoods and in the strong village and kinship networks that connect them.

While the relationships that owners have to their property differ markedly across both cities, what these cases demonstrate is that in both Istanbul and Cairo, class—and the property relations that constitute it—is made through the spatial-material-affective transformations of the city. Through a constellation of geopolitical, infrastructural, affective, environmental, sensorial, and legal-politico institutional dynamics, some of the city's most lucrative property came to be owned by the city's working classes, clustered into ethnic and regional enclaves. Rather than access to wealth or political clout, it was the transforming materiality of the built environment that produced the unique class makeup that positioned the city's working classes as sought-after property owners, and that manufactured how class struggle would unfold as the city's property came into the limelight with the rise of a corporate-developer class in a globalizing Istanbul. The making of class formations is not a static process determined by access to wealth and political clout but rather a fluid process shaped by ever-transforming urban built-environments, among other processes.

In its quest to transfer lucrative property to its economic-elite base, the Turkish ruling regime did not simply expropriate property outright. Instead, it latched onto localized conflicts, situational crises, and grassroots movements to enable forced expropriation. The state manipulated long-developing dynamics and conflicts in the city to attempt to mask the violence of their expropriative regime, at least to a voter base sitting outside immediately affected property owners. Tracing how the AKP-led regime mobilized a depoliticized and aesthetics-focused notion of "urban crisis" to mask a political conflict around morality in Sulukule, elide a dispossessive infrastructural project in Tarlabaşı, and hijack a grassroots movement seeking political accountability for the city's vulnerability to earthquake damage brings to light the *work* that goes into "liberating" property for corporate-capitalist accumulation. Searle (2016) insightfully argues and demonstrates the ways in which that work latches onto and manipulates localized political dynamics and struggles with long histories in the city. Capitalist accumulation in a neoliberal era thrives on its ability to latch onto and manipulate long-existing struggles.

Reading side by side how the "liberation" of property from the shackles of rent control and urban decay (among other factors) enabled the making of "healthy" markets in Egypt and Turkey puts the violence of this process in sharp relief in both contexts. Seeing how, in Cairo, the seemingly nonviolent trappings of property "deregulation" with the gradual reversal of rent control enabled a wholesale and violent transfer of property from overburdened property owners to a heavily capitalized developer class demonstrates that the Turkish state is not unique in its violence, nor is it deviating from a neoliberal ideal of property deregulation. The making of "healthy" property markets and the tool kit of "deregulation" that often accompanies that process is seldom about facilitating property exchange.[39] Deregulation is a process that is being mobilized around the globe to violently transfer property to a rising corporate-capitalist class. What differs among these states is not the political project they are working to enable but the tactics afforded to them depending on how the spatial-material-affective histories of these property terrains have shaped the relationship between city dwellers and their property. Moreover, as I'll show in coming chapters, once they do gain access to this property, corporate-capitalist classes and the states that enable them are constantly working to find ways to *distort* "free market" dynamics in order to multiply the capital they accumulate through property development.

While chapters 1 and 2 have illuminated the intricacies of the violent processes underlying the unleashing of "healthy" property markets in central Cairo and Istanbul, and how they work to transfer property to a rising corporate-capitalist class, the story of neoliberalization does not end here. Alongside this familiar story of "accumulation by dispossession," other actors are waging a battle for housing in Cairo and Istanbul, and they are manipulating hegemonic market logics to enable a host of political projects, including securing affordable housing in city centers. The next three chapters unpack the intricacies of that nonlinear political struggle. They map out how struggles over redistribution and access to property continue to rage in the city rather than being unequivocally settled in favor of this corporate-developer class and trace how the violent *making* of "liberated" property markets has transformed *how* redistributive struggles over property are unfolding in a neoliberal Istanbul and Cairo.

PART II

Redistributive Markets

Heritage 3

ZEYNEP AND HER HUSBAND HIKMET LIVE IN FENER, Istanbul, in a home built by a Greek family at the turn of the twentieth century. They applied for a housing restoration grant from the European Union (EU) as part of the EU's rehabilitation program in the adjoining neighborhoods of Fener and Balat. After much negotiation with the EU's team, they decided to agree that the EU restore only the exteriors of their home and forgo the restorations the EU would have funded for the interior. They turned down the opportunity to restore their interiors because they had several disagreements with the EU team about the restoration plans. Zeynep described what they saw as one of the most egregious of the EU's proposals:

> The biggest disagreement we had was about exposing electric wiring from inside [the walls] to the outside. [The EU] said let's install exposed electric wiring as they did in old times. We objected and said it would look very ugly exposed. Nowadays there is no such thing. This may have been done in the past but now... in Turkey there is no longer any of the old original sturdy materials. Wasn't it made of steel back then [looking at her husband]?

Hikmet then chimed in:

> In the past, at one point, electric wiring was installed on the walls [pointing to the top edge of the walls] in steel rods.... Of course there are no pure steel rods to be found today... and the electric cables were made of plastic on the surface and paper insulation inside [back then]. These cables don't exist anymore. They stopped producing them.... [Our decision] was about safety. If you install short-circuit cables insulated by a layer of paper and plastic that is in immediate contact with the iron rod, mostly copper really, it would be bound to heat up. Common knowledge is that this sort of cable should be covered [within the walls]. Would you want this sort of cable exposed in your home?!... In addition, in our wooden houses you don't use the same electrical installations as normal houses. Our wiring has to be thicker and safer, especially if you're insured.... So, with a television, a refrigerator, and other things we need at least three to four different wire installations around the house.... And because this is a wooden house a fire hazard is even more serious, as a fire would quickly spread to all our neighbors before the fire department gets here, especially with our narrow streets... so that was one of the main disagreements we had with the project.

Exposed, ugly, and potentially unsafe electric wiring was a deal-breaker for Zeynep and her husband. Demonstrating remarkably detailed knowledge of their home's wiring, they simply couldn't understand why the EU was so intransigent about installing such outdated electrical systems after technological advances had resolved so many of these concerns. Exposed electrical wires weren't the only reason Zeynep and Hikmet decided to forgo the opportunity to restore their home at no cost, however. The other deal-breaker was the EU's proposal to remove their cherished bathroom.

Originally, the home was built with only one bathroom on the top floor where the master bedroom is located. When they moved in, Zeynep and Hikmet constructed a second bathroom on the second floor where the living and guest rooms are located. They built the bathroom into the stairwell that was used as closet space by the previous owners. The EU team saw that the bathroom was not part of the original plan for the house during its preliminary survey and said that the bathroom would have to be removed as part of the restorations. Hikmet saw the EU's demand as unreasonable: "If we have visitors they stay [on the second floor], and it gets pretty crowded. Past owners may not have had the same need for a bathroom. I mean, in a way, this setup meets [our] Islamic values." For Hikmet, having a bathroom that was accessible to guests was crucial for a family and their guests who made ablutions ahead of prayer five times a day, a concern that he was not sure their Greek Christian predecessors shared, nor would the EU experts knocking on their door today necessarily appreciate.[1] Ultimately, the EU lost the opportunity to restore a historical home in Fener after having invested so much of their resources in setting up the neighborhood rehabilitation project because they couldn't compromise on wires and bathrooms. The historical accuracy of the restoration reigned supreme.

Introduction

How did the historical accuracy of electrical wiring and a stairwell bathroom become the conflict that prompted Zeynep and Hikmet to refuse a fully paid grant to restore the interiors and structural foundations of their home? Stairwell bathrooms and electrical wires do not typically spring to mind as sites where the politics of heritage unfold. Their intimacy and everydayness hardly evoke the monumental heritage associated with political projects to valorize one history over another. Their private interiority makes them *invisible* from outsider gazing revenue-generating tourists or national public. Yet electrical wires and bathrooms did produce the impasse over which Zeynep and Hikmet refused a fully paid restoration grant. With the EU's arrival at Zeynep and Hikmet's doorstep and their refusal to compromise on the historical accuracy of private home interiors, the everyday and intimate space of a private bathroom became burdened with the weight of identity politics. How did the politics of identity, heritage, and memory seep into the city's most intimate and private spaces?

Tracing the forces, practices, and actors that bring an EU team, intransigent on the historical accuracy of electrical wires and bathrooms, to Zeynep and Hikmet's doorstep, I argue that the seepage of heritage and identity politics into the city's most intimate and invisible spaces is galvanized not by a politics of memory but by a politics of *redistribution*. The project that brought the EU to Fener-Balat was born out of a redistributive initiative to safeguard affordable housing, increasingly vulnerable in a neoliberalizing Istanbul. With housing subsidies, rent control, public housing, and other extra-market redistributive mechanisms on the wane, coalitions championing redistributive agendas turned to the market itself and deployed its logics to claim affordable housing as *valuable*. Within historical neighborhoods, where many low-income communities dwell in cities like Istanbul and Cairo, affordable housing is claimed valuable as *heritage*. Although public monuments had historically garnered the most attention as heritage worthy of preservation, by the turn of the millennium, private property was increasingly valued as heritage to be restored and preserved. A number of processes had come together during the second half of the twentieth century to produce a shift away from treating heritage as *monumental* sites that individually commemorate particular histories over others and toward seeing heritage as *environmental* landscapes valued in their totality, including the private properties that constitute that landscape, regardless of the history they may commemorate. The movement pushing for the environmental shift in heritage was working to extricate heritage preservation as a practice from the politics of memory and identity that had plagued a monumental approach to heritage, reframing it as an apolitical *technical* practice of conserving all of humanity's treasured historical landscapes. An environmental shift that worked to extricate heritage from identity politics coincided with market-driven, political-economic transformation in a neoliberalizing Middle East. Private property, including low-income housing, within historical urban fabrics once contested as battlegrounds for identity politics were reclaimed as spaces of special "value creation" on the open market. Redistributive coalitions capitalized on that newfound worth and sought to mobilize it in ways that would particularly harness that value for the benefit of low-income residents at the exclusion of others. They were fostering *particularistic value* by claiming value for safeguarding low-income housing in the city as heritage. In this chapter, I follow the processes that brought together an unlikely coalition of redistributive activists and the heritage industry to Istanbul's historical districts where activists succeeded in attracting considerable funding toward the upgrading of low-income housing in the Fener and Balat neighborhoods by turning to logics of market value creation in order to claim low-income housing in the district worthy of restoration as prized heritage. Tracing the frictions that animated the work of that unlikely coalition in Fener-Balat as planners, property owners, activists, bureaucrats, tenants, and investors made claims to what should be valued as worthy of preservation and how, I unpack how redistribution materialized on the ground as it was channeled through heritage preservation and how it came to reshape the politics of memory in the city.

Unsurprisingly, I find that channeling redistribution through heritage preservation skewed the redistribution of material resources away from traditional needs-based logics, prioritizing the worth of the neighborhood's historic and aesthetic materiality and redrawing hierarchies of power in the neighborhood. The skewing of redistributive efforts was neither unidirectional nor uniform, however. The project didn't simply unidirectionally force these skewed redistributive effects on a passive, unsuspecting neighborhood of residents. Rather, neighborhood residents, owners of commerce, and the project's own planners maneuvered around the conditioning of redistribution on prioritizing the historic and aesthetic in their quest to access those resources on their own terms and protect what they saw as most valuable about the neighborhood. To maneuver around these conditions, they physically transformed the materiality of their property by hiding artifacts, skirting around Conservation Board regulations and their professional codes, and mobilizing their capabilities as neighborhood brokers to access the opportunities for material gain as well as communal power that the project opened up. Not only did they reconfigure how access to that power and those economic resources were distributed in the neighborhood and sabotage the material landscape of heritage that was so prized for creating new market value in the city, but their defiant maneuvers also repoliticized the project with the identity politics the coalition had been working so hard to evade. Their challenge of the conditions through which redistribution came to the neighborhood didn't reproduce traditional identity politics that simply contested the elevation of one identity group over another. Instead, they invested seemingly technical decisions about the restoration of the city's most intimate and personal spaces with the weight of identity politics, as Hikmet had done. Rather than extricating heritage from identity politics, the environmental shift that enabled the channeling of redistribution through heritage preservation had *displaced* the weight of identity politics onto the city's most intimate and private crevices, with unmistakable ramifications for how the polity would come to grapple with the politics of memory in an era of neoliberalization.

Heritage and Markets: An Environmental Perspective

The shift toward an environmental view of heritage, or what Andreas Huyssen (2003) describes as a "voracious museal culture" (1) where "the form in which we think of the past is increasingly memory without borders rather than national histories within borders" (4), gradually took root as several processes came together throughout the twentieth century. I trace here how psychological experiences with modernity, Cold War politics, postindustrial political economies, and globalizing cities worked together to supplant a monumental view of heritage with an environmental one.

First, a long line of thinkers (e.g., Benjamin 1968; Anderson 1983; Derrida 1998; Nora 1996) have argued that an obsession with archiving the historical trace is a hallmark of a psychological experience of modernity and even more so "super-modernity" (Augé 1995). Pierre Nora (1996) characterizes the experience:

> The "acceleration of history" [thus] brings us face to face with the enormous distance that separates real memory—the kind of inviolate social memory that primitive and archaic societies embodied, and whose secret died with them—from history, which is how modern societies organize a past they are condemned to forget because they are driven by change.... If we still dwelled among our memories, there would be no need to consecrate sites embodying them. *Lieux de mémoire* would not exist, because memory would not have been swept away by history. (2)

For Nora, the disconnect with "real memory" has led modern humanity toward the frenzy of commemorating vanishing historical traces to somehow salvage this lost memory. Walter Benjamin (1968) interrogates the same processes through his study of the dying art of storytelling. The supplanting of the art of storytelling with the novel is emblematic of a shift similar to the one depicted by Nora, "where experience has fallen in value" (83–84). Benjamin argues that this shift is not simply a "'modern' symptom. It is, rather, only a concomitant symptom of the secular productive forces of history, a concomitant that has quite gradually removed narrative from the realm of living speech and at the same time is making it possible to see new beauty in what is vanishing" (87). Ultimately Benjamin (and later Benedict Anderson [1983]) argues that secularism produces the shift toward "homogenous empty time" (262; Anderson 1983, 24). Although Benjamin and Nora may not agree on what causes it, they both document a shift away from living real memory and valued repeated experiences that produce a different and new embodiment of "memory." In the words of Nora (1996), this "modern memory is first of all archival. It relies entirely on the specificity of the trace, the materiality of the vestige, the concreteness of the recording, the visibility of the image ... the less memory is experienced from within, the greater its need for external props and tangible reminders ... hence the obsession with the archive" (8). While these collective psychological experiences are essential to understanding a modern obsession with the historical trace, grounding those experiences in the actors, flows, and political struggles shaping *how* heritage preservation materializes in practice illuminates whether those historical traces are then memorialized as individual *monuments* or totalized *environments*.

Tracing the shift toward a modern memorialization of heritage as totalized environments, scholars first associate that shift with changing international norms that manifest through organizations like the League of Nations and the United Nations (UN). Notably, Lucia Allais (2018) argues that the environmental turn was a political project borne out of the fighting of World War II and Cold War politics that culminated in the adoption of the 1972 World Heritage Convention by the United Nations Educational, Scientific and Cultural Organization (UNESCO), which widely expanded the purview of "universal heritage of mankind" to all historical landscapes that came to be valued as total "environments" rather than individual monuments.[2] Transforming norms around heritage first developed as ethical codes shaped by the experiences of fighting World War II, with the unprecedented scale at which the war threatened heritage. The political project behind the environmental turn became even more pronounced and deliberate as the Cold War unfolded and an expansion of "universal heritage of mankind" to all historical environments, regardless of the history they may represent, produced more spaces for liberal international cooperation in cultural spheres (alongside scientific cooperation) to counter the expansion of the communist bloc. Heritage preservation expanded the jurisdiction of organizations such as UNESCO that were deployed as liberal antidotes to the spread of communism (Allais 2018). The geopolitics of World War II and the Cold War gradually but surely cultivated an international regime of norms that valorized heritagescapes as total historical environments rather than individual monuments commemorating particular histories over others.

In tandem with changing international norms, a second scholarship traced the environmental turn to a transformation of heritage preservation from an almost exclusively top-down practice into one that is largely espoused and practiced by the popular masses of "amateurs and ordinary citizens." Jordan Sand (2013) described this development as "the turn from the monumental to the vernacular" where "more amateurs and ordinary citizens became engaged in [the] preservation . . . [of a] vernacular city connected directly to their lives in a way public monuments [were] not" (3). Expanding what these activist-citizens viewed as valuable heritage beyond the monumental and into the realms of the "vernacular" slowly but surely transformed its scale, moving preservation into the spaces of the private and everyday. Moreover, the grassroots nature of this advocacy transformed heritage preservation from a national or international practice into one that was heavily rooted in *local* histories and experiences, one that eschewed a unifying national project and instead connected local heritage preservation efforts to other local efforts across national boundaries, producing the "memory without borders" Huyssen described above.

In their study of grassroots heritage preservation movements in Tokyo and Brooklyn, Jordan Sand (2013) and Suleiman Osman (2011), respectively, traced the development of local preservationism to postindustrial political economics. Grassroots preservationism was gaining ground in the 1970s and 1980s as a reaction to the suburbanization that accompanied mass industrialization in the two contexts. In Tokyo, industrialization was orchestrated through state-led development coupled with a nationalist project that produced an aggressive monumentalism to heritage preservation that coincided with a valorization of individual private property through suburban home ideals, termed "my homeism" (Sand 2013, 7-8). Sand then argues that "running through all the interpretations of vernacular heritage in the late twentieth century was the ideal of a city constructed and inhabited according to terms other than those dictated by capitalism and state-led development" (3). Specifically, "The closure of the national public sphere and the nuclear-family private sphere as spaces of utopian hope [in a postindustrial mass society] thus permitted new spaces to open in between. The mass politics of the public and intimate phenomenology of the private were brought together in mobilizations for the small common spaces of local community" (10). Osman makes a similar argument about grassroots preservationism in Brooklyn as a spatial manifestation of a postindustrial middle class waging battle against New Deal liberalism. Preservationism was born out of a new localism that "expressed a deep distrust of large institutions, expertise, universal social programs, and public-private consensus . . . [and] championed voluntary service, homeownership, privatism, ethnic heritage, history, self-determination, and do-it-yourself bootstrap neighborhood rehabilitation" (Osman 2011, 14). Such preservationism then found itself allied with a politics of anti-statist, conservative neoliberalism springing from both the Left and the Right. For both Osman and Sand, grassroots preservationism that valorized private, everyday spaces grew out of mass disillusionment with the industrial regimes of the New Deal in the United States and state-led development in Japan. Postindustrial political economics were driving the valorization of the vernacular, moving heritage into the private and everyday *environments* in which the vernacular dwells.

Finally, global tourism further entrenched an environmental view of heritagescapes. An established scholarship on the "global city" (e.g., Harvey 1989; Boyer 1996; Zukin 1996; Keyder 1999; Sassen 2001) has argued that technological and political economic transformations that compressed distances for a global middle class with disposable income produced unprecedented global tourism in the 1970s and beyond. With cities competing with one another to attract tourists, each city worked to carve out a niche for itself among its competitors, and a city's heritage often became central to producing that peculiar persona. Sand expands that idea to argue that urban heritage was preserved to attract not only global but also local tourists with newfound disposable income who had migrated to the suburbs during mass industrialization and now saw the heritage in city centers as exotic spectacles (Sand 2013, 18–23). When heritage is preserved in order to attract tourists rather than memorialize national or identity-based histories, what becomes accepted as heritage expands beyond the monumental to the entirety of *visible* (rather than intimate) historical landscapes that may attract tourists, further solidifying the environmental turn. Psychological experiences of modernity, Cold War politics, postindustrial suburban disenchantment, and global tourism gradually but surely entrenched an environmental view of heritage with far-reaching consequences for private property markets in urban historical cores.

The Fener-Balat Project: Heritage as Redistribution

The seeds of the project that obsessed over the historical accuracy of electrical wiring in Zeynep and Hikmet's home were planted not at a heritage or conservation convention but at the United Nations Conference on Human Settlements: Habitat II. In 1996, planners, government officials, lawyers, academics, and leaders of nongovernmental organizations (NGOs) the world over flocked to Istanbul to craft an agenda that would secure "adequate shelter for all"[3] and "mak[e] human settlements safer, healthier and more livable, equitable, sustainable, and productive."[4] A group of local stakeholders (hereafter "the Habitat coalition") saw Habitat II as an opportunity to build momentum for safeguarding affordable housing in Istanbul, as its residents became increasingly vulnerable to the city's deindustrialization and neoliberalization. As they crafted their campaign, the coalition identified residents of Istanbul's historical core, and especially the Golden Horn region, as one of the most vulnerable groups in the city. As seen in chapter 2, some of the city's most vulnerable populations in the 1990s were migrants who had lived and worked on the Golden Horn and were left unemployed with the city's aggressive deindustrialization and redevelopment into a "global city." Acting upon that urgency, the Habitat coalition focused their campaign on protecting affordable housing in the historical core, choosing the neighborhoods of Fener and Balat as the first site for their intervention.

By 1996 political support for extra-market redistributive policies such as housing subsidies and public housing projects was fast disappearing in Turkey, so the coalition avoided these unpopular demands and got creative. They claimed that housing in the historical core of the city was worthy of protection on terms legible through the logics of the market itself and called for recognizing its worth not simply as the home of some of the city's most vulnerable residents but also as valorized *heritage*. To frame the safeguarding of low-income housing and heritage as integral to one another, they argued, "There is [a] solution ... where the inhabitants of this ancient centre, who are of modest means, can have decent life standards, preserving their heritage, protecting their environment and ensuring the amelioration of their life styles" (Altınsay 2009, 1). The preservation of heritage and protection of the environment now became integral to securing a decent standard of living and "adequate shelter" for the historical core's working-class residents. Putting that integrated approach into action, the Habitat coalition turned to the heritage arm of UNESCO to implement their intervention.

UNESCO jumped at the opportunity to head a heritage preservation project in Istanbul's historical center, and after swiftly conducting a socioenvironmental survey of the neighborhood in 1997, it enlisted the EU and the local Fatih Municipality to jointly sponsor the rehabilitation of Fener-Balat.[5] In 1998, both the EU and the municipality pledged €7 million to the project.[6] As they embarked on the project, all three actors—UNESCO, the EU, and the Fatih Municipality—actively espoused the Habitat coalition's social justice agenda. Rather than seeing a social housing project as a burden that would limit the potential for creating new market value in the city, they found grounding heritage preservation within a social justice framework a welcome and attractive opportunity. A social justice agenda has the potential to distance heritage preservation from a politics of identity/memory and instead open up space for actors historically seen as politically taboo to preserve heritage in hotly contested environments. As shown in chapter 2, Fener and Balat were historically home to mostly non-Muslim communities, with a high concentration of Greek residents in Fener and Jewish residents in Balat, with Fener being home to the Greek Orthodox Patriarchate (or *Patrikhane*) since 1601. With that history, the historical preservation of Fener and Balat can easily be pulled into a politics of memory around Greek-Turkish relations, Muslim-Christian-Jewish relations, and the anti-minority violence that erupted in Istanbul in the 1950s and 1960s, among other conflicts. When the actors restoring the neighborhood are international and European, like UNESCO and the EU, their intentions and relationship to the history of that conflict become especially salient. Emphasizing a social justice mandate, whether or not they did so genuinely, then had the potential to elide that politics and open up space for long tabooed organizations such as the EU and UNESCO to preserve the city's European and non-Muslim community heritage, and do it in partnership with the elected local Fatih Municipality. Over a decade later, UNESCO still claimed that social justice agenda through, for example, its evaluation of the project through the 2008 World Heritage Report where it continued to emphasize that "the Rehabilitation of Fener and Balat Districts Programme grew out of the UN Habitat Conference II, held in 1996 in Istanbul."[7] The Fatih Municipality found it just as important to distance their collaboration with the EU and UNESCO from any suspicions that they were empowering a European narrative of Istanbul's history, and they emphasized time and again the developmental motivation of the project. The municipality's website introduced the project as follows, "As the 1996 Habitat Conference that took place in Istanbul adopted a resolution to 'adopt urban policies that respect social and environmental rights,' the Fener and Balat Neighborhood Rehabilitation Program was envisioned as a model for implementing this resolution."[8]

The commitment to safeguarding affordable housing moved beyond rhetoric to the legal instruments the EU's team mobilized. Alongside the funding that the heritage machine had attracted to the neighborhood, the EU brought with them legal protocols that became instrumental in *regulating* the real estate market against gentrification that could threaten the neighborhood's affordable housing. To get access to restoration grants that the EU offered residents, property owners had to sign a contract that regulated their control over their building after restoration (figure 3.1). These contracts largely mirrored the protocols in the 1983 Law on the Conservation of Cultural and Natural Property, decreed by the Turkish state to protect against the loss of privately owned heritage.[9] Through these protocols, property owners promised not to tamper with any of the restoration work that the EU's team had done or change the building in ways that would jeopardize its historical integrity by, for example, closing off balconies into their indoor living space or installing air-conditioning. Alongside protecting the restoration work, these protocols afforded the Habitat coalition a legal infrastructure for regulating property markets against gentrification. Built into the contract, the EU team embedded decrees that not only protected against the loss of heritage but also regulated the exchange of the restored buildings on real estate markets. One of the main stipulations the EU made was that property owners agree not to sell their property, nor increase rental costs beyond inflation, for

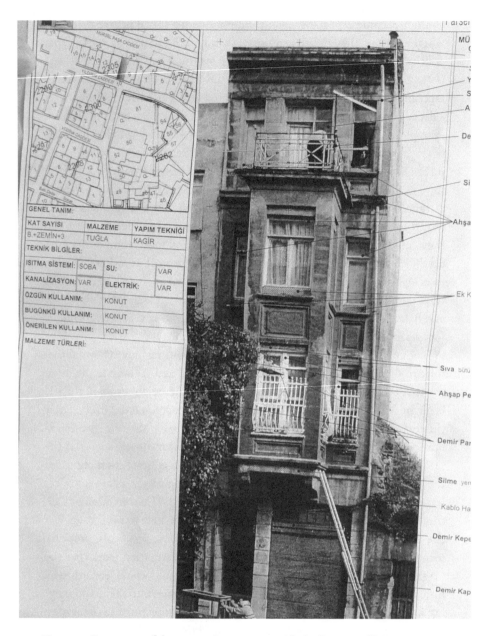

Figure 3.1. Front page of the restoration contract with the European Union. Source: author, May 2012.

the next five years in order to receive the EU's restoration grant. According to Elif, a planner with the EU's team, they included that stipulation because: "All our efforts were geared towards trying to keep that area's current population living in it. That was the principle that they had at the [Habitat II] conference. That's why we had all these protocols. We didn't want to create real estate speculation through our project."[10] Rather than being typical of a heritage protocol, these stipulations were purposefully added to the EU contracts to safeguard affordable housing in Fener-Balat. Elif and her team were consciously working toward stemming the outmigration of neighborhood residents (and especially tenants). Even as layers of actors filtered its social justice agenda to the ground, the commitments the coalition forged at Habitat II remained integral to the compass Elif and her team were working with, and they deployed the regulatory environment created through heritage protocols and their financial leverage in the neighborhood to intervene in its real estate market and stem gentrification. The Habitat coalition likely would have preferred a time frame longer than five years for those protocols, but regulating property, even within that limited time frame, was quite an achievement within Turkey's deregulatory environment. The Habitat coalition had successfully brought much-needed funding and regulatory legal protocols to Fener-Balat's low-income housing.

Rumors and Ghosts: Identity Politics Strike Back

The translation of that funding and regulatory infrastructure into housing upgrades was not so seamless, however. On a most basic level, it proved surprisingly difficult to convince Fener-Balat's residents to accept the fully funded grants to restore their homes. As the EU team went knocking on doors to convince residents, they met considerable resistance from dwellers with strong beliefs about what the EU were *really* doing in the neighborhood. The neighborhood was buzzing with rumors that the EU was funding the project to bring Greeks back to Fener-Balat. As we wrapped and stuffed grape leaves in the basement of a women's association, Emine Hanım told us that the EU project was not to be trusted because they were restoring homes to return them to the Greek populations that used to live in the neighborhood (before the 1955 anti-minority riots). This work, she said, was actually part of a larger plan in collaboration with the *Patrikhane*, or Patriarchate, to turn Fener-Balat into an isolated Christian stronghold in the middle of Istanbul in the same fashion as the Vatican. Özlem Hanım was in agreement, nodding as she heard Emine's warnings. Melek Hanım vehemently retorted that this allegation was not even logical. She explained that the EU project was actually so keen on ensuring that current residents stay in their homes after the restorations that they had the residents, and especially owners, sign a contract that ensured that they would not sell the home in the five years following the restorations. Melek Hanım then implored that the EU could not possibly be working to bring back the Greeks if it did not allow owners to sell their homes for five years after restoration. To that, Emine Hanım responded that this was a long-term project meant to attract the Greeks back to a rejuvenated Fener in the next decade or so.[11]

Emine and Özlem Hanım were not alone in believing and circulating that rumor. I encountered it time and again throughout my fieldwork, and it wasn't just the EU funding but also the legal trappings of the contract that fueled the rumors. For many, rather than a reassurance, the contract that Melek Hanım was sure would put these rumors to rest threw even more suspicion on the project. Many believed that there must be a clause embedded in that contract that would be signing their property away to their former Greek (or non-Muslim) owners. Aynur Hanım brought this up as she explained to me the winding process through which her family ultimately decided to accept the grant and restore the interiors and exteriors of their home with the EU. She recounted that after her family initially showed interest in the grant, her neighbors warned them of the circulating rumors that claimed they would be effectively signing their property away to the EU and implored them not to take the grant. Growing suspicious, the family considered refusing the grant, but then she explained that they had the good fortune of having a lawyer in the family (her niece), who read and reread the contract to put these suspicions to rest. Eventually, because their niece was family, they trusted her reassurances that the EU would not be taking over their property and that the fully funded grant would indeed restore and upgrade their three-story home at no cost to the family, and they signed on. Try as she might, though, Aynur Hanım had a hard time convincing her neighbors and friends that the EU was not going to take over their homes and turn the neighborhood into a Greek enclave in the city, but she also didn't blame them. It was hard to trust anyone but family to decipher the obscure legal language of the contract with the strong suspicions that come with the EU restoring Greek heritage.[12]

These suspicions gained special potency in the neighborhood as they were layered upon how residents experienced the materiality of their neighborhood and its ghosts. Most of the residents who were being offered restoration grants were of the generation that had moved (as children or adults) into these homes in place of minority families fleeing violence and persecution in the 1950s and 1960s, as related in chapter 2. They often knew the stories of the families they had replaced firsthand or through their neighbors' stories and knew full well who would be entitled to that property, were it returned to its previous owners. Like the ghosts that haunted the women and men who dwelled in homes vacated by Greek Cypriots in Northern Cyprus in Navaro-Yashin's (2012, esp. ch. 8) incisive account, Fener-Balat's residents were living in "phantomic spaces" haunted by the ghosts of the fleeing minorities whose homes they had occupied. The ghosts textured the identity politics that flared up in the neighborhood by grounding the circulating rumors about the EU in the materiality of living in homes haunted by ghosts that had known names and faces. Like in Northern Cyprus, the ghosts gain special potency because of the claims they can still make today on their property that was illegally occupied when they fled the city and was retroactively titled by opportunistic electioneering politicians. In some cases, residents (or their neighbors) knew the family members who would be entitled to these properties and may one day come knocking on their door, making claims to their abandoned property, especially if real estate becomes more lucrative in their neighborhood. Residents were especially aware of the precarity of those retroactive deeds in a world where Istanbul may be reckoning with its violent past and reclaiming its cosmopolitanism and openness in a quest to become a European and global cultural hub, starting with winning the bid as the European Capital of Culture in 2010. The descent of the EU onto the neighborhood and its phantomic spaces in the midst of (and as part of the production of) a shifting political climate brought with it a potent identity politics that sabotaged the Habitat coalition's core mission to upgrade low-income housing. One could imagine a very different reaction to the project had it been framed as a social housing subsidy led by a known state actor such as the Mass Housing Authority, aka TOKİ (before its transformation into a predatory developer).

The EU's team confirmed the sabotaging effect of that identity politics on the project's ability to reach some of the neighborhood's most needy families and ailing buildings. Senem, a social expert on the EU's team, recounted that the rumors were a real obstacle to getting people to sign on with the project for their home restorations and that the team dedicated many hours to group and one-on-one meetings to build trust and dispel the rumors "because [neighborhood residents] were actually afraid that they would lose their houses." More frustrating was the fact that many people withdrew from the project after having initially agreed to restore their homes with the EU. According to Senem, the most poignant force behind these withdrawals was that "they heard from their neighbor or they heard from a real-estate speculator that we [the EU team] would buy their house and give it to the *Patrikhane* [or Patriarchate]."[13] In addition to stalling redistribution by discouraging people from accepting the grant, the strength of the rumors actually pushed the EU team to change their designs for the neighborhood to attract people to the project despite the rumors. Elif, the planner seen above, explained that dynamic: "Our criteria towards the end got a little flexed I would say. We were trying to find people who would consent [and accept the grant], so some of our criteria were compromised."[14] However successful the environmental shift and impetus of a social justice agenda may have been in depoliticizing the EU's restoration of formerly Greek housing in Istanbul within official circles, it had not protected the project from that politics once it hit the ground. The neighborhood's dormant ghosts rose to reinvest the project with the identity politics it had worked so hard to extricate itself from. As the ghosts brought potent rumors with them, though, the fear of return of Greek and Jewish communities didn't materialize through familiar geopolitical concerns about war or population exchanges but through the power of title deeds and a slow infiltration of property markets. As the heritage industry's technical-legal instruments were mobilized as an apolitical subtle modality for manipulating real estate markets, the identity politics it claimed to have outgrown came back with a vengeance to both sabotage that social justice agenda and open up a new field through which those politics would operate in Istanbul. Channeling redistribution through the logics of a market that valued heritage over social welfare provision sabotaged the core tenets of the Habitat coalition's social justice agenda by driving its most needy beneficiaries away. As heritage worked to intervene in property markets through seemingly apolitical technical-legal instruments, a struggle over the city's property and its ownership transformed into the battleground where identity politics was feared to be playing out. It was not materializing as a public struggle over a negotiation of history and memory, such as the struggle over recognizing the Armenian Genocide, but was instead traveling to the realm of the private to play out as a fear of a slow and subtle infiltration of private property markets.

The Bricks and Mortar of Identity Politics

The dormant ghosts of the neighborhood's Greek and Jewish communities not only materialized as fear over the future of the neighborhood's property, but also haunted intricate design decisions once the EU team managed to convince some residents to accept the grants and started conserving the neighborhood's buildings (see example of restored building in figure 3.2). Time and again I saw them seep into debates over the design of the most intricate and intimate of spaces within residents' homes. Turning back to Zeynep and Hikmet from the opening vignette, the neighborhood's dormant ghosts subtly appear when Hikmet defended their second bathroom. Rather than resort to everyday comforts as justification, he evoked religion when he said, "If we have visitors they stay [on the second floor], and it gets pretty crowded. Past owners may not have had the same need for a bathroom. I mean, in a way, this setup meets [our] Islamic values." He framed this everyday comfort through the prism of religion, as a value embodied in his home's spaces. In addition to regular needs, Muslims need to use bathrooms to perform ablutions (cleansing rituals) before they pray five times a day. Thus, traffic would be even heavier on bathrooms, especially when visitors stay over, in the homes of practicing Muslims. Hikmet argues that this religious need sets him and his household apart from their Greek non-Muslim predecessors who did not have the same religious needs and thus did not design their house to accommodate them. He also felt that the EU team would similarly be incapable of understanding or valuing that religious need, assuming they were not practicing Muslims. As he brought up the cultural and religious differences that set his family apart from their Greek predecessors to defend his stairwell bathroom, Hikmet reinvested the project with the identity politics (manifesting here around religion-based identity groups) that the EU and UNESCO had worked so hard to extricate themselves from.

Interestingly, Hikmet framed his critique of those identity politics not in terms of a traditional concern over the elevation of one identity group over another (that often erupts during conflict over monumental heritage) but through the groups' divergent experiences of the city in its most intimate of spaces. Conscious of the EU's efforts to distance their project from identity politics through their technical, depoliticizing focus on the accuracy of all historical environments, Hikmet drew strength in his critique by reintroducing the very same identity politics the EU was fleeing within those technical details and intimate spaces. In repoliticizing the technical practices through which heritage had been depoliticized and mobilized to intervene in the struggle over property markets, Hikmet hadn't simply reignited the identity-based political struggles that the EU was hoping to bury but had also displaced where and how they materialized. The specter of minorities' ghosts was now quietly, and perhaps insidiously, rearing its head through the city's most intimate and personal of spaces rather than through the traditional facets of the public sphere where these struggles had traditionally unfolded.

The dynamics behind the displacement of identity politics onto the city's personal and intimate spaces manifested again as one of the residents debated the paint colors of her home's exteriors with the EU team, as explained by Elif:

> For example, one lady wanted her balconies to be painted a particular color. You know I was fully dedicated to her because she was involved with her house and she wanted her say in it. She of course created a lot of problems during the construction, but I liked the way she *owned* her house. So, we tried to do what she wanted but we couldn't because she wanted [a color that was] too bright. Later she did paint the color she wanted, and that's all right.... We gave them a range of colors and had them choose. If they thought the colors were foreign colors, well the houses were originally foreign. What can I do? They would prefer bright pinks, bright oranges.[15]

This confrontation is revealing on multiple levels. First, as this negotiation unfolded, it became clear that paint colors didn't simply satisfy personal aesthetic preferences but also worked to code buildings as foreign or local in the city. This resident wanted to paint her home a bright pink or orange not simply because that was her aesthetic preference but because it coded her home as "local" within an urban fabric riddled with the imprint of the "foreign." The city's urban materiality, down to the minute detail of a building's paint color or sartorial aesthetics as described in chapter 2, was one of the main theaters upon which identity politics was performed in the city, and interventions that would transform that materiality would inevitably step into the throes of that politics. Coding buildings as "foreign" or "local" could simply be an urban dweller's way of declaring their belonging to one group or another. Since Fener-Balat is quite religiously homogeneous, with an overwhelming majority of Muslim Turks after the non-Muslim exodus, such coding likely carries an even deeper meaning in the neighborhood. Buildings that were once painted in "foreign" colors were likely inhabited in the past by non-Muslims, including the Greek Orthodox and Jewish communities that dominated these neighborhoods before their exodus. As I discussed in chapter 2, rural migrants who moved to Istanbul after the non-Muslim exodus of the 1950s and 1960s often illegally occupied vacant housing and were only given rights to their homes retroactively by electioneering politicians. Continuing to live in homes coded as "foreign" by their paint colors is a constant reminder of the violent history through which Fener-Balat's residents had come to occupy prime real estate in the city's center. Although probably not entirely consciously, painting their homes "local" colors helps residents distance themselves from that violent history and their own complicity in it as beneficiaries of its fallout, or what Northern Cypriots in Navarro-Yashin's (2012, ch. 6) account referred to as the "loot" or "*ganimet*" upon which their political community was built. Restoring homes to their original paint colors marks these homes as ones that were once illegally occupied loot, and has the power to reassociate its owners with that violent history. Again, the technical details, operating at the most personal of levels, through which the environmental turn was working to depoliticize heritage were repoliticized when the EU's team was reminded that paint colors were not simply aesthetic choices but coded buildings within the neighborhood's history with identity politics. The move toward the technical restoration of all historical landscapes as equally valuable was not depoliticizing heritage preservation meant to intervene in market struggles. It was displacing the weight of identity politics onto the city's most intimate and personal crevices.

The subtle displacement of identity politics as the specters of the neighborhood's ghosts manifested in debates over stairwell bathrooms or paint colors transformed not just where identity-based political struggles appeared but also how they were experienced in the polity. Repoliticizing the technical details of restoration compelled identity politics to manifest more subtly, and perhaps insidiously, through the logistics of everyday life within the city's intimate spaces and away from public arenas now claiming cosmopolitanism and inclusiveness, especially in the wake of Istanbul's declaration as European Capital of Culture in 2010. The dissonance that was brewing in how identity politics were experienced in public and private realms carried the potential of an even more explosive political backlash (perhaps foregrounding the growing appeal of populism soon to plague Turkish politics) borne from its festering within spaces and crevices impossible to excavate and grapple with in their subtlety within such a dissonant political climate.

Ignorance, Environmental Care, and the Classed Politics of Conservation

The Denizli family's three-story home was also built by a Greek family at the turn of the twentieth century. They applied for a restoration grant from the EU in 2003–4 and started negotiations with the team from there. Three years before the Denizli family had encountered the EU, their living room walls had

Figure 3.2. Example of a home restored by the European Union.
Source: author, May 2012.

suffered from water leakage and they had to replaster them. As they removed the gypsum and paint layers of the wall, they made an unexpected discovery. Instead of uncovering layers of ugly brick, they were astounded to find colorful walls beneath the gypsum. Emel Hanım and her son Hüseyin attempted to describe what they found in great detail as I sat in their living room.

"The bricks were covered with a white lime-based plastering material.... We don't know this plastering material today," started Hüseyin. The plaster was covered by handcrafted designs that came together to form what Hüseyin described as "an enormous, richly adorned *tablo* (painting)." According to Emel Hanım, they found such *tablos* in several rooms of the house, not just the living room: "The painting would cover the wall from top to bottom and in the middle a different *desen* [or design/pattern] would be found. In other words, it was like a painting. Each wall had a different design at the center... for example, this room's [pointing to the adjacent room] design was different.... They used at least three to four colors. There was yellow, green." Hüseyin then expressed their marvel at the preservation of the colors where "decades had passed and yet the colors remained vivid [*canlı renkler*]. Truly, we were astonished by the vivid colors!" After much deliberation with my research associate Cem, we came to the conclusion that what the Denizli family had uncovered beneath layers of paint and gypsum were most likely fresco-based murals.

The reason why Emel Hanım and her son Hüseyin had to go to such lengths to describe the murals to me was that I could not see them. As I sat in their living room in June 2012, all I could see were plain walls covered in white paint. The question then became: Where are the murals?

The Denizli family had actively covered the murals. Emel Hanım explained, "They were so beautiful that we covered the walls to ensure that the UNESCO not see them... because they would not have given us permission to plaster over them. They would have forced us to restore them." Hüseyin then explained that when they had originally uncovered the murals, they had contemplated restoring them themselves but that neither the original materials nor the craftsmen (*ustalar*) necessary to restore the walls were to be found: "It would have required archeologists or specialized university students.... [I]t would have required both a long time commitment and a large financial investment to restore. Perhaps if we had the resources, we would have done it, but who is capable of that?" As a result, once they heard rumors that the EU (whom they referred to as UNESCO) was going to start the implementation phase of their project in 2003, they immediately covered the murals because "the UNESCO... could not see it. Had they seen it, for sure they would have restored it."[16]

Emel Hanım then emphatically made her case against involving the EU architects. She argued,

> They had found similar artifacts in several houses before ours. As soon as they saw them, they would immediately start restoring. I mean, in our case, they took around one year and a half [to restore the exteriors of the home].... If they were to restore these paintings, it would last at least five years of them working inside of our home. In other words, for five years there would be men from UNESCO working inside my home, and it would be impossible to be comfortable. It would be very difficult because their restorations are very involved [çok ağır yapılıyor].

Having to live outside her home for five years was too costly of a choice for Emel Hanım to make in order to restore the murals. Ultimately, in fear of the EU restoration team's zeal, the Denizli family rushed to cover the murals adorning their home's original walls.[17]

While she narrated the uncovering and covering of the murals, Emel Hanım walked me from room to room on their home's main floor, vividly describing the designs and colors of the murals that covered each wall. As she painted the murals into our imaginations, she radiated with pride. Her home was not like any other home in the district. Hers was the distinguished home adorned by rare and beautiful murals on every wall, even if not visible. Twinned with her pride was a visible agitation. She was distraught by a sense of loss for the murals we could no longer see. The Denizli family did not cover the murals out of simple ignorance of their historical or aesthetic value. Far from it. They had such a deep appreciation for their value that they shared with me the story of their uncovering and covering at the risk of sounding ignorant of the murals' value or of that information going back to zealous conservationists to impress upon me just how special their home was. Theirs was hardly the work of ignorant laymen inadvertently destroying heritage as they went about their daily lives with no appreciation for the historical. The Denizli family was making a pragmatic decision to cover the murals and challenging an order that put the murals above their well-being.

Yet in spite of Emel Hanım's agitation over losing the murals and the many encounters I had with residents who had intricate knowledge and appreciation for the histories of their homes and their materials, many of the conservationists I met believed that the people living within historical buildings were the biggest threat to heritage. They repeatedly lamented that residents did not have the awareness (*farkındalık* or *kültür* in Turkish or *waʿey* in Arabic) to appreciate or care for historical buildings. For example, an Egyptian conservationist who had worked on several state- and internationally funded conservation projects in Islamic Cairo told me, "Unfortunately [the population's] *waʿey* here is backward [or *motakhalef*]."[18] Another conservationist went a step further to suggest that only people with the intellectual capacity to appreciate heritage should live in historical neighborhoods. He had been working on the state's conservation project in Gamaliyya, Cairo, and told me that if he had his way he would evacuate all of Gamaliyya's residents and replace them with new residents who are "above average intellectually [or *mothaqaf*] and ... are youth in order to liven up [or *yeḥyi*] the neighborhood."[19] Such beliefs were echoed across the board, even by conservationists working on projects embracing a social justice agenda. One of the planners on the AKTC's redistributive project told me, "We had a problem in the housing program because people weren't fit to use their houses after their rehabilitation."[20] Conservationists often couched these beliefs within discussions about the need for environmental awareness campaigns, but it is not hard to see how these beliefs would judge, even subconsciously, some residents as more worthy of restoration grants than others.

Circling back to Fener-Balat, I saw the subtle ways these judgments of worth could develop through a conversation I had with Duygu, a member of the EU's team. Duygu explained to me why she found working with Fener-Balat's residents quite difficult sometimes:

> I was really amazed with the lack of tidiness [in the neighborhood]. One house, we went in there, and you know my colleague, he's a man, and we went in this house, and there was underwear everywhere. I mean, they knew we would be there the next day. You could actually tidy your house. I was ashamed going into the house. You would look at the house, and this was a middle-class family ... such things personally bothered me, maybe they shouldn't, [but] the level of poverty and dirt and other things. And these houses had running water. I mean, I did projects in rural Southeast Anatolia, and I saw people who did not have anything, but as long as they had running water, their houses would be clean. I have seen poverty, but this was something else.... If you know you're expecting a guest, at least get rid of your underwear.... I was really ashamed. It was everywhere.[21]

When Duygu and her colleagues walked into people's intimate home spaces to do their work, they brought with them their beliefs about decent behavior, what it takes to care for homes (especially historical ones), what sets people within the same class (of poverty) apart from each other and more or less worthy of a helping hand, and so on. Becoming privy to people's intimate lives, and possibly their (dirty?) laundry, then lends itself to, at least a subconscious, exercise in judging how people measured up to those beliefs. Whether they would admit it or not, those judgments stayed with EU experts as they made difficult decisions about who would be receiving EU funding and who would be turned away. Such judgments of character and decency (often tinged with strong class connotations) generally have the potential to impact development work, but it gains special potency when couched through heritage preservation. Heritage preservation centers the protection of historical buildings and artifacts alongside, if not in priority to, alleviating the inequality and poverty that ails their residents. Centering the building gives creed to judgments about people's worthiness of grant money because it justifies asking questions about people's cleanliness, intellectual awareness, and decency in relation to their ability to care for these invaluable buildings. As a language of care gives credence to these questions, it opens up space for the complicated class, racial, and religious politics that shape and color those judgments.

When the Denizli family covered the murals but then took great care to narrate the story of the uncovering and covering of the murals to their (non-EU) visitors, they laid bare the hypocrisy of classed beliefs about ignorance and environmental care when entwined with systemic shifts toward neoliberal market-making. Rather than being an unconditional subsidy, getting access to funding that would secure the safety of their home's structures and beautify its fixtures was conditioned on the obsessively accurate conservation of their home's historical materiality. While they covered the murals to outmaneuver an order that put the worth of buildings and their historical materiality above people, the Denizli family had undermined the essence of that order by remaking their physical world and actively hiding the artifacts that the market had prized as the neighborhood's most valuable of assets.

In an interesting twist, while the outside world lost access to the historical murals the family had hidden, the Denizli family found a way to recover the privileged status in their community that they derived from the murals. As they narrated the covering of the murals to me and countless others, and painted the murals back to life before our eyes, they slowly reconstructed their distinction in the neighborhood as owners of the home adorned with beautiful, historical murals. In fact, the allure of hidden historical artifacts (and treasures) possibly even added to the value of the covered murals. They had mobilized the power of narration to defy the logics through which value was being calculated in a sight-centric world and recovered the murals' power to distinguish their family in the neighborhood. The Denizli family had not lost their murals after all.

Conflicted Planning: Self-Reflexive Experts
and Neoliberal Redistribution

Neighborhood residents were not the only ones challenging the project's tenets in Fener-Balat. The architects, planners, and social liaisons working on the EU's team were also defiant in their own ways. Earlier in the chapter, I discussed fissures in the edifice of an EU team intransigent on the historical accuracy of their restorations when discussing the paint colors of building façades. There, one of the EU team's own planners, Elif, defied the project's fixation on historical accuracy to satisfy the homeowner's preferences for façade colors. Any compromises on historical accuracy are worth investigating, but this one was particularly interesting because it was not made to satisfy any of the resident's essential needs in everyday life. Instead, Elif turned a blind eye as the woman painted the house an inaccurate bright color because she "liked the way [this woman] *owned* her house." Elif valued the strong emotional bonds that this resident had with her home and didn't want to see conservation rules dilute them. Elif's belief in the value of the emotional bonds residents fostered with their home, as what I term a *self-reflexive expert*, complicated the project's elevation of historical worth.[22] I focus here on Elif's ideas, planning priorities, and relationship to the project as a microcosm through which one can see the layers and fissures operating within projects wedding redistribution and heritage preservation, because she amassed quite a bit of authority within the EU's team over time and took an illuminating, circuitous path as she did so.

Elif's defiance of a rigid understanding of conservation manifests again in how she dealt with discrepancies between current and original home layouts. She explained how her team dealt with modified balcony spaces as follows:

> They have small balconies . . . they usually closed them to make room. . . . They didn't want to go back to open terraces, because they could create an extra room. The Conservation Board tells us that you have to knock this off because this is illegal, so we didn't listen because I can't knock someone's bedroom. It's not our issue. We didn't want to beautify something that is illegal, but we just tried to be plain on that level. Keep it simple and just repair and go away. But in some balconies where they had

extended, we went back to the original size with the railings and top shade and everything, because they made really horrible and unsafe extensions.[23]

Elif painted a picture of a team highly attuned to the everyday needs of dwellers that worked toward minimizing the discomforts of restoration rather than an intransigent team that was deaf to the concerns Zeynep, Hikmet, and many others had as they applied for restoration grants. She was especially keen to avoid invading the privacy and comfort of people's bedrooms. Despite her professional commitment to accurate conservation, she would rather maneuver around a few conservation rules than see families become so frustrated with the discomfort of living within the confines of historical homes that they would leave the neighborhood—something the Habitat coalition meant to avoid. Elif's maneuvers around those conditions was not universally accepted within the team, however. For example, when I talked to Tuna, another conservationist on the team, he was emphatic about the inflexibility of layout and explained that any and all extensions had to be dismantled, with no exceptions. The discrepancy between the approaches Elif and Tuna took to the accuracy of restorations points not only to the obvious conclusion that the EU's team was not a harmonious monolith but also illuminates the unstable and uneven conditions residents encountered as they tried to access redistributive restoration grants, and how dependent the process was on the personalities and layers that shaped the EU's team at any given time. The extent of those layers becomes even clearer when delving into the plans Elif had for the neighborhood's social spaces.

Elif worked to foster strong emotional and social bonds in the neighborhood—not just through housing restorations but also through the plans she devised for its shared and social spaces. That commitment shined through as Elif explained to me how she saw her relationship to the neighborhood: "You live there five and a half years and that's how we got to know the heart and soul of the place. It's not something where you can go and do some research and ask people certain things and then decide for planning. It's almost impossible."[24] From that experience, Elif and (some of) her colleagues learned a lot about the intricacies of social life in the neighborhood and developed several plans meant to preserve and perhaps even strengthen its sociality. Her first set of proposals remained close to the designs of restored homes and their fixtures:

> There are interesting needs of such areas.... For example, they wash carpets on the street all the time. I think they also [wash carpets] commercially apart from their own carpets.... You have to provide [carpet-

cleaning facilities] if they need it. Of course, we didn't because it's not nice. Also, we meant to reestablish all those clotheslines but make them a bit better. We meant to use a similar system but with . . . better pulleys and cords. You could make a stainless cord . . . but that didn't happen. The budget was spent on [other considerations]. . . . I believe we could've [restored] a fewer number of houses and [spent more] on these important [additions]. The EU [was so focused on numbers]. They said . . . the 121 houses [we restored] were not enough [because they didn't reach the plan's target] of 200. That's [misguided], I think.[25]

Elif's perceptive eye had recognized Fener-Balat's clotheslines and alleyways right outside building doorsteps as particularly valuable social spaces. In Fener-Balat, women clean carpets together, whether for personal use or commercially, leaving behind small rivers of soapy water flowing down the neighborhood's hilly streets no matter the season. Elif and her team wanted to make sure that there would be a place for that soapy water to go, so that carpet cleaning would survive the changes that were bringing more and more tourists and municipal regulations to the neighborhood. The alleyways as spaces for carpet cleaning would be valuable, both as places of sociality that build stronger bonds between neighbors and as sources of income. Stronger social bonds and access to income keep people invested in their neighborhood against the forces that may push for their outmigration. In a similar vein, Elif valued the banal materiality of the neighborhood's clotheslines. Clotheslines hover above streets, crossing from one side to another as they connect buildings on opposite sides of the street (see figure 3.3). To hang their clothes, residents pull on their side of the line, aided by a pulley, to bring the line closer to their window and hang their clothes. As they do so, residents on opposite sides of the street are constantly coordinating and sharing the intimate space where they dry their clothes. Here, again, Elif and her team saw that the best way to sustain the neighborhood's social bonds was to ensure these practices survived by making them more resilient to change. Unlike her success with maneuvering around the Conservation Board during home restorations, these plans never saw the light of day. Both plans came up against her employers' heritage priorities and aesthetic ideas about what was considered "nice" in a neighborhood and what was meant to attract tourists to the city. The first layer of pushback Elif encountered as she set about to strengthen social bonds in the neighborhood came from within the organization, as her supervisors turned down her proposals.

Her supervisors didn't turn down all her proposals, however. As Elif moved away from building fixtures like clotheslines or the soapy trails left from their

Figure 3.3. Image from Fener-Balat with cleaned carpets hanging on clotheslines that connect buildings across the street. Source: author, July 2015.

doorsteps to more traditional public spaces like proposing a public garden, Elif found traction with her supervisors:

> We identified an area for a park that was owned by the *vakıflar* [or religious endowments], but [it was] occupied by someone who was using it as a paper storage area. It was almost like a wasteland. So, our financial director worked hard, and went out to Ankara and so on, and got this area to be given to the Municipality for a certain period of time.... We designed the area and started the construction, but a lot of money went into [restoring] the retaining walls so we couldn't finish the final park servicing, the gate, and so on. So, we gave it to the Municipality and [sadly] the first thing they did was pave it with [cobblestones]... and rent it out as a private tea garden.[26]

Although she had an easier time convincing her superiors that creating a public garden would align with the project's social goals, the perversities of

134   Chapter Three

embarking on socially-attuned projects through the workings of a heritage preservation project soon reared their head. Instead of building up the park's infrastructure, the EU invested most of the park's budget in the restoration and beautification of its outer gates, betraying their prioritization of the aesthetic above all else. Then, the plan saw its final blow as the municipality, the EU's partner and now official owner of the space of the park, decided to turn it into a private tea garden that would collect immediate revenue from paying tourists rather than contribute to the social justice agenda that they claim to prioritize on their website. Elif's plan to sustain and thicken social bonds in the neighborhood was thwarted by the complicated web of actors enacting the Fener-Balat rehabilitation project on the ground.

The stakeholders Elif encountered weren't confined to those within that web of actors, however. As Elif put forth a final proposal to strengthen social bonds in the neighborhood, yet another group appeared to stifle her plans. Alongside the public garden, Elif had envisioned a much larger public parks project for the area when she learned that "the ladies [in the neighborhood] don't go out on to the waterfront because there is a huge traffic road [separating the neighborhood and the waterfront] that they can't cross easily, and they can't leave their house because they cook something and sit in front of their home [watching] their children play. So, I thought we could make temporary corner parks for them [on empty lots where demolished buildings once stood], but we couldn't get the permissions from the landowners."[27] This time, when she managed to get support from her superiors for dedicating time and energy to a project so finely attuned to the rhythms and needs of the neighborhood's women, Elif and her team encountered yet another roadblock: property owners. While it's understandable that property owners would fear that the temporariness of the project would eventually gain unwelcome permanence or confound more immediate sales opportunities, this encounter suggests that neighborhood landowners and residents are not simply on the receiving end of interventions such as the EU's. They often wield a lot of power as enablers or obstructers of plans designed to incorporate their property in one way or another. Rather than view them romantically as challenging a dispossessive order, it is important to conceptualize the positionality of neighborhood dwellers and property owners as one that is deeply intertwined with the web of power relations that shapes these projects.

By the end of her time working with a project, Elif had amassed a lot of authority in shaping its trajectory, but she came upon that authority circuitously. Early in the project, Elif had been hired as a member of the technical team on the ground in Fener-Balat. By the time the project was exiting

Fener-Balat, Elif had been promoted to become one of the directors of that technical team. In the middle, though, Elif had been fired from the project, rehired a year or so later, and then eventually promoted. How do we make sense of that circuitous path? She described her firing as follows,

> [There was] a stage when I was not on the project. I was talking too much, I think, so they sent me off, and then they brought me back. The management was not very good at the beginning. It was never very good, really. These companies that work for EU projects are really too commercial, and they don't understand. The EU itself did not understand this project, because they had no experience in it.... They said, "Repair around two hundred buildings," and I was saying, "What do you mean by repair? These buildings are not buildings that you go touch and then go away. If you touch them, things will happen."[28]

It is hard to know the exact circumstances behind Elif's firing and rehiring, but her account indicates that she had a self-image as someone who was critical of some aspects of the project and vocal about that criticism. It's clear from the account of Elif's many proposals that she was constantly pushing leadership to expand what they understood as social dimensions of the project beyond their focus on restoring a countable number of buildings enumerated in donor reports. If not the whole story, it is clear that Elif was someone who experienced a lot of friction with her supervisors, and that could have been at least one of the reasons she was initially fired.

In spite of that friction, Elif was soon rehired and eventually promoted to lead the project. The timing of Elif's rehiring is telling. Elif was fired early on in the project, but soon after, the project faced backlash in the neighborhood. It is then not surprising that the EU turned to experts like Elif to help them regain the neighborhood's trust and overcome the power of rumors and suspicion. Elif's dedication to an expansive understanding of social implications had been the source of the friction she had with her supervisors but now became the reason they saw her as valuable. Her knowledge of minute details such as the sociality of clotheslines or the coding of building paint colors set her apart from other experts as an especially effective *broker* between those funding the project and the residents who needed to accept that funding for the project to succeed. Her expertise was particularly valuable because unlike neighborhood dwellers or "social liaisons" who could and did serve as brokers, she combined that intimate knowledge of the neighborhood with professional training and expertise in conservation. With that amassed authority, Elif's beliefs and political proclivities gained unforeseen power in shaping how the project would unfold in the neighborhood. In exercising that power, she actively destabilized from within the conditionalities obstructing the Habitat coalition's redistributive vision as it was being forced through the confines of a heritage preservation project.

The Architect's Guide

Experts on payroll aren't the only brokers who mediate between the multiple layers of a project. As rumors spread and the project stalled, the EU enlisted residents as brokers who would assure their neighbors that they could entrust their homes to the EU for restoration. Kemal Bey, from chapter 2's opening vignette, became just such a broker in Fener-Balat. He was one of the first residents to agree to restore his home with the EU. As restorations on his home progressed, he became quite engrossed in the team's work, spending a lot of time with the architects, learning about the history they hoped to restore, and the architectural intricacies of the restoration process. With time, Kemal Bey had acquired elaborate knowledge of the process and, most importantly, he had seen the EU meticulously restore the inside and outside of his home and return it to him without threatening his ownership or tenure in his home in any way. When the EU team started having trouble enlisting more residents to accept restoration grants, Kemal Bey was well positioned to become a broker who could help build trust between the EU's team and his neighbors. Soon he was standing side by side with EU architects and conservationists at town hall meetings that the EU had organized to dispel myths about the project, assuring his neighbors that it was safe to restore their homes with the EU and mediating their concerns to the EU team. He was even, on occasion, invited to join the team during one-on-one negotiations with residents considering restoring their homes with the EU. The time and effort he put into that mediation soon became worth its while. Kemal Bey slowly transformed from a retired schoolteacher into a neighborhood gatekeeper. The more he appeared alongside the EU's team, the more Kemal Bey gained a reputation as someone who could directly connect residents to EU architects and help them sidestep the intimidating formal application process, and perhaps even get them special attention from the team as friends. He became a gateway to some of the most coveted resources to come to the neighborhood in a long time.

On their end, the EU rewarded Kemal Bey. Not only did they give him visibility within the neighborhood as a trusted liaison but soon gave him that visibility outside the neighborhood as well. Kemal Bey received his greatest endorsement as a neighborhood broker when the EU team chose him as one of three members of the Fener-Balat community to be featured in a short documentary film about the EU's project airing on Turkish television. When I visited Kemal Bey, the most important element of the visit for him was showing me the entire documentary film. As we watched, he paid little attention to what was being said about the project and focused instead on explaining to me that the EU had chosen only the most important members of the community to be featured in the documentary. He, a retired schoolteacher of modest means, was on national television alongside two recognized community leaders who had gained that status through extensive property ownership in the neighborhood.[29] Kemal Bey had steadily but surely accumulated power as a community leader—not through access to wealth, family networks, or elected office but through mediating the community's access to the EU's housing grants, some of the most coveted resources to land in the neighborhood since its deindustrialization. I myself encountered Kemal Bey's renown as I was repeatedly referred to him by other residents as the person to talk to about the EU's project in the neighborhood. As the EU enlisted brokers to overcome the rumors that had politicized and stalled their project, they were not only redistributing access to safe, affordable housing but also redrawing hierarchies of power in the neighborhood.

Urban Archiving and Communal Power

Enlisting residents as brokers wasn't the only way that a project like the EU's redrew hierarchies of power in the neighborhood. In this final section, I step outside Fener-Balat and cross the bridge over the Golden Horn to the neighborhood of Tarlabaşı, where as seen in chapter 2, a public-private partnership with Çalik Holding was implementing a violently dispossessive urban renewal project. Here, I examine how urban dwellers have cultivated power in their communities through the relationships they fostered with their neighborhood's histories, and especially through the practice of *archiving*. I then explore how the prioritization of narrow understandings of the historic and aesthetic value of a city's urban fabric that comes with heritage preservation can disrupt those archives and the communal power that urban dwellers accumulate through them.

Figure 3.4. Barbershop mirror fixtures in Tarlabaşı, Istanbul.
Source: author, June 2012.

HEADSHOTS

Mustafa and Emre Bey have been collecting headshots of their friends and clients for twenty-eight years. The dozens of passport-size photographs they've collected are displayed on the mirror fixtures (figure 3.4) of the barbershop they run in the center of the zone evacuated in preparation for the urban renewal project in Tarlabaşı. As Cem and I wandered through the evacuated, pillaged, and in some cases burned buildings in the urban renewal zone and talked to the few remaining residents and establishments operating on the periphery, we were repeatedly referred to Mustafa Bey's barbershop, still operating in the renewal zone in spite of the evacuations.

The buzz inside the barbershop contrasted sharply with the dead quiet outside its doors. There were several clients under Mustafa and Emre Bey's razors as well as a friend in another chair chatting with them casually. What struck me most though were the headshots arranged side by side on the mirrors of the shop. When I asked about the photos, Mustafa Bey explained that his father had started collecting photographs when he ran the shop and that he had continued the tradition, along with his business partner Emre Bey. The pictures included extended family members, his father's friends and clients, and their own friends. One of the pictures was of a researcher who had been living in Tarlabaşı for two years now and came to the barbershop often.

As Mustafa and Emre Bey explained who was who on the wall of photos and their life stories over the past three decades, Cem could not help but exclaim, "Müze gibi ya!" translatable to, "Wow! It's like a museum!"[30]

As I heard Mustafa and Emre Bey relate the life stories of the people in the photographs, I started to appreciate why Cem and I had been referred to their barbershop. As they meticulously archived and displayed the neighborhood's social universe on their mirror fixtures, their barbershop had developed into an anchor for the neighborhood that kept track of the community's past and present. Because they had been there for twenty-eight years, many of the photographs on the mirror were of people who were no longer living in Tarlabaşı. This is particularly important in this neighborhood, given the somewhat itinerant nature of its community. Since the 1980s, Tarlabaşı has acted as the first landing for many new migrants into Istanbul, and especially Kurdish migrants coming from the Eastern provinces, and more recently a population of migrants from Africa and Syria. Although for many Tarlabaşı became a permanent home, there was relatively more turnover than in other neighborhoods in Istanbul's city center. The photographs kept track of that movement.

The barbershop documented the intricate networks that shaped the community, but more importantly it became a place where stories that relate these connections came to life. The power of the materiality of the photographs to evoke stories designated the barbershop an anchoring place, where people came to not only learn about these people and their histories but also relate their own. While we were in the barbershop, we were introduced to Selim Bey, who had already gotten his shave and was sitting casually on a chair to the side, chatting with Mustafa and Emre as well as some of the clients who came in who seemed to know him well. Selim had lived in Tarlabaşı for many years before moving away a decade or so before our visit to the barbershop. Yet he told us that he comes back to the barbershop almost on a weekly basis on his day off to see his friends and share life updates.[31] The barbershop had become the anchor through which people built and maintained their social universe—not just in Tarlabaşı but in Istanbul—for most of the people whose headshots adorned its mirror. The meticulous collection and tracking of these photographs gave Mustafa and Emre Bey particular power in shaping how the community's social universe was commemorated and the narratives that became central to its shared identity.

The power that the photographs cultivated in shaping the neighborhood's shared narrative also allowed the barbershop owners to wield power in other domains of everyday life. The barbershop's mirror was a very important marker of neighborhood status. Making it onto the mirror signaled one's centrality to the neighborhood and its imagined narrative and gave Mustafa and Emre Bey remarkable gatekeeping powers. It was not an accident that the researcher who had been living in Tarlabaşı for two years had her photograph displayed. As I conducted my interviews, several residents told me I should get in touch with the researcher (which I eventually did) who had her photograph hanging in Mustafa Bey's barbershop. She had been vetted by the neighborhood's gatekeepers, and they would be my best connectors to my fellow and now trustworthy researcher. I myself felt that the barbershop owners had vetted me for the rest of the neighborhood. Mentioning that I had interviewed Mustafa and Emre Bey and spent many hours in their barbershop was in many cases helpful in gaining others' trust. Along with gatekeeping power, such relational power gave Emre and Mustafa Bey recognition as neighborhood arbitrators. Although I had not witnessed Mustafa or Emre Bey arbitrate disputes between residents, they had cultivated claims to neighborhood histories, and the barbershop was an anchoring place where people congregated in a way that accumulated the relational power that sets particular people and places apart as neighborhood arbiters in Middle Eastern cities.[32] The kind of relational power that the barbershop owners had cultivated was not accidental. It was built on meticulous archiving through the materiality of the headshots adorning their visible mirror fixtures.

DRAWERS

Walking down the hill, leaving behind us the zone designated for Calik Holding's urban renewal project, we came upon a wide street at the bottom in Tarlabaşı that was lively with commercial activity, contrasting sharply with the deadening quiet of the evacuated zones up the hill. When Cem and I walked into several of the street's stores and bakeries to talk to dwellers and shop owners about the neighborhood's history, we were repeatedly directed to Murat Bey's hardware shop. The moment we entered the store, we knew why we had been led there. Every fixture in the store, from the decaying wooden ceiling to the green wooden shelves to the archaic balance scale used to measure the goods sold there, felt like it came from another era. The most dramatic experience of all was seeing the drawers (figure 3.5). There were more than a hundred old green drawers that looked like they were built into the walls the day the shop was built and had been in continuous use ever since. It was an experience that evoked every captivation the "old" can possibly evoke. Not only was it the perfect aesthetic of old fixtures and unending

Figure 3.5. Drawers from a hardware store in Tarlabaşı, Istanbul. Source: author, June 2012.

old drawers with just the right amount of discoloration and disrepair to give it an unmistakable patina, but more importantly the decaying fixtures were still in use in the same way I imagined them to be used a century or more ago. It would have been hard for even the most ardently immune to not feel at least a tinge of nostalgic joy creep up on them at the sight of the drawers. Murat Bey had meticulously worked to produce an aesthetic of the past that primed his guests for the historical narratives he was always ready to deliver. As soon as we started snapping photographs of the shop, Murat Bey narrated its history. The shop was originally a grocery run by a Greek man in the early 1900s. The shop was attacked during the anti-minority riots of September 6–7, 1955 (known as the *olaylar*, or "events"; see chapter 2). The Greek owner decided to stay despite the *olaylar* but transformed the grocery into a hardware shop to capitalize on the construction boom of the time. This was at the start of the rural migration into Istanbul discussed in chapter 2. Ten years later, in the mid-1960s, the owner of the shop decided to sell his assets in Istanbul. According to Murat Bey, this was kismet, or fate, because that's when Murat Bey had migrated to Istanbul from Diyarbakır in Eastern Turkey seeking a store of his own.[33] The Greek owner transferred ownership to him forty-five years ago, and sure enough, Murat Bey kept all the fixtures in place as the previous Greek owner had installed them. As he was narrating the shop's history, Murat Bey went to great lengths to show us that he was using the shop's furniture and fixtures in the same way that the previous owner had used them.

We then eventually settled down with our tea and started listening to the history of Istanbul. Although I had asked Murat Bey about the neighborhood's history, he started with a history of nineteenth-century Istanbul that he had clearly narrated many times before. His account came with evidence from a map that he had ready in his cabinet to show his visitors. After a long discussion with Murat Bey about the city and neighborhood, he pointed us in the direction of two shops where we would meet some of the neighborhood's oldest and "original" dwellers.[34] At our first stop, a furniture manufacturing workshop, we met Dimitri Bey, who identified himself as a Christian Albanian/Greek, and Artoun Bey, who was of Armenian descent.[35] At our second stop, we met Mert Bey, whose wife was of Greek descent, at his car repair shop.[36] I later learned through a common acquaintance that Murat Bey himself was of Armenian descent, despite his Turkish-sounding name. Murat Bey had guided me toward a very particular narration of the neighborhood's history.

Murat Bey had long invested in creating a reputation as the neighborhood's history guide. He maintained strong relationships with neighboring store owners. He took every opportunity to share tidbits of the city's past with clients and neighbors alike. Most importantly, he invested in his store's historical aesthetic. His shop's materiality and the patina of its fixtures took on a life of their own, creating an expectation that the store's owner and artifacts' caretaker would be knowledgeable of the neighborhood's history. In time, Murat Bey's relationship to his decaying environment cultivated for him a claim to authenticity few in the neighborhood could match and ensured that several neighborhood dwellers sent us his way. With a claim to authenticity came a claim to historical narrative.

The historical narrative that Murat Bey related to us was a very particular one. It did not document the lived histories of relatively recent migrants to Istanbul and their movements as did the universe represented in the barbershop's headshots. Instead, for Murat Bey, the only people who could give us an accurate history of the neighborhood were the city's few remaining non-Muslim dwellers. His mental map of historical informants led Cem and me into long conversations about the city's "cosmopolitan age" and anti-minority violence with Dimitri, Artoun, and Mert that were very different from the stories of itinerant migrants we had heard in the barbershop. It was not Murat's identity as an Armenian that led us to this narrative, however. Murat Bey had changed his name to a Turkish-sounding one, likely to avoid violence, and was not keen on revealing his Armenian origins as he built relations of neighborliness in Tarlabaşı. It is the evocative materiality of the hardware shop that attracts Muslim and non-Muslim Turks alike to Murat Bey's shop and his historical narrative, and not any claims to minority identity. It was through a long relationship with archiving the historical fixtures of his shop that Murat Bey gained the power to claim knowledge of the neighborhood's history and guide us to this particular narration of it.

Although when we met them, both the barbershop and hardware store owners could wield the power they had cultivated through long-term relationships with the materiality of their shop interiors, I am suggesting that the increased embrace of heritage preservation as a redistributive practice would reorder those power dynamics. Channeling redistribution through heritage preservation in a neighborhood like Tarlabaşı would divert funding for the physical restoration of private buildings toward "historically valuable" buildings and interiors, such as the hardware shop, and away from buildings that could not claim such narrowly defined historical worth, such as the barbershop. In its most benign sense, that would ensure that buildings such as the hardware shop would survive longer and be marked as safer structures, creating the visible hierarchies that I analyze in chapter 4. Such preference for historical worth could also mean that the owners of a building like the barbershop's would terminate their lease and bring in stores with more relevance to a heritage zone. In short, prioritizing the historical worth and aesthetic beauty that creates stature with heritage preservation as a redistributive practice (as well as vernacularization more generally) would multiply the power that Murat Bey cultivated through his shop's patina while undermining or even erasing the power the barbershop owners had cultivated through the headshots on their mirror fixtures and thus reordering power in the neighborhood.

The reality that Tarlabaşı's residents are facing is not so subtle in its reordering of power dynamics fostered through the EU's project. Through the violent urban renewal that Çalık was orchestrating in the neighborhood, the barbershop's lease was terminated, and they had already planned to relocate to a space in neighboring Kasımpaşa, about one and a half kilometers away. It remains to be seen if they would be able to build the same kind of relational power once they relocated to a new neighborhood with new power dynamics and away from the community represented on their mirrors. The hardware shop was spared from the violent renewal project, but if the project were to expand down the hill, all the shops, including the hardware store, would be evacuated, since Çalık's focus on renewal was not committed to the preservation of interiors. In fact, the mobile headshots might be more resilient in the face of such violent displacement than the hardware fixtures. All in all, urban dwellers cultivate unmistakable power through archiving a wide array of the city's materialities and the narratives they tell. The enactment of redistribution through the heritage industry would valorize particular aesthetic and historical materialities over others to significantly reorder power dynamics in the city.

Conclusion

A stairwell bathroom creaked under the weight of identity politics, property title deeds became haunted by the long-dormant ghosts of fleeing minorities, beautiful historical murals vanished under a thick layer of plain white paint, clotheslines were elevated to the rank of a neighborhood's social glue, and a home's exterior paint colors resignified it as "local" or "foreign" as the European Union invested €7 million in the restoration of a historically Greek and Jewish neighborhood on Istanbul's arterial Golden Horn. Each of these acts *repoliticized* practices that had been touted as apolitical technical practices when redistribution through heritage preservation had brought the EU to Fener-Balat. As Turkey's neoliberal transition coincided with a global shift toward environmental heritage, an unlikely coalition of stakeholders channeled a redistributive campaign via heritage preservation as an opportunity to bury the politics that had plagued the plans they had for the city.

For the Habitat coalition, heritage preservation would bury the now unpopular class politics underlying redistribution to protect and upgrade low-income housing. Heritage preservation would circumvent the success of the corporate class in bankrupting the welfare state and tabooing redistributive campaigns that subsidized the working class by rendering low-income housing worthy of protection as revenue-generating heritage. The more the environmental turn succeeded in extricating heritage preservation from identity politics, the more heritage was seen as a valued generator of new market value through tourism and real estate. For the heritage industry, represented in UNESCO and the EU, a social justice agenda would solidify the work the environmental turn had been doing to extricate both organizations from the civilizational and identity politics that would normally plague the preservation of formerly Greek and Jewish neighborhoods in Istanbul. Similarly, the Fatih Municipality, and a Turkish state working toward accession to the EU at the time, found a social justice agenda to be a great opportunity to bury the politics involved in cooperating with the EU on preserving Greek and Jewish heritage in the city as it sought immediate windfall from tourist revenues. It also helped reposition Istanbul as a cosmopolitan city poised to win the bid for European Capital of Culture 2010 (which it did). Finally, channeling redistribution through heritage preservation buried an almost reverse class politics that often infuses initiatives in support of low-income populations in the Global South. Even as they execute redistributive campaigns meant to reverse urban inequality, some experts bring with them ingrained beliefs about who deserves such support and what sets them apart from the undeserving. While such beliefs distort all developmental work in the Global South, heritage preservation provides a particularly powerful tool kit for burying that politics behind the language of *care* for what are considered valuable heritage environments. The deserving poor are labeled *ignorant* of the value of heritage and incapable of caring for their environments, and the importance accorded to buildings within heritage preservation projects becomes a powerful tool for burying the reverse class politics involved in determining who the deserving poor are in neoliberalizing economies.

The burying of these political projects did not go unchallenged, however. Throughout the chapter, residents and planners on the EU project's payroll alike *repoliticized* the project as they challenged the conditioning of redistribution on the preservation of heritage. What was interesting about the work of repoliticization is that it manifested through the very technical practices and intimate spaces that the various stakeholders had mobilized to depoliticize the project. To illustrate, the Denizli family had challenged access to housing grants on intricate, time-consuming conservation by hiding valuable historical murals under a thick layer of paint. On the one hand, hiding the murals enabled the family to circumvent the conditions that limited their access to the grant, which challenged the politics through which support for low-income housing had to be couched through the practice of heritage preservation rather than distributed unconditionally. On the other hand, hiding the murals also challenged the reverse class politics that hid beneath conservationists' concerns about residents' ignorance of the value of heritage and their inability to care for it. By hiding the murals and then narrating the story of their uncovering and covering to their (non-EU team) visitors, they showcased their full appreciation for the value of the murals that they still believed distinguished their home and family in the neighborhood, even when invisible. In hiding the murals, they were protesting the elevation of their value, and that of similar artifacts, above their own well-being. To protest and lay bare that politics, however, they had turned to the very artifacts in whose name conservationists had mobilized the innocuous language of care to depoliticize the class politics underlying their project and their public imaginary for the city.

In a similar vein, Hikmet reinvested the intimate space of his stairwell bathroom with religious politics, rumor campaigns in Fener-Balat repositioned title deeds—rather than war or geopolitical conflict—as the battlefront through which non-Muslim communities surreptitiously reentered and infiltrated the city, and homeowners recoded their building's paint colors as "foreign" or "local" as they all infused the city's logistical, private, and intimate spaces with the politics of identity that the EU and UNESCO had been working so hard to circumvent. Neither class nor ethnic or religious identity politics had disappeared from the city, as redistribution was channeled through heritage preservation in an era when neoliberal political economics coincided with an environmental turn in heritage. Rather than disappear, that politics had been displaced, perhaps more insidiously, onto the subtle everyday logistical and intimate crevices of the city. The displacement of class and identity politics leaves those political struggles to fester and brew within the city's crevices without recourse to public outlets for confronting and channeling them into collective negotiations of the struggles facing the polity. Instead, the displacement of such political struggles onto private and intimate spaces creates dissonance between their manifestation in private arenas and public imaginaries of the polity, such as the imaginary of Istanbul as a cosmopolitan city ahead of the bid for the European Capital of Culture 2010. Such dissonance carries the potential of an even more explosive political backlash (perhaps foregrounding the growing appeal of populism soon to plague Turkish [and Egyptian] politics) borne from festering identity politics within spaces and crevices impossible to excavate and grapple with in their subtlety within such a dissonant political climate.

Community 4

WALEED AND AMIR ARE YOUNG MEN in their early twenties who grew up in Darb El-Ahmar in Historic Cairo and continue to live and work in the neighborhood. They work in a furniture workshop where we met, along with two of their coworkers, to discuss the neighborhood and its recent transformation. During our conversation, I learned that Waleed, Amir, and their families had applied for home restoration grants offered by the Aga Khan Trust for Culture (AKTC) in the mid-2000s. Through the grant, the AKTC would design and execute the full rehabilitation of homes and fund 70 percent of the cost while the residents would pay the remaining 30 percent. By the time it exited in 2012, the AKTC and its partners had invested E£86 million (around $13.9 million at the time) in the restoration of 121 residential buildings and hundreds of apartments within those buildings.[1] While Amir's application was accepted, and his building restored, Waleed's application was rejected.

Digging into why Amir's family was awarded the grant while Waleed's was rejected, I was surprised to learn that the decision was not rooted in technical logics. Waleed's building wasn't rejected on the basis of its architectural attributes, the building materials necessary to restore it, or its claims to heritage status (or lack thereof). The reasoning for its rejection was a sociopolitical one. The residents of Waleed's building weren't *collaborative* enough to win the grant.

The AKTC required that residents of a building apply for the grant as one unit with the full consent of all residents (whether tenants or owners) who must agree to pay their share of the 30 percent remaining costs not covered by the AKTC. Waleed's mother-in-law, who also lived in the building, did not agree to the restorations, and so everyone else in the building lost access to the grant. Amir ran into a similar issue when his family applied to restore the building. Their downstairs neighbor, who was renting a small room, refused to pay the E£5,000 that she would have had to pay as her contribution. Because they couldn't get the tenant to agree, Amir's family decided to find a way to restore their apartment through a private contractor rather than the AKTC and found that it would cost them E£25,000 just to restore the interiors while it would only have cost them E£17,000 to have the AKTC completely rebuild the foundation of the building and rehabilitate both its interiors and exteriors. Building residents then collectively decided to pay the tenant E£6,000 as compensation to vacate her room, and were awarded the AKTC's restoration grant.[2]

When I asked Samy, the AKTC urban planner from the introduction, why the AKTC required that all building residents agree to the restorations and to shouldering their portion of the cost as a condition for the grant, he explained: "Even if residents had the money, they can't just come and restore the building on their own. That wasn't what we were aiming for at all. Our purpose was that you get to know your neighbors."[3] The buildings chosen for restoration were the ones where neighbors managed to communicate with one another and jointly invest in the future of their building. The logics behind a decision as crucial as who won the restoration grant lottery in Darb El-Ahmar sounded a lot like Samy's explanation for designing inconvenient shared water pumps from the introduction: "Our purpose was that you learn to coordinate with your neighbors."[4] Above and beyond the many technical and logistical logics that shaped the AKTC's work in Darb El-Ahmar, the AKTC were working to engineer collaborative "community," and they turned to the planning and design of home restorations to perform that work.

As they engineered community, the AKTC's team were not simply displacing the responsibilities of a retreating welfare state onto coresponsible citizens, as most scholarship on the "development industry" in a neoliberal moment would argue.[5] Rather, the AKTC was mobilizing "community" to manipulate real estate markets as a redistributive strategy to secure affordable housing in the city, and they were not alone in doing so. Tracing the work of the AKTC in Darb El-Ahmar and the Ismailia Consortium in Wust El-Balad (aka downtown Cairo), I found that both protagonists deployed urban planning and design to manipulate real estate markets in the two neighborhoods. The AKTC was working to corner real estate markets downward in an effort to secure affordable housing while the Ismailia Consortium worked to corner markets upward for a luxury clientele. Their turn to engineering "community" was not coincidental. The spatial and othering dynamics created through fostering local particularistic community are particularly affinitive with projects working to manipulate markets and limit property exchange to a tightly bounded group. The particularistic dynamics of community work to manipulate *value* differently for different groups in the city, making neighborhood property more attractive for one group over another and thus limiting access to that group. They were intervening in property markets through crafting what I have termed *particularistic value*.

Specifically, on the upper end of the market, the Ismailia Consortium, a private corporation capitalizing on the opportunities created by the 1996 law, mobilized the "authenticity" of the aesthetics and commercial environment of Wust El-Balad to foster what I call a *community of strangers*.[6] Fostering a community of strangers produced dynamics that would ensure the exclusivity and security necessary to attract a high-paying clientele without resorting to physical and visible barriers that diminish the attraction of living within the seeming urban messiness of the city's center. On the other end of the redistributive struggle, the AKTC mobilized community to stem the displacement of the urban poor from Historic Cairo, as the reversal of rent control and other dynamics were gradually pushing the city's low-income communities to the city's periphery (see chapter 1). A collaborative community *invested* in its neighborhood would ensure that local residents would service and care for their shared environment. Because such services were *contingently* provided by local residents, a serviced neighborhood would make property more lucrative for existing residents but less attractive for potential gentrifying outsiders who would not be guaranteed such services by an entity like the state. The particularistic relationship between the invested community and its neighborhood would stem both gentrification and out-migration from the neighborhood. Fostering local, particularistic community was meant to manipulate real estate markets and not simply displace the responsibilities of a welfare state onto coresponsible citizens.

As they deployed community to manipulate property markets, both actors were reorganizing the political around community in ways that mirror the neoliberal transformations, presciently described by Nikolas Rose

(1996): "[Under advanced liberal rule] individuals are to be governed through their freedom, but neither as isolated atoms of classical political economy, nor as citizens of society, but as members of heterogeneous communities of allegiance, as 'community' emerges as a new way of conceptualizing and administering moral relations amongst persons" (41). Community could be envisioned and configured in a variety of ways, however. The ways that our protagonists understood community encompassed a wide spectrum of understandings of the relationality between community members. AKTC planners were mostly working to foster communal ties among a group of residents already existing in Darb El-Ahmar. In a sense, they mobilized an understanding of community most familiar to scholars of the "local" and its emphasis on face-to-face relationality. Leaders of the Ismailia Consortium understood community quite differently. They believed that strangers, who did not necessarily reside in Wust El-Balad, could still come to see themselves as a "community" with a special affinity to Wust El-Balad's spaces. In fact, the consortium's CEO, Karim Shafei, saw that a limited understanding of community would be doing a disservice to the neighborhood's future and to the much broader set of Egyptians who viewed themselves as Wust El-Balad's community. When discussing his plans for community input in the consortium's plans for Wust El-Balad, he explained,

> Definitely now is the time to bring the community's input into our planning process. It's not only about the neighborhood, in the sense that Wust El-Balad is regarded by many Egyptians as the property of all Egyptians. In other words, you can't go ask the people living next to the pyramids in Nazlet El Seman [neighborhood] whether or not they want to paint the pyramids pink. The pyramids are owned by all of Egypt, so if we're going to make a decision about it, we would need to take a referendum. [Similarly,] Wust El-Balad has a very small number of residents. The actual people who live in downtown are a minority. On the other hand, all Egyptians love Wust El-Balad and have an opinion about it. So, we need representation from the entire community across the board. We needed to talk to artists, shoppers who come downtown to buy a suit for [the low cost of] E£200, and so on.[7]

This broader understanding of "community" reflects how theorists such as Benedict Anderson, Jane Jacobs, and Miranda Joseph have conceptualized the term. In the broadest sense, in Anderson's *Imagined Communities* (1983), one of the main contentions is that the making of nations was provoked by the ways in which print capitalism enabled strangers with almost no daily contact to see each other as members of the same community, as a nation. Closer even to the ways that the consortium mobilized community is Joseph's (2002) distillation of the relationship between community and capitalism. In her analysis of that relationship, she conceptualizes community as a "social formation" with shared values articulated as "particular desires for particular commodities, produced by particular acts of labor" (15) rather than as strictly defined by face-to-face relationality. For Joseph, it is the particularity of those desires that specifies a social formation as a "community" rather than whether or not they are strangers. Similarly, for Jacobs (1961), strangers define the sociality of urban neighborhoods in ways that mirror how the consortium understands the relationality of strangers (discussed later). Building on Shafei's own understanding of community and this scholarly genealogy, I came to term the consortium's work in Wust El-Balad as engineering a *community of strangers*.

While the AKTC and the Ismailia Consortium do deploy different understandings of the relationality of members of a community, adopting Joseph's conceptual flexibility exposes the ways in which both deployments of community are performing similar work in the making of markets. Both sets of protagonists fostered communities that were *particularistic*, with a shared set of tastes and common fates striving to attract one another to that market and keep outsiders out, and that were *spatially situated* around real estate and would physically demarcate those boundaries. The Ismailia Consortium worked to ensure that a group of Cairenes who shared a distinct set of high-end tastes came to see the spaces of Wust El-Balad as a secure and exclusive hub. In Darb El-Ahmar, the AKTC worked to ensure that a group of residents who were already situated in those spaces would identify as one community with a shared set of vulnerabilities and a common fate. In short, it is community's *particularism* that not only produces its affinity to capitalist markets (as insightfully argued by Joseph) but enables the manipulation and cornering of those markets through the crafting of particularistic value. It is thus not the trust or welfare support that communities might produce that is crucial to the neoliberal revalorization of community. By extension, in manipulating market value, these actors were also accentuating *difference* among communities of particular destinies, tastes, and values. Redistribution through market manipulation in neoliberalizing economies is thus the work of political differentiation and division—not simply the accentuation of the local over other forms of political allegiance.

As the manipulation of market value accentuates difference and particularism among communities in neoliberalizing economies, it also transforms power dynamics within groups that become identified as communities. Engineering spatially situated particularistic communities develops from a belief that "community" is a technical field that planners can identify as an object of intervention, one that they themselves are external to and can transform. Drawing on Timothy Mitchell's (2002) insights about the politics of the expert production of such objects of intervention, the chapter also investigates the assumptions that urban planners made in Cairo about community, its coherence, and its preexistent nature; the contradictions inherent to interventions based on those assumptions; and their ramifications on political and power dynamics in the neighborhood.[8]

An Invested Community: The Aga Khan Trust for Culture

The Aga Khan Foundation, founded and led by the Aga Khan (imam of the Imami Ismaili Shi'ite sect of Muslims), first turned its attention to Darb El-Ahmar and its environs in Historic Cairo in 1984, when plans were first hatched for creating the seventy-four-acre Azhar Park. The foundation hosted a conference in Cairo that year entitled "The Expanding Metropolis: Coping with the Urban Growth of Cairo." The conference was the ninth in a series of workshops the foundation was hosting, entitled "Architectural Transformations in the Islamic World," and brought together some of Egypt's most renowned architects, planners, and conservationists. During the conference's opening ceremony, the Aga Khan himself pledged to gift Cairo a massive green space in the city's center (Ahmet 1985). Soon after, the foundation identified the five-hundred-year-old garbage dump bordering Darb El-Ahmar as the site it would convert into a park (the same dump that Haga Samia, from the introduction, could see from her living room). Initially, the project stalled for over a decade. Then, when the 1992 earthquake hit, the urgency it created around safeguarding Historic Cairo's built environment helped the foundation overcome the many bureaucratic hurdles it had been facing. By the mid-1990s, the foundation was able to secure rights from the Egyptian state to excavate the seventy-four-acre garbage dump, and its subsidiary, the Aga Khan Trust for Culture (AKTC), started transforming it into what would be inaugurated in 2005 as Azhar Park (see figure 4.1).[9]

As the AKTC's team excavated the garbage dump in the mid-1990s, they realized that even though it gave Cairo a new lung, their project was compounding the vulnerabilities experienced by low-income residents living on the dump's edge. This was especially the case because their work coincided with the aftermath of the 1992 earthquake and the reversal of rent controls in

Figure 4.1. Aerial view of Azhar Park after its opening. Photo by Gary Otte. Source: "Creating an Urban Oasis: Al-Azhar Park, Cairo, Egypt," Aga Khan Development Network, December 4, 2017, https://www.akdn.org/gallery/creating-urban-oasis-al-azhar-park-cairo-egypt.

1996. Homes sitting on the edge of the dump, like Haga Samia's, had been on the lowest rungs of the real estate market and were long slated as low-income housing. Over time, with the gradual movement of Historic Cairo's property owners to neighborhoods outside the core, as discussed in chapter 1, most of Darb El-Ahmar's residents came to be tenants rather than owners. With the enforcement of rent controls in the 1950s and 1960s, most of those tenants came in possession of long-term rent control contracts that they passed onto their inheritors. By the time the AKTC were excavating the garbage dump, almost 70 percent of Darb El-Ahmar's residents were tenants living in rent-controlled housing.[10] Similar to Umm Mustafa's building in chapter 1, most rent-controlled units in buildings owned by absentee landlords were left unmaintained for decades and were hardest hit by the earthquake. When the 1996 rent control laws gave landlords incentive to vacate their buildings of tenants with rent control contracts—primarily by vacating collapsed buildings so they could bring in new tenants on unrestricted rental contracts—Darb El-Ahmar's tenants were already experiencing unprecedented insecurity in their debilitated buildings.

Building the park only compounded that insecurity. Real estate that had been on the lowest rungs of the market would be overlooking one of the best views in the city with direct access to one of the rare, large green spaces in central Cairo. Landlords were now doubly motivated to find ways to expel their rent-controlled tenants. Not only would new rentals be unrestricted but the value of their property overlooking the park would skyrocket. Both the tenants and the neighborhood's urban fabric were now under threat, as owners started bringing down Mamluk-style three- to four-story buildings and replacing them with high-rises that would capitalize on the park's view. Samy, the AKTC urban planner, likened the threat to what happened when the Fustat Garden was constructed in Cairo. He explained, "There was an urban fabric there that was demolished in its entirety to make way for the high-rises that [now] overlook [Fustat Garden]."[11]

In response to these compounding threats, in 1997, the AKTC decided to implement an urban rehabilitation project in the neighborhood that would work against the layered vulnerabilities that they were now drawn into (see restoration work, figure 4.2). In a published report, the AKTC described the project as one meant to "preserve [the neighborhood's] urban qualities, as well as the potential to regenerate its economy" (Aga Khan Trust for Culture 2005, 2). In Samy's words, "Our goal was to create a suitable environment for the people to invest and feel that there is hope in the neighborhood, defeating the salient insecurity that stopped people from investing in their neighborhood, and leaving as soon as they could afford to."[12] In a published article, two members of the AKTC further explained, "If the present pattern of disinvestment [from Darb El-Ahmar] persists, it can only pave the way for further deterioration and the eventual loss of irreplaceable social, economic, and cultural assets" (Shehayeb and Mikawi 2003, 1.) The AKTC team was working to stem the out-migration (voluntary and forced) of Darb El-Ahmar's residents from their secure and central affordable housing. They saw fostering a sense of ownership among residents, whether tenants or owners, that would push them to *invest* in their neighborhood and its future as key to stemming out-migration. A collaborative community of residents with strong emotional bonds to one another and the physical spaces of their neighborhood would gradually but surely spur a sense of collective ownership and investment through which residents would resist the many forces working to push them out of their affordable homes.[13] I turn now to tracing the intricacies of how the AKTC team worked to engineer an "invested community" in Darb El-Ahmar.

Figure 4.2. An alleyway in Darb El-Ahmar in the early 2000s before (*right*) and after (*left*) restoration work was performed by the Aga Khan Development Network. Source: "Al-Darb al-Aḥmar Housing Rehabilitation Programme: Housing Rehabilitation beyond Physical Upgrading," Tadamun, March 30, 2017, http://www.tadamun.co/?post_type=initiative&p=8465&lang=en&lang=en#.YwY28uxBwc-.

Redistributive Funding and Its Logics

One of the most crucial decisions that the AKTC would make was *who* would receive funding to restore their homes in Darb El-Ahmar. The AKTC would only ultimately restore 121 buildings out of the thousands in the neighborhood. As the opening vignette illustrated, one of the main criteria for accepted applications was the degree to which a building's residents (tenants and owners) could collaborate. From the very first step of the restoration project, the AKTC was mobilizing its home restoration program to foster communal bonds in the neighborhood.

Layered onto that challenging demand, the AKTC deployed an unorthodox method for calculating the financial shares each resident would contribute to the overall restoration costs. The AKTC only allowed building residents to divide shares of their financial responsibility into increments of 0.5 of a share, and residents couldn't resort to smaller fractions to gain perfect equality. For example, if an apartment occupied 1.15 shares of the building's space and another only 0.85, both residents would pay for 1.0 full share of the financial burden of the restorations. Even though calculating more accurate shares would not have been too difficult to achieve, Samy again resorted to sociopolitical logics when explaining why the team insisted on uneven shares:

> We didn't divide their shares very accurately, so there would be debates where residents would say, "Your apartment is a little bit bigger and mine is a bit smaller," and so on. We worked to make sure that people at the end of the day felt that they were one unit and that the unit was not their apartment.... We wanted to instill in them the concept that the *community* is made up of interconnected units and that it's not the apartment that's the home. Rather it's a residential building all connected and that they have to see it as a residential unit. Then, after a while we would start to talk to them about public spaces and that they are living around open spaces that they have to start taking care of. So, you create larger and larger units and larger networks connecting the *community*.[14]

Again, the AKTC saw urban planning as engineering community. Even something as intricate as how a building's shares were being calculated was expected to perform the sociopolitical work of manufacturing community. What is remarkable about Samy's description of the units is their relationship to neighborhood spaces. Community would develop from a shared sense of investment and ownership in private spaces that are now interconnected. Eventually, connections multiply as property owners realize that the fate of their private properties are linked to the fate of the shared spaces (public or private) that surround them and the community members who share these spaces. For the team, it was in a shared sense of responsibility for spaces in which residents had invested that community would be born, and it was only through strong communal ties that this shared responsibility would be shouldered and neighborhood spaces cared for. Ultimately, the experience of collective care for neighborhood spaces could evoke emotional bonds of belonging to both place and people that would make the neighborhood not only more livable but infinitely more valuable to residents as multiple forces conspire to push them out.

Autonomous Community: Fleeing the Predatory State

As the AKTC worked to foster collaborative community, it was also interested in fostering a sense of independence from the state in the neighborhood. Beyond concerns about the state's neglect of the neighborhood's infrastructure or mismanagement of the 1992 earthquake (see chapter 1), AKTC team members saw the state as a potential predatory threat to the neighborhood as it transformed. Particularly troubling to the team was the Egyptian state's penchant for what Asher Ghertner (2015) conceptualizes as "rule by aesthetics." The Egyptian state has a history (especially since Sadat's open-door or Infitah policies of the 1970s) of making arbitrary decisions that led to thousands of evictions based on housing aesthetics as it haphazardly became visible to the authorities. Two notable examples of such "rule by aesthetics" materialized during the bread riots and the construction of the Ring Road. When the bread riots erupted in January 1977—protests against the removal of government subsidies on daily staples such as flour—police forces followed protesters into the "popular" neighborhood of Bulaq that sat on the Nile, adjacent to downtown. Once inside, the police lost their footing in a neighborhood that was illegible to them (à la Scott 1998, ch. 2), and the marked debilitation of a neighborhood that sat on prime real estate by the Nile River became starkly visible to the state. In the aftermath of the bread riots, hundreds of residents were forcibly evicted and relocated to mass housing on the city's periphery.[15] Similarly, Cairo's first Ring Road was constructed in the mid-1990s. It would redirect considerable traffic away from the city's inner roads, bridges, and tunnels to a highway that circled around the city's (then) outskirts. As David Sims (2010) documents, soon after state functionaries started traveling along the Ring Road and saw the extent of the city's informal housing and its debilitation, it became targeted for demolition (69-71). Building on those experiences, AKTC team members worried that the debilitation of Darb El-Ahmar's buildings would similarly be exposed with the construction of Azhar Park.

Fear of that visible exposure then became another logic through which the AKTC chose buildings for restoration. The team saw restored homes as a physical barrier that would secure the neighborhood from the state's predatory eye and focused the first phase of their project on restoring homes on the border with the park and that would be most visible from it (see figure 4.3 for restorations to the park's border). In that vein, team members spent many hours in their first years in Darb El-Ahmar convincing those

Figure 4.3. A view of Darb El-Ahmar from the park before and after restoration. Source: "Al-Darb al-Aḥmar Housing Rehabilitation Programme: Housing Rehabilitation beyond Physical Upgrading," Tadamun, March 30, 2017, http://www.tadamun.co/?post_type=initiative&p=8465&lang=en&lang=en#.YwY28uxBwc-.

residents to restore their homes. In a published interview, one of the team's leaders explained that one of the tactics she used to convince residents was to show them panoramic pictures she took of their run-down homes from the grounds of Azhar Park (top half of figure 4.3) and saying:

> I told them, "Seriously, if [the First Lady] Susan Mubarak is invited to the opening of this park, which she will be, and she stands there, during construction or something, this is what she will see of you guys. These are the backs of your houses; they gave their backs to a garbage heap for hundreds of years. Would you blame her if she said, 'Poor people, we have to move them to new cities, to better housing?' You can't blame her." And they were convinced. (Shehayeb 2011, 114)

She was impressing upon the residents that the aesthetic that their homes produced from the park put them in a position of shared vulnerability to a state obsessed with imagery. It was also from that shared fate that their salvation would come. To fend off the threat, they would need to identify as a community and work together to beautify not one or two of the houses but all of the homes and public spaces that produced that aesthetic vulnerability. Protection from a predatory state depended on maintaining the aesthetic beauty of their buildings and autonomously caring for their shared spaces as one communal unit. Chapter 5 delves deeper into how aesthetics and the visibility of the built environment became entangled in redistributive projects, but it is clear from this example that the making of "community" in opposition to a threatening state was entwined with the visible aesthetics of the neighborhood and was shaping the logics behind how the AKTC disbursed its limited funding. Maintaining independence from the state via that visible physical barrier was not only about an impending threat of relocation. It also maintained the community's autonomy in a way that would ensure they saw themselves as servicing the neighborhood rather than relying on the state. The contingent services provided by an autonomous community would then keep gentrifiers away and manipulate property markets in favor of existing residents.

Rumors: Repoliticization and Stolen Treasures

While the AKTC's team had a vision for how the logics behind distributing funds would ultimately secure affordable housing, to neighborhood residents those logics remained obscure and funding decisions seemed arbitrary and haphazard at best. What residents could see was that some families—like Amir's—were getting their life completely transformed through restoration grants while others—like Waleed's—were denied, even when willing to make the 30 percent investment in restoration costs. Amir and Waleed could not see what set their families apart from one another to warrant such different outcomes. With obscurity came suspicion, and that suspicion soon creeped into my conversations with neighborhood residents, especially young men in their twenties.

Coming back to the conversation I had with the four young craftsmen in the furniture workshop, such suspicion of the AKTC's true motives crept into our conversation when Waleed and Maged, another of the young craftsmen who was also born and raised in Darb El-Ahmar, started describing their long personal history with the AKTC. Waleed and Maged were both teenagers when the AKTC arrived in the neighborhood. As young teenagers, they joined the many field trips that the Aga Khan's social program arranged for children from Darb El-Ahmar. They went to museums, the amusement park called Gero Land, and even on a four-day field trip to Alexandria that included accommodation and food. Waleed and Maged explained that they had initially enjoyed the field trips until they saw their pictures in the Aga Khan Foundation's brochures and in their headquarters. Waleed expressed with indignation, "We later learned that they took pictures of us and put the pictures up on their office walls and brochures ... as if we were street children (*'eyal tassawol*) and the Aga Khan was feeding us, whereas we are educated and working." Maged interjected that the Aga Khan Foundation was not really interested in the well-being of the community. In fact, they only restored homes "because they wanted to beautify the Azhar Park's façade" or interface with the neighborhood. Maged explained that if they really cared about the families, "they would have reconstructed the homes with sturdy structures rather than leaving them without structures and needing constant maintenance. What they really care about is the park's façade." Ultimately, Waleed interjected: "only the people near the park benefited, and many people in Darb El-Ahmar, in other alleys such as Haret El-Roum and many others, didn't benefit because the housing reconstruction was only done on the interface with the park, because when the tourists exit the park, they will only see houses on the path from Bab El-Wazir to the hospital [at the exit from Darb El-Ahmar]." (This view does mirror the AKTC's tourist routes, discussed in chapter 5.) Ultimately, the conversation between the young men showed that they all mistrusted, to some degree or another, that the Aga Khan Foundation's project was ultimately designed for the good of the neighborhood. Maged finally verbalized this self-interest when he said, "We have all seen with our own eyes [Waleed nodding] the Aga Khan digging out treasures, and we saw planes come and lift antiquities out of the neighborhood."[16] In an interesting twist, the young men in the furniture workshop believed that the Aga Khan was stealing archeological treasures from the area. For these young men, the AKTC wasn't simply inept at running a development program. It was deliberately stealing Egypt's national treasures under the guise of restoration.

This was not the first time I had encountered this theory. In fact, I first heard it when I was visiting a fully restored home in the neighborhood. After I visited with different families to learn about the restoration work, Samir, also in his twenties, took me on a tour of their shared and newly constructed rooftop. During the tour, he shared with me what he thought was the true nature of the Aga Khan's project. Samir insisted that the foundation was not in the neighborhood to selflessly develop it. Rather, they were there out of *masslaḥa*, or self-interest. According to Samir, the Aga Khan was actually there to steal the antiquities beneath people's homes. He had personally seen from his roof (and he pointed to the exact spot) workers digging into the ground at

2:30 a.m. to produce boxes surrounding the Ayyubid Wall, a historic wall that the AKTC unearthed and restored while building Azhar Park. He then narrated that he saw bulletproof (*mossafaḥa*) trucks pull up to take the boxes at around 3 a.m. He was sure that if any of these antiquities were being recovered legitimately, the transport of the boxes would have occurred in daylight.

Moreover, Samir argued that the Aga Khan Foundation's people were so determined to steal treasures that they were willing to kill for them. He then recounted the story of his friend Anwar's death. Anwar had worked for the AKTC in Azhar Park. One day, Anwar told Samir that he had found a statue that he described as small (he gestured to around eight inches in height), made of gold and of pharaonic origins. Anwar told him that he was going to report the statue to the authorities the next day. Anwar was found dead the next day. According to Samir, the Aga Khan Foundation reported that he had died from an accident with exposed electrical wires. Samir, however, argued that the truth of the matter is that the foundation had killed Anwar because he wanted to report the statue to the authorities and they wanted to steal it instead.[17] At a later interview during my fieldwork, Youssef, a member of the AKTC's team, relayed the story of a young man from the neighborhood who had decided to work with the Aga Khan Foundation and was tragically found dead in a garden near Cairo's Citadel. According to Youssef, the police reported the death as a suicide. Youssef's opinion, and he emphasized it was not a scientific opinion but rather his own observation, was that the young man's suicide was a product of his confusion after working with the Aga Khan for a few years. The young man was somewhat conservative and, according to Youssef, his sudden exposure to different worldviews and experiences that he could not reconcile with his background may have eventually led him to have a psychological break and commit suicide.[18] In Youssef's words, "This is one aspect of developing society, that you open people up to ideas that are not their own, and then it ended up that one day we found [the young man] dead in a park near the Citadel."[19] It is most likely that Samir's friend Anwar is the same young man that Youssef referred to. While members of the AKTC team such as Youssef interpreted the young man's death as a tragic fallout from intense developmental work, for Samir and whoever else was espousing this theory in the neighborhood, the Aga Khan were so suspect in their activities that they were capable of murder to support their quest to steal the country's treasures.

Finally, on yet another occasion, Amin and Tarek, who worked in a shoemaking workshop in Darb El-Ahmar, shared the same theory about the Aga Khan Foundation's interest in the neighborhood. Amin in particular, also in his early twenties, argued that the Aga Khan chose to work in Darb El-Ahmar because they knew of the treasures underneath. He then described the treasures in detail. Amin shared: "If you dig, you'll find gold. There was a well in the courtyard of one of the mosques where we used to play as children. If you dug under that well, you'd find gold.... Darb El-Ahmar has tunnels [*saradeeb*] that could connect you to other gates [of the old city].... The Aga Khan has unearthed a lot of antiquities from under the park, and they have another park in Aswan. They are doing all this to find antiquities." Amin then compared the Aga Khan Foundation's project to that of Gamal Mubarak's (the son of the then president Hosni Mubarak). Amin narrated that Gamal Mubarak had bought the whole of Upper Egypt looking for treasures but didn't find anything satisfactory. Like Gamal Mubarak, the Aga Khan won't be very successful in Darb El-Ahmar because, according to Amin, the treasures are enchanted. He went on to say that under his grandmother's home, where he lives, there is gold, and "the home brings blessings to those who enter it but hurts those who try to dig."[20] The rumors circulating among Darb El-Ahmar's young men carried both an indictment of the foundation and talismanic protection for the neighborhood.

The obscurity of the work that the AKTC was undertaking in Darb El-Ahmar and the logics behind it had created enough confusion, unanswered questions, and resentment among those left out of its immediate rewards that it shrouded the project in a cloud of suspicion. Burying a socially minded initiative to secure affordable housing in Cairo's center under layers of the subtle, quiet work of engineering community through careful urban design performed the work of depoliticization necessary to manipulate market dynamics, but it also obscured that politics so effectively as to render it unreadable for its supposed main beneficiaries. Faced with that ambiguity, residents pushed back. They forced a repoliticization of the project by circulating rumors that positioned the project within a more familiar narrative of pillaging and corruption. The foundation was not pulled into the wide web of corrupt actors pillaging Egypt's future haphazardly, however. The rumors intricately mapped onto the young men's experiences of the materiality of their neighborhood and Egypt's political-economic realities.

In all three accounts of the rumors, the young men turned to the city's subterranean topography to animate their narratives. They imagined a rich terrain of buried treasures, gold, and secret tunnels (*saradeeb*) sitting under their corner of Historic Cairo. The young men circulating these rumors were not alone. Several times during my fieldwork, interlocutors would travel with their narratives to the subterranean city as they remembered playing as children in tunnels that connected Gamaliyya with the Citadel or recounted a story about a distant cousin who found gold under their home and moved away to a much grander life. Although most of these narratives map onto Cairo's medieval (especially Mamluk) history, the making of the subterranean city is also salient in reminiscences of a more modern Cairo. The vividness of underground tunnels in how Cairenes imagine and experience their city comes through, for example, in how residents of Antikhana alleyway in the more modern terrain of Wust El-Balad narrate their history. As introduced in chapter 1, the Model Citizens project that the Dutch artists Uitentuis and Osterholt undertook in Antikhana recorded how the alleyway's residents remembered different sites/buildings in the neighborhood. *Saradeeb*, or underground tunnels, made a repeated appearance in how residents remembered the red palace of Antikhana. For example, one of the residents related, "There were lots of legends about the palace. Some people said that it is a Mamluki palace, and this allegation was proved by the tunnels [*saradeeb*] found along the Nile bank, because those tunnels helped the Mamluk or his family escape."[21] On the other hand, others told a different story. One resident narrated, "Said Pasha Halim was a member of the king's [one of Mehmed Ali's heirs] family. He was supposed to marry a Turkish princess, and he built this palace especially so that she would live in it,"[22] and another said that the "owner's wife was a princess and she wanted to live on the Nile, so he dug her a tunnel connecting the palace to the Nile's banks in Kasr El-Nil."[23] Finally, another resident relayed his firsthand experience of those *saradeeb*:

> I took a friend of mine and told him, let's go explore the tunnel. . . . So, we entered, and there were many rooms to the left and to the right. There were railway tracks. . . . We walked for twenty or thirty minutes and were surprised to find ourselves in the middle of Tahrir. This tunnel continues to the Nile and at its end you can find the palace of the diplomatic authority these days. But when the underground metro was built, they separated [*fassalo*] the tunnel. . . . We also found a train car that supposedly moved on these tracks, and we discovered that this was Champollion's daughter's kitchen. The train car would carry food from the kitchen, in Champollion's [palace], and go all the way up to the river with the food staying piping hot till it got there.[24]

A rich and textured underground terrain of treasures and tunnels has long animated how Cairenes imagine and experience their city's historical center, within and outside its medieval gates. Darb El-Ahmar's young men built upon the specific materiality of their historical neighborhood and the world they imagined beneath it, as they developed and circulated rumors about the AKTC when faced with the project's many ambiguities and contradictions. The rumors didn't appear out of thin air. They carefully mapped onto these young men's material experiences of their neighborhood and city. Embedding the rumors within the textured materiality of their neighborhood's underground terrain rather than circulating trite corruption allegations gave the rumors more potency as a powerful (and for some believable) challenge to the AKTC.

In many ways, the circulation of rumors about the AKTC mirrors how rumors repoliticized the European Union's (EU) work in Fener-Balat, Istanbul (chapter 3). In both cases, concerted rumor campaigns questioned and challenged the work that outside interveners were doing by the very residents who were supposed to be the projects' primary beneficiaries. The substance of the two rumor campaigns and their politics differed in important ways, however. Seeing the rumor campaigns develop side by side shows how human-environment interactions—as insightfully theorized by Navaro-Yashin (2012, 18–20)—can carry different political implications in different environments. Whereas in Fener-Balat residents' lived experiences with a neighborhood haunted by ghosts of the minority communities once pushed out of the city animated the rumors that reinvested the EU's project with the *identity politics* it had been working so hard to elide, in Darb El-Ahmar, the environmental irritabilities and enchantments that shaped the rumor campaign pushed for a different repoliticization of the AKTC's work.[25] Darb El-Ahmar's young men developed their theories about the AKTC from a combination of the irritabilities and allure that their experiences of the neighborhood's underground terrain evoked, carrying both the potential for blessings and curses, and the haunting of their young lives by the everyday experiences of the constant pillaging of the country's resources by a corrupt ruling class. The salience of the politics of pillaging and the materiality of their neighborhood's terrain pushed them to make sense of the ambiguities of the AKTC's work through the lens of corruption but to develop very potent rumors about stolen historical treasures as they did so. They were repoliticizing the AKTC's work around the *class politics* the foundation had been eliding as it deployed its battle for housing through the mechanics of the market, accusing the AKTC of sitting on the wrong side of that battle by siphoning resources from the have-nots to the haves. Even though residents in both Cairo and Istanbul found rumor campaigns a potent challenge to contradictory outsider interventions, their material and affective experiences of the city shaped not only the substance of the rumors but the nature of the politics that the residents reinfused into these supposedly apolitical interventions.[26]

Designing Community

Once the AKTC chose their grant awardees, their dedication to engineering community continued to shape their *modus operandi*, influencing technical design decisions throughout the physical restorations phase. As the book's introduction illustrated, features as basic as water and sewage infrastructures were designed to foster communal cohesion in the neighborhood. As a refresher, the AKTC decided to install shared water pumps that only one apartment unit could use at a time within a building, and the team justified the inconvenience not through technical reasoning but through sociopolitical logics. Shared water pumps would force residents to communicate and coordinate around using them, fostering more cohesion among building residents who would then act as a unit. Water pumps were expected to perform the sociopolitical work of engineering communal cohesion.

Shared water pumps weren't the only building features designed to engineer collaborative community in Darb El-Ahmar. The AKTC's commitment to fostering communal cohesion also shaped their design of one of the most important shared spaces in Cairo (and especially in low-income communities): the rooftop. I refer here to a tale of two rooftops I encountered during my fieldwork to illuminate their importance and how they figured in the AKTC's intervention.

Umm Hassan, introduced in chapter 1, narrated life on the rooftop of the large courtyard house, Beit El-Kharazaty (c. 1881):

> In the winter, everyone would go up to the roof in the morning and spend the day there. We would have breakfast together, and if one woman has something sweet she would add it, and if another woman has something she would add it. In the summer, we would go up to the roof at night after sunset, and the girls would play together, and the men and youth would play cards together, and the older women would sit together chattering away.

She remembered those days nostalgically as we climbed the stairs up to the rooftop. Umm Hassan's was one of twenty-five families that once lived in the building in Gamaliyya neighborhood in Historic Cairo.[27] Unfortunately for the families, they were evacuated from the house during a restoration project and lost access to their rooftop.

Climbing up the stairs to see Haga Samia's new rooftop in Darb El-Ahmar was a much more joyful experience. She stood by with pride as I absorbed the views of Azhar Park to the east and Cairo's "thousand minarets" to the west (see this book's introduction). She then walked me to the other side of the roof to show me the vegetable garden she had cultivated with her neighbors and the now defunct solar panels in the corner. She explained that the rooftop's vegetable basins and solar panels were newly built and installed by the AKTC when they restored the building.[28]

Haga Samia's roof wasn't the only one to be rehabilitated. The AKTC created more than a hundred such rooftops. Samy, with the AKTC, explained that the decision to create accessible roofs was a complicated one. The architectural team was originally divided on the issue. A faction of the team was worried that the rooftops would turn into dumpsters and chicken coops that would harm the rehabilitated buildings, while the other half argued that the rooftop would be valued by residents and provide coveted communal space. The team then experimented with building a few rooftops and found that "when the rooftops became accessible ... a lot of people would take up living room furniture and spend their evenings there, and some even pitched sun canopies. It was in buildings where the roofs were not accessible that people threw their rubbish on the rooftop. It was rare that anybody would ruin their rooftop. . . . There were those who would raise chickens. They still raise chickens but the situation is so much better than it used to be."[29] Thus, vibrant rooftops came to light up Darb El-Ahmar's nightscape.

Umm Hassan's lamentations about her lost rooftop and Haga Samia's joy emphasize the importance of the rooftop as a communal space in Cairo and how attuned the AKTC team was to their value as shared spaces as they mobilized architectural design to produce collaborative community. A commitment to engineering community was not the only thing that drove the AKTC to invest in rooftops, however. They were also devising mechanisms for protecting the physical integrity of newly restored buildings. In designing shared rooftops, the AKTC was motivating a larger contingent of residents to maintain building rooftops, protecting them from being misused or trashed. In cooperating to care for their rooftops, not only would residents become more tightly knit as a communal unit but they would also maintain the value of their newly restored buildings, making it more costly to buy them out.

Existent Community: Real or Imagined?

Even though the engineering of collaborative community drove so many of the decisions that the AKTC's team was making, with time I came to realize that the team did not have a unified understanding of the notion of "community." They differed on who they identified as the neighborhood's community, whether they were building upon preexisting cohesion in the community, and whether they needed to enlist communal leaders as allies (and who those leaders would be), among other things. "Community" was not a clear predefined entity they were working toward but was slippery and mutating, constantly evading their grasp, even as it sat at the core of their project's raison d'être.

The team demonstrated confusion around perceptions of "community" when they expressed differing views on whether Darb El-Ahmar's residents were already a cohesive social unit with significant social capital or whether the AKTC was building such cohesion from scratch. On one extreme, one of the project's team members agreed with the project's official line in its published reports, that "what is needed is an incremental improvement of what is already in place, and a strengthening of the available social capital" (Aga Khan Trust for Culture 2005, 2). In a published piece, she argued that communities in Cairo's "popular neighborhoods" like Darb El-Ahmar were quite cohesive and much stronger than ones in "new cities" built on Cairo's periphery for mass housing projects (Shehayeb and Eid 2007). Moreover, in a published interview she asserted, "When [community members in Darb El-Ahmar] are sure they are getting the benefit, there is this positive collaboration. They do a lot of positive collaboration together. At the smallest scale in order to clean the building or share the rooftop. Workshops do it all the time to bring new raw material or even share power tools" (Shehayeb 2011, 118). By contrast, Rania, a member of the team who was born and raised in Darb El-Ahmar, held the exact opposite view. According to her: "The community in Darb El-Ahmar is considered a bit different from any other, even the community in Gamaliyya that lives directly adjacent to it.... You feel that they have this trait of being arrogant and feel that there is no one else quite like them.... The other thing is that [members of Darb El-Ahmar's community] don't like each other, and this in itself is a problem."[30] For Rania, positive communal ties are almost nonexistent in the neighborhood. Mounir, another member of the AKTC team, and who unlike Rania saw himself as an outsider to the community, shared Rania's perspective on communal cohesion in Darb El-Ahmar. He explained, "You'll find people here very strange in that they all fear each other. In other words, he'll come say that it was so and so who transgressed, and when we ask why he didn't stop him, he'll say, 'I don't want any trouble.' And that is the main problem."[31] He goes a step further though and argues that mistrust is a trait common to all Egyptians.[32] Hence, for Rania and Mounir, the AKTC was not simply building upon a wealth of social capital in Darb El-Ahmar. It would have to cultivate most of it from scratch. Samy, the urban planner discussed earlier, straddled the two extremes. He believed that there existed social ties between Darb El-Ahmar's residents but not a culture of collaboration and cooperation among them necessary for the creation of community in the neighborhood. He argued that resorting to microcredit and rotational savings mechanisms for financing housing restorations was ideal in Darb El-Ahmar because "people know each other and trust one another."[33] As explained previously, however, he saw that people in the neighborhood were not "talking to each other" or cooperating in resolving their neighborhood's problems, and that it was the AKTC's role to cultivate such cooperation.[34] For him, the AKTC was transforming latent social ties into active communal networks. The very team that was expecting a collaborative community to intervene in the workings of real estate markets held no consensus around what community was and whether it existed in Darb El-Ahmar. From the team's contradictory perceptions appears a nebulous, slippery notion of community rather than the well-defined entity one would expect from the engine tasked with waging a battle for affordable housing.

Community and Hierarchy

The slipperiness of community followed the team as they grappled with the many hierarchies they encountered in the neighborhood. The lack of clarity around preexisting hierarchies and how they should be navigated became especially salient when the team led participatory planning exercises around the neighborhood's public spaces. For example, when the AKTC team started participatory planning around Tablita Market, they soon realized that there were significant hierarchies affecting whose voices were heard in the sessions. Working around that dynamic, the team divided the planning process into two sessions where one included powerful vendors in the market and the other one included less influential, mostly female, vendors in the market. In a publication, they argued that the idea behind stratifying the process according to power hierarchies "was to give an opportunity for the less influential vendors to express their opinion and not be dominated by the more powerful leaders of the vendor community" (Shehayeb and Abdel Hafiz 2006, 70). Confronted with the market's hierarchies, the team decided to work around (and possibly reify) those hierarchies rather than disrupt them.

The planning of Aslam Square was similarly layered. Samy explained that the team stratified planning sessions into layers of children, women, men, store owners, residents of buildings overseeing the square, and service providers (in particular, the man who owned and operated a pay-for-use children's swing set in the square).³⁵ Mounir elaborated that within the stratified sessions, participants were chosen deliberately according to their influence in the neighborhood. He said, "We would invite the people that they call 'community leaders' or heads of the neighborhood [*kebar el manteqa*] and gather them together, either in the square itself or in our offices, and discuss their requests."³⁶ Eventually it became clear that identifying community leaders would not be so straightforward and would generate a lot of contestation around the planning process. Mounir described these challenges as follows:

> That didn't stop the people with whom we negotiated from arguing with us as we implemented [the designs] because it was exactly as we saw with the [25th of January] revolution with personal agendas and factional demands.... We would implore the supposed community leaders to intervene and some would succeed and some wouldn't... because even if you resort to the community leaders, we don't follow the notion of a head [*kebeer*] of a place anymore here in Egypt, and especially in these neighborhoods. In other words, in the past you would go and reach an agreement with the head and nobody would contradict it, but now they bring you someone and say that he's the head and as soon as they turn around someone else shows up and you try to convince them that you had an agreement, and they say, "Who told you he was the head?"³⁷

As they worked to engineer community, the AKTC's team turned to (what they thought) were existing hierarchies. In leaning on those hierarchies, they once again met a messy and slippery field. Rather than celebrating the unmaking of what others may have seen as problematic hierarchies, Mounir deplored that the Egyptian mentality that would have once facilitated following the village or neighborhood head or *kebeer* was disappearing and making the production of autonomous communities more challenging.

Finally, the ways in which the AKTC reified existent communal relations traveled to how their physical design of Aslam Square reified gendered dynamics. The team found that women felt particularly unsafe passing through the square, as they were threatened by lingering youth in nearby coffee shops who often made inappropriate remarks and harassed them as they passed by. To address that insecurity, they devised a new walkway parallel to the mosque for the women to use that was on the other side of the square from the coffee shops and so protected the women from such harassment.³⁸ Although creating the pathway for women most likely increased their ability to navigate the square and interact with a wider variety of neighborhood dwellers, it was also designed to work around existing practices of male-female interactions, and the insecurities they produced, rather than disrupt them. The square's design only removes the women from hearing the harassment but doesn't change the fact that men sitting at the coffee shops would continue to harass women. The AKTC was not molding new values for gender relations in the neighborhood. Rather, they were working to produce a self-governing community that would stem out-migration from the neighborhood within power structures and values already practiced, however problematic.

New Communal Hierarchies

As it reified some hierarchies in the neighborhood, the AKTC disrupted others. When cooperation among building residents becomes one of the key criteria for homes that receive rehabilitation grants, the resulting image is that of visible differentiation. Some buildings are beautifully restored and others remain debilitated. The unintended consequence of such visual differentiation is the transformation of communal hierarchies in the neighborhood. First, it is known that the residents of any renovated home contributed financially to the renovation. In phases two and three of the project, people contributed 30 percent of the cost.[39] With that, renovated homes came to visually mark those financially able to contribute to the restorations, and a new marker of wealth was born in the neighborhood. Second, given their structural superiority, renovated homes came to be known as those that were safe and accommodating to visitors. Almost all my respondents expressed that after renovating their homes, they became much more comfortable inviting guests inside. For Haga Samia, this was especially true after the governor of Cairo visited her home during his tour of the AKTC's achievements. For her, if the home had become aesthetically beautiful and safe enough to be visited and celebrated by the governor, then it must be safe and inviting to all her acquaintances.[40] Thus, visual hierarchies signaled which homes became safer and more inviting for women and men to gather and share gossip and neighborhood news as they cooked, sewed, watched their children, or watched football matches together. Gradually, hosting such gatherings could have far-reaching implications on the hosts' power over the dissemination of information, setting agendas for the community and dispute resolution in the neighborhood.[41] Slowly but surely, the new and differentiated visible aesthetic translates into new communal hierarchies in the neighborhood.

Engineering the bonds that would foster a community of residents attached to and invested in their neighborhood and its physical spaces worked on one level to foster a particularistic community that was clearly demarcated from other Cairenes, and especially gentrifiers and a predatory state. As they embarked on that work, the team also constantly grappled with how slippery "community" was, relying on conflicting ideas of who that community was or what bonds and hierarchies existed within it, even as they sought to work with it as a clearly demarcated object of intervention. The distance between an imagined object of intervention and the slipperiness of communal bonds and hierarchies in Darb El-Ahmar speaks to the messiness and contradictions inherent to displacing redistributive work onto the quiet machinations of urban design practices.

A Community of Strangers: The Ismailia Consortium

On the other end of the market, the corporate developer Ismailia Consortium saw the 1996 rent control laws as an opportunity rather than a threat. Funded by Egyptian, Saudi Arabian, and Kuwaiti investors—including the Egyptian real estate tycoon Samih Sawiris and Saudi real estate tycoon Sulaiman Abanumay's family—the consortium saw an especially lucrative investment in reviving Wust El-Balad's real estate market as rent control laws were changing. In 2008, when most real estate developers were developing desert lands they acquired cheaply on the suburban periphery of Cairo,[42] the Ismailia Consortium decided to forgo the immediate financial windfall of suburban development and invested around E£400 million toward transforming Wust El-Balad into a space for luxury real estate.[43]

As suburban gated communities on the city's periphery marketed exclusivity and security as their hallmark attractions, affluent residents of Cairo saw themselves facing a difficult choice. They were choosing between the comforts of security and exclusivity in the suburbs and the attractive dynamism as well as geographic convenience of living in the city's center. The Ismailia Consortium embarked on an ambitious project that aimed to provide both. They were designing luxury real estate that would provide the exclusivity and security of suburban enclaves within the dynamic urban messiness of central Cairo. Their answer for achieving that balance was to foster what I have termed a *community of strangers* in Wust El-Balad. They worked to attract a group of Cairenes with a shared set of high-end tastes who were scattered around the city into downtown, as a secure spatial hub for their exclusive tastes. It was this particularistic community of strangers that would elevate the value of Wust El-Balad's real estate.

Although the 1996 rent control laws had created a new opportunity for owners to rent out their units, it was still quite costly to get buildings dominated by rent-controlled units onto the open market, as discussed in chapter 1. Tenants expected significant sums of money (known as key money) in return for relinquishing their inheritable rent-controlled contracts. Securing and coordinating the dispersal of the considerable capital needed for key money was then further complicated by the fact that most of Wust El-Balad's buildings were owned by dozens of (if not over a hundred) absentee owners through inheritance laws. Moreover, most owners had relocated from Wust El-Balad and left their buildings unmaintained, as it transformed from an upper-middle-class residential neighborhood in the 1960s to a neighborhood with ailing infrastructures dominated by rented commercial offices and workshops within debilitated buildings. Transforming the neighborhood into a built environment fit for luxury residences and commerce would require significant capital investment up front. It was then not surprising that few people saw investing in Wust El-Balad's property immediately lucrative after the reversal of rent control laws. With others shying away from Wust El-Balad's property market, Ismailia Consortium saw it as the perfect opportunity for their project.

They embarked on a project that would buy at least forty of the buildings known as 'emarat Wust El-Balad (see figure 4.4) and renovate them into luxury residential and commercial real estate. They sought to buy buildings that would be geographically clustered in such a way that the consortium would be able to upgrade and manage the infrastructural foundations and commercial activity surrounding them. Ismailia undertook the challenges and costs necessary for rejuvenating 'emarat Wust El-Balad in particular because they saw that these buildings were uniquely capable of performing the cultural work essential for attracting Cairenes who identified with particular high-end tastes to Wust El-Balad.

Karim Shafei, the consortium's CEO, provided the first clue about that cultural work when he explained to me why the consortium chose to rejuvenate Wust El-Balad in particular:

> A very important development took place in the last five to seven years, and that was the Egyptianization of Egypt. Until about eight years ago, all the new brands that were created would be called Daly Dress, or Mohm, and then in the past few years, brands started to adopt [Arabic names] like El Diwan, Alef Bookstores, and Makani. In other words, there was a move

Figure 4.4. Image of some of ʿemarat Wust El-Balad in Talaʿat Harb Square. Source: Hengameh Ziai, August 2022.

towards a more national, a more Egyptian, identity and not the very confused mutated Westernized identity of Egypt. Part of that identity was represented in Wust El-Balad. For example, most TV ads from the past two years have been filmed in Wust El-Balad. . . . So, I think [Wust El-Balad] represents a certain nostalgia towards better times when Egypt was living a much better life, when everyone was respectable, and *kol el nas kanet nedheefa* [people were classy or cultured]. All of these were factors that made downtown attractive to us.[44]

Ismailia chose to work in Wust El-Balad because the materiality of ʿemarat Wust El-Balad had become associated with cultural production. It had become associated with a revival working toward the "Egyptianization of Egypt" and its purification from a "mutated Westernized identity." Interestingly, for Shafei, the very same spaces of Wust El-Balad that evoked that cultural revival evoked nostalgia for a time when people were *nedheefa*. *Nedheefa* literally translates to "clean" in Arabic but colloquially in this context it has strong class connotations. It refers to a class of people who are wealthy but

174 Chapter Four

also cultured and civilized. In other words, Shafei saw the materiality of Wust El-Balad evoking a nationalist cultural revival, but this revival is especially important because he saw it not only as purification from Westernized identity but also as a socioeconomic cleansing of sorts that would bring back *el nas el nedheefa* to Wust El-Balad.

Culture, Community, and Exclusion

Ismailia's profit-making scheme would only work, however, if a wealthy clientele feels at home and safe in Wust El-Balad and decides to migrate back into the city's center.[45] The amenities promised to wealthier clients in peripheral suburbia include isolation from other socioeconomic classes in day-to-day life, and this is often enforced through erecting walls high enough to produce a physical barrier that polices entry and exit but low enough to show off the compound's luxury to outsiders, as Eric Denis (2006) insightfully observed. As Shafei noted, "We are not building a compound in the desert."[46] Ismailia cannot and actually does not want to build the physical barrier of a wall to control who their clientele interact with on a daily basis. The concept that sets luxurious living in Wust El-Balad apart from suburbia is not only the central location but more importantly the experience of engaging with the lived messiness of the city versus the stale, manufactured life of the compound. The consortium needed to reassure its clientele that they would be surrounded by civilized *nas nedheefa* and maintain that exclusivity while selling them the promise of an exciting urban experience. Instead of physical walls and barriers, or an "aesthetics of security" that Teresa Caldeira (2008) insightfully argued develops in neoliberalizing cities to produce that segregation and safety in lieu of the state, they needed to find new modalities of exclusion that would resolve the tension between maintaining the illusion of urban messiness and ensuring the comforts of security and exclusivity their clientele would expect. For Ismailia, the answer was twofold. First, they aimed to produce a cultural and artistic environment, which they saw as self-policing against lower-income populations they believed were uninterested and incapable of engaging with that cultural environment. Second, they worked to foster an "authentic" or "organic" commercial space that mirrored the commercial environment that Jane Jacobs (1961) and the "new urbanism" school saw as the key to producing the "eyes on the street" (45) that gave neighborhoods safety and rootedness within the bustling city.

Shafei explained the centrality of producing cultural revival to Ismailia's project:

> We think that downtown, like all downtowns around the world, should be accessible to all socioeconomic segments of the society.... What we're trying to do is bring all these people together around positive activities. The key focus for us is art and culture. We believe that art and culture is nondiscriminatory and it attracts people from all segments of society but with a positive reason to come downtown. We don't believe that shopping is a positive activity.... Cultural spaces like El-Sawy Culturewheel and Azhar Park's El-Geneena Theater are good examples of how a space can bring together a wide diversity of people.... There are very specific coffee shops in Wust El-Balad, for example, that we want to keep, and we don't want them to ... [become too expensive], because this will drive away a segment of artists that we think are very enriching for the place.[47]

Fostering a cultural space would produce the "diverse" urban experience that Ismailia's clientele would be seeking without breaching the neighborhood's exclusivity. This cultural space would only welcome the specific "segment of artists" and people who have the capacity to appreciate that culture, even if from the lower classes; to be *nedheefa* and desirable dwellers of Wust El-Balad. To accelerate the production of this cultural space, Ismailia invested in subsidizing the arts and controlling commercial activities so that they would be attractive and affordable for those artists.

To achieve that control, they suspended the "invisible hand" of the market in the buildings they bought and refurbished. Ismailia's plan was that refurbished units in their buildings would only be available for rent but never resold to owners outside the consortium. Renting units through short-term contracts would allow the consortium to control how each unit was used. They then decided to forgo the immediate profits they may get from other tenants and set aside spaces within their building clusters for artists and cultural organizations who would rent them at subsidized rates.[48] For example, they offered Townhouse Gallery (an arts and theater space that had operated in Wust El-Balad for a decade before Ismailia bought their building) continued residence at reasonable rental rates.[49] Moreover, they ensured that some spaces would be set aside for services—such as specific, cheap coffee shops—that would attract the right segment of artists to the neighborhood.

The consortium also invested in sponsoring cultural events staged in the streets and buildings of Wust El-Balad as part of their cultural program. Most notable of these events is the Downtown Contemporary Arts Festival, or D-CAF, that at the time of this book's publication was ongoing and held its tenth festival in 2022. The festival lasts for around two weeks every year and hosts a number of local and international theatrical, musical, and artistic performers who stage their work in the buildings and streets of Wust El-Balad.[50] On the event's website, D-CAF's organizers explained that they had chosen Wust El-Balad specifically because "one of the main aims of D-CAF is the revival and reclamation of downtown Cairo as a vibrant cultural center, capitalizing on its unique architectural and social heritage."[51] In other words, cultural production was identified as a performative as well as a spatial practice. The authenticity of the aesthetics of downtown's buildings would produce a particular spatially situated cultural revival that was not just reproducible anywhere. Authenticity as a spatial-cultural practice then became a soft rather than physical modality through which Ismailia policed its boundaries. In seeing how culture operates both to attract potential gentrifiers and as a spatial modality of exclusion, I build upon work that highlights the importance of interplay between authenticity and culture to the neoliberalization of cities (e.g., Zukin 1996 and 2009), but I emphasize the specific *spatial* modalities through which culture and aesthetic authenticity operate to physically demarcate exclusivity.

Interestingly, D-CAF provoked a lot of controversy in 2015 since most of its performers were from international theater and dance companies who were allowed to perform in the streets under the auspices of D-CAF while El-Fan Midan's (Art Is a Square's) monthly festival that was born out of the Egyptian revolution in 2011 and took place in Wust El-Balad had been banned.[52] When the grassroots El-Fan Midan was banned, the consortium showed allegiance to the state and its security services by displaying large images of Egypt's president Abdel Fattah El-Sisi during the D-CAF festival. In the face of cultural censorship, the consortium was forced to mobilize the hyper-visible trappings of securitization and declare their politics openly, undermining the subtle soft modalities of securitization they had hoped to mobilize. The cracks inherent to a project mobilizing soft trappings of exclusion and securitization were already showing as it was barely taking off.

Commerce, Community, and Securitization

In addition to investing in cultural revival as a modality of exclusion, the consortium sought to engineer an "authentic" or "organic" commercial environment. Karim Shafei described these commercial activities as follows:

I would like cosmopolitan from a completely different perspective than, for example, City Stars [a shopping mall built on the outskirts of Cairo in 2003–4]. City Stars is a very American mall-like experience, which is completely different from what downtown can offer. I'd like cosmopolitan in the sense of a pizzeria, for instance, operated by an Italian living in Egypt or an Egyptian who lived in Italy for thirty years and married an Italian woman. I'm not interested in Pizza Hut.... I'm not interested in having Zara and Mango [international chain clothing stores]. I'm interested in having Azza Fahmy [an Egyptian high-end jeweler specializing in silver products] or Mounaya, who sells items from Morocco, Lebanon, and Turkey and all over the region, but it's not mass production like Zara and Mango.[53]

On the one hand, controlling the commercial environment to produce the intimate and "authentic" experiences produced through Azza Fahmy or the Egyptian-Italian family-run pizzeria can be seen as fostering the cultural revival evoked by the aesthetics of Wust El-Balad's buildings. The commercial environment could be seen as producing the unique cultural experience that attracts the clientele interested in urban messiness as well as exclusivity and the artists necessary for creating the neighborhood's soft, spatial-cultural boundaries.

More importantly, however, an "organic" and intimate commercial environment would produce another dynamic crucial to the consortium's project of producing a luxurious oasis in Wust El-Balad: the need for security. To provide the illusion of urban messiness, the Ismailia Consortium needed to find soft modalities that would go beyond the state's security presence or physical barriers for security provision. Unlike the suburban compounds described by Denis (2006) or the individualized efforts to produce physical barriers of protection or "aesthetics of security" described in Caldeira's 2008 study of São Paulo, the consortium needed to find nonphysical modalities that would produce familiarity and a sense of security within the allure of urban immersion. The answer was to create a "community of strangers" that would provide a sense of rootedness and familiarity in the city but also provide stable surveillance mechanisms without reliance on the state. The key to building this community of strangers was in cultivating the right commercial environment in the neighborhood. For Jane Jacobs (1961) and the "new urbanism" school, an urban area's "eyes on the street" are anchored in its commercial culture. It is through the small shops (aka mom-and-pop stores) or intimate restaurants and bars that neighborhoods gain onlookers who are either the known owners of establishments (like the Egyptian-Italian pizzeria owners) or their clients who regularly frequent these establishments and maintain a level of familiarity and surveillance of outsiders on the street. Thus, intimate stores can provide the spatial mechanisms needed to guarantee a stable group of onlookers, and hence its security, but also a regular, familiar group that frequents the neighborhood's streets and gives the anonymous city of strangers a sense of rootedness (Jacobs 1961, ch. 3). Anonymous mass establishments with rotating clerks and an irregular clientele cannot provide that community. In other words, the "authentic" cosmopolitan-yet-Egyptianized commercial environment may work to elicit a unique cultural experience in Wust El-Balad, but more importantly it was also a spatial modality of producing a *community of strangers* essential for maintaining the safety guaranteed to high-end consumers in suburban enclaves without the physical trappings of the gates and walls upon which that safety is guaranteed. For the consortium, cultural revival and the "authenticity" of Wust El-Balad's commercial environment would produce the community of strangers that would resolve the tension of desired exclusivity and security within the urban messiness of the city.

Conclusion

The AKTC and Ismailia Consortium were engineering particularistic communities through urban design as they manipulated real estate markets in the aftermath of the deregulation of Cairo's property market. On the upper end of the market, the Ismailia Consortium was fostering a "community of strangers" as it aimed to create new value in Wust El-Balad through luxury real estate that guaranteed its clientele both the exclusivity and security found in gated compounds and the dynamism of living amid the city's messiness. On the lower end of the market, the AKTC was fostering collaborative, autonomous community with a shared sense of vulnerability and a common fate that cared for the neighborhood's shared spaces. Rather than reading the AKTC's investment in community as an attempt to simply replace a retreating welfare state, I argue for seeing community here as manipulating property market value by striking a careful balance of providing much-needed services to neighborhood insiders invested in their neighborhood without attracting potential gentrifiers. By harnessing the particularism of communities to corner markets, these protagonists challenge existing scholarship on the relationship between fostering communities and neoliberalization. They challenge both the celebratory claim that fostering communal ties generates the *trust* crucial to thriving market economies and the critical claim that communities are fostered in market-driven economies to produce a coresponsible citizenry that *replaces* a welfare distributive state.

In *Making Democracy Work* (1993) and *Bowling Alone* (2000), Robert Putnam argued that strong communal ties and networks are crucial to thriving market economies and democracies because of the *trust* they generate. A strong associational life fostered through sports clubs, music groups, or volunteer associations creates cross-cutting ties and *generalized* trust among strangers who would not have naturally met through family or religious networks. For Putnam, such generalized trust or "social capital" is essential to sustaining repeated market transactions that rely on mutual respect for contracts and property rights among strangers. Putnam's alluring argument spurred a long line of scholarship investigating the politics of trust (e.g., Uslaner 2002; Jamal 2007) and was seen by several critical theorists (see Joseph 2002; Elyachar 2005; Li 2007) as causal of the growing investment in communities or social capital that accompanied transitions to market-driven economies.[54]

Mobilizing piercing ethnographies of community development across market-driven economies, this critical scholarship (e.g., Elyachar 2005; Li 2007; Muehlebach 2012; Zencirci 2015) argued that Putnam's (and similar) work had obfuscated the dispossessive politics of fostering community and social capital. Rather than benignly cultivating more efficient markets, fostering community shifts the burden of public goods provision from a distributive welfare state to coresponsible citizens, paving the way for dismantling the official safety net. In Muehlebach's (2012) words, "As the state shifts the burden of the reproduction of solidarity onto a citizenry conceptualized as active and dutiful, solidarity is outsourced . . . onto citizens, every one of which is now coresponsible for the public good" (11–12). Arguing that communities are being fostered to replace a disappearing welfare state, this scholarship drew attention to the fact that the centering of market logics as the engine of development in fact shifts the economic burden of development onto those most reliant on the nonmarket safety nets now being dismantled. Thus, investing in social capital rather than safety nets further entrenches that equation by holding those most disadvantaged by the shift responsible for public goods provision.

In *Markets of Dispossession*, Julia Elyachar takes that critique further. Working in Egypt, she argues that the valorization of social capital as the key to efficient markets produced a different mechanism for the dispossession of the poor: cycles of indebtedness. Rather than fostering social capital where none existed, it was discovered that the poor, or the informal economy, relied for decades on social capital to survive in the face of inept states. Formalizing the informal economy through loans was claimed to multiply the impact of such "indigenous" social capital—or, in the words of Hernando de Soto (1989), "dead capital"—as it became incorporated into the logics of the formal market. In Elyachar's words:

> The notion of social capital helped to effect the movement of programs about the empowerment of marginal individuals in the informal economy to the center of debates about the economy at large. It was discovered that the informal economy, and the important ability of the poor to survive without help from the state, had at their core social networks built around community reservoirs of trust. The social networks that lay behind the entity called "the informal economy," it had been found, were a form of "capital." Giving loans to support this reservoir of social trust thus became a way of investing in the economy. (186)

Thus, Elyachar importantly moves the conversation about the larger political-economic and potentially dispossessive implications of the valorization of social capital from one that strictly revolves around replacing nonmarket public goods provision to one that interrogates the inner workings of market logics themselves. For her, the market's logics of accumulation rely on incorporating the "indigenous" social capital cultivated by an economy's most vulnerable populations and work through dispossessive cycles of indebtedness to unearth that "dead capital."

Like scholars arguing that community replaces a welfare state, Elyachar's work remained wedded to seeing community being strictly valorized for the relational trust networks it may create, however. As demonstrated, though, the AKTC and the Ismailia Consortium were not working to foster communities because of the trust networks they may produce. As they sought to corner real estate markets, they accentuated the particularism and spatial tactics of boundary-setting that local communities cultivate. In the case of the AKTC, relational networks of collaboration did play an important role, but the ways in which those relational networks were linked to specific spatial tactics of boundary-setting as well as a shared fate particular to neighborhood residents emphasized that it was not *generalized* trust as an abstract concept that was most valued. Far from it. Instead, both actors were cultivating the particular, and not generalized, communal networks that Putnam saw as the bane of efficient markets. Their interest in particularism is reminiscent of Miranda Joseph's (2002) insight, discussed in the chapter's introduction, about the relationship between consumption and particularism. To reiterate, Joseph articulated that relationship as follows: "Consumption ... can only occur within a particular social formation, in which particular desires for particular commodities, produced by particular acts of labor, are operative.... The particularities of historically and socially determined use values, which include particular social relations and 'values' supplement the discontinuous circuit of abstract value, enabling its circulation. In this structural account, 'community' is quite crucial to capitalism" (15). For Joseph, particularism was not necessarily produced through the family or religious networks that Putnam derided but from a shared set of consumer tastes or positions of vulnerability that were nonetheless particularistic and antithetical to generalized trust. In other words, transitions to market-driven economies are cultivating *difference* and an accentuation of what sets communities apart from one another within the city rather than relations of trust.

The key to understanding the cultivation of communal particularism is in realizing that actors like the AKTC and Ismailia Consortium are not interested in the efficiency of markets per se. Their reaction to the "unleashing" of markets is not to maximize their efficiency but to distort and manipulate them. The Ismailia Consortium's main concern when the real estate market was "liberated" from rent controls was to corner it so that only the highest-paying clientele would be attracted to Wust El-Balad. Similarly, the AKTC's reaction to the vulnerability of low-income tenants was to be exclusively attractive to low-income residents and to ensure that they invested more rather than less in the neighborhood as their vulnerability increased. In other words, transitions to neoliberalism—in Egypt, Turkey, and beyond—provoke market-distorting behavior even by those who stand to gain the most from it. The logics of capital accumulation inherently incentivize market distortion and not just, or even mainly, efficiency, as authors such as Putnam or the school of new institutional economics would suggest. Communal particularism is being mobilized as a soft, and undetectable, modality for producing such distortion. Thus, empirically speaking, the most natural affinity between communities and markets is one that fosters division and particularism in service of market distortion rather than one that fosters relational trust for the sake of market efficiency, especially as market modalities become the dominant space through which redistributive politics are channeled. It is only through recognizing the strength of the incentives created by capital accumulation toward market distortion that we come to appreciate the multiplying forces at work in reorganizing the political around local particularistic communities that accentuate *difference* and produce profound transformations in power dynamics in neoliberalizing cities around the globe.

Visible Publics 5

THE AGA KHAN'S PLEDGE TO CONVERT the five-hundred-year-old garbage dump that bordered Haga Samia's home into a seventy-four-acre green space was finally fulfilled when Azhar Park opened its doors to the public in 2005. When I visited the park after a long absence on a Wednesday afternoon in the summer of 2011, I was struck by the sound of utensils banging on metal pots as throngs of families, mostly of modest means, spread out picnics on the park's lawn. My initial reaction was of pleasant surprise that the park was proving accessible to low-income Cairenes despite the E£5 entrance fee, accessibility mainly by car, and sparse public transit there. I later learned that most of the families I had seen were from Darb El-Ahmar neighborhood, who entered the park through a special entrance that connected the neighborhood directly to the park and charged tickets at the discounted rate of E£1. Unlike most well-maintained green spaces in the city, the park was proving accessible and attractive to low-income, if only local, Cairenes.

In the midst of the throngs, I then noticed a strange, fleeting scene. A young boy had started doing cartwheels a few yards away from his family on a patch of green that he seemed to have all to himself. Right when I glimpsed the boy's vivacious cartwheels, a man dressed as a security guard appeared very suddenly, as if he had been hiding behind a bush, ready to pounce, and started yelling at the boy. I was too far away to hear the man's words but saw the boy quickly retreat back to his family and their picnic. I found it very odd that cartwheels would be policed in an open, outdoor park but then thought there may have been an angle to the interaction between the boy and guard that I had missed and continued on with my walk.

At the end of my stroll, I decided to visit the gallery that the Aga Khan Trust for Culture (AKTC) had set up to sell handicrafts produced by Darb El-Ahmar's residents (see chapter 1). The gallery was located in a building overlooking the park that housed several upscale restaurants. Heading toward the building, I walked through the park's center fields and climbed a short set of steps up a hill that opened onto a large green expanse in front of the building. The moment I set foot on the green fields between the steps and the building, a security guard suddenly appeared out of nowhere, again as if hiding behind a bush ready to pounce, and started quickly heading toward me with a grave look of alarm on his face. The security guard then explained that I had to turn around and leave the area immediately. People were not allowed in this area of the park. I looked around and sure enough I was the only one in the area. Moreover, I noticed that the young boy I had seen doing cartwheels had been playing on the edge of this large green field in the center of the park. It wasn't that cartwheels were policed in the park but that this entire area of the park was off limits to the public. This was puzzling since there were no visible gates or signs signaling that it was against the rules to walk, sit, or do cartwheels on these fields. What was so special about this area of the park? And why was it policed through invisible security guards rather than the more common use of fences or signs to regulate the park?

Twenty minutes later, I finally made my way to the gallery's only entrance through the restaurants' designated parking lot. The restaurants' patrons were expected to come by car rather than walking through the park. Before entering the gallery, I was struck by the view from the outdoor veranda. The upscale clientele saw a huge green expanse with the shimmering water from a lake on the other side of the park and the minarets of Islamic Cairo on the horizon. The picturesque view was completely clear, without a single person in sight. The security guard was clearing the view for the restaurants' clientele, and the topography of the park's design facilitated the postcard effect. The building was perched on a hill surrounded by a large green expanse invisibly policed against public use that seamlessly weaved into the image of the lake and minarets beyond. The restaurant's clientele could enjoy their meal and picturesque view without encountering a single one of the families picnicking on the park's lawns or even know of their existence.

The boundaries between the exclusive private space of the restaurant and the (fairly) accessible public space of the park were governed not by ownership structures or the territorial and functional boundaries of each space but by lines of *sight*. Azhar Park is an important pillar of the redistributive project that the AKTC embarked upon in central Cairo. In addition to ensuring that low-income Cairenes have access to a public space in the city's central neighborhood, the park had direct connections to the AKTC's project to safeguard affordable housing in Darb El-Ahmar. Living next to a picturesque, accessible green space in the midst of a congested city incentivized residents' attachment to and investment in their neighborhood. Moreover, the park proved an engine of economic growth. In Samy's (the AKTC urban planner met in previous chapters) words, "One of the goals of the Aga Khan for the park was that it would become an engine for economic development . . . and that the people would start coming down from the park to visit the neighborhood bringing along economic revival."[1] The very people for whom the view from the restaurant's veranda was being sanitized were to serve as an engine of growth. Revenues from the restaurant would maintain the park and even some of the neighborhood's rehabilitation. As the AKTC write on their website: "With nearly two million visitors a year, the US $30 million Azhar Park . . . not only generates enough funds for its own maintenance (through gate and restaurant receipts), but has proven to be a powerful catalyst for urban renewal in the neighboring district of Darb al-Ahmar."[2] More directly, restaurant patrons would buy handicrafts from the neighborhood from the gallery in the restaurant complex or even go on guided tours from the park into the neighborhood and patronize service providers there by buying handicrafts directly from local sellers. Azhar Park visitors, and especially well-off restaurant clients, would become an important financial engine for the redistribution that would keep residents invested in their neighborhood and safeguard affordable housing in Darb El-Ahmar. Producing that redistributive mechanism is greatly reliant, however, on aesthetics, vantage points, and the picturesque. In a way, similar to how mobilizing heritage preservation as a redistributive practice centers the importance of aesthetics and historical worth in the city, mobilizing the tourism machine as part and parcel of a redistributive project places great emphasis on aesthetic and visible topographies. In this chapter, I analyze the impact of these projects on *public/private boundaries*. Among the political implications of public/private boundaries are the accessibility of space and the allocation of responsibility for urban services or the urban "commons." This chapter focuses on how the fixation on visible *aesthetics* that comes with crafting *particularistic value* as a redistributive practice redraws public/private boundaries and its consequences on the accessibility of urban space and responsibility for its servicing.

Visible Aesthetics and Societal Engineering

The political importance of visual topographies has long captured the imagination of scholars of the modern city. A foundational literature on modern (colonial and independent) state-making projects emphasized the centrality of the design of visual topographies to a modern governing order based on discipline and population control obsessed with molding the ideal productive society (see Foucault 1977; Mitchell 1988; Holston 1989; Scott 1998; Benjamin 1999). Visual order became essential for placing the productive society under surveillance (Foucault 1977) and rendering cities legible and accessible to high modernist states (Holston 1989; Scott 1998). Surveillance and legibility came to the modern cityscape through urban spectacle and a more general fixation on "representing" visual order (Mitchell 1988; Benjamin 1999). The main audience gazing onto the city's disciplining and representational spaces was a local population to be molded into ideal modern and productive national citizens.

Visual topographies are just as central to the neoliberal marketization of politics as they once were to the making of productive capitalist subjects, but the logics governing their design have transformed dramatically. The prolific literature on "global cities" (see Harvey 1989; Boyer 1996; Zukin 1996; Keyder 1999; Sassen 2001; Caldeira 2008) has mostly argued that the deployment of visual aesthetics as modalities of societal engineering receded when states turned their attention toward attracting global audiences and deployed urban visual aesthetics to market their cities to those outsiders. That shift is then seen to elicit an unfettered commodification of urban landscapes that entrenches market logics in how cities are (un)planned. In David Harvey's (1989) words, this shifts governance from "urban managerialism" to "urban entrepreneurialism." Taking that analysis a step further, Asher Ghertner (2015) argues that such aesthetic-based marketing and commodification of the urban built-environment then transforms how states govern their own citizens, shifting away from Foucauldian practices of disciplinary governmentality and toward a "rule by aesthetics" that deploys the visual as a guiding principle for understanding, categorizing, and ultimately governing society.

While the literature on "global cities" documents an important shift in how audiences now gaze upon a city's visible landscape, it underestimates the continued importance of societal engineering in shaping the design of visible urban landscapes.[3] Societal engineering remains an important logic motivating the design of visible and invisible urban built-environments, as discussed in the previous chapters, but the expanding audience of "global cities" has indeed transformed the emphasis of such work. Rather than a strict focus on molding *bodies*, the manipulation of market value as redistributive practice has mobilized the design of the built environment to engineer "community," marshal the power and wealth of the heritage industry, and capitalize on tourism in ways that are qualitatively different from the focus of modernizing state-making projects on the making of productive *society*. Nevertheless, the intricate design of visual topographies is still central to mobilizing political struggles through market-making practices in ways that focus on the study of societal engineering through urban design relevant to our understanding of contemporary cities. In this chapter, I unpack how visual topographies are embroiled in societal engineering practices and how they are redrawing public/private boundaries in neoliberalizing "global" cities.

Tourism and Redistribution

Tourism has a complicated relationship with redistributive projects that work through the modalities of the market, especially ones dedicated to safeguarding affordable housing. In some regards, fostering tourism is seen as one of the pillars of such redistributive work. As Samy explained, tourism operates as an engine of "economic revival" when tourists spend money on neighborhood services or buy locally produced goods and handicrafts. Similarly, tourists' entrance fees—whether to a space like Azhar Park or local monuments—could directly support a neighborhood's physical rehabilitation in lieu of taxes. On a psychological level, I was told by several conservationists that they believed people developed *pride* when they saw outsiders flocking to their neighborhoods, attracted to their natural or heritage endowments. One of the residents of Gamaliyya in historic Cairo, Umm Amira, articulated this sentiment a little differently. Umm Amira told me that knowing that outsiders were choosing to come to her neighborhood signaled to her that it had finally become safe and secure enough for them to visit.[4] Seeing others value their neighborhoods' built and natural environments would motivate residents to invest in their own neighborhoods rather than flee them.

Specific to heritage preservation, a long-term trajectory of global tourism is one of the main structural transformations that galvanized and continues to empower an "environmental turn" in heritage preservation, essential to enabling it as a redistributive practice. More immediately, the allure of tourism is one of the main incentives motivating local government partners to join and support efforts to rehabilitate low-income neighborhoods through heritage preservation projects.

When tourism is valorized as a pillar in the redistributive battle in this way, tourists represent a category distinct from feared gentrifiers. Tourists are transient visitors whose money circulates in the neighborhood without encroaching upon its real estate markets and threatening affordable housing. Of course even if they are distinct populations, one of the biggest critiques of tourism-attracting projects is that they produce neighborhood conditions that make not only Umm Amir feel safer in her neighborhood but potential gentrifiers as well, and scholars have already written extensively about these risks and the gentrifying effects of tourism (e.g., Zukin 1996; Keyder 1999). To gain a more holistic understanding of tourism's place within the battle for housing, I move beyond an exclusive focus on its gentrifying effects and unpack how projects navigate the complicated opportunities and risks that tourism affords redistributive work, specifically through the lens of transforming visual topographies and public/private boundaries within neighborhoods.

Visual Topographies and Public/Private Boundaries

GAMALIYYA

In Historic Cairo's Gamaliyya neighborhood, Umm Ayman had saved enough money to install aluminum windowpanes in the mid-2000s. The reflecting glass provided Umm Ayman an unobstructed view of the outside world without being seen, and the insect screen kept out uninvited guests. Most importantly, for Umm Ayman, as for many others in Gamaliyya, her aluminum windows signaled wealth and the ability to afford such a luxury.[5]

In 2009, the Egyptian Ministry of Culture demanded from Umm Ayman that she remove her aluminum windows. The Ministry of Culture, through a subsidiary called the Historic Cairo Organization (HCO), had started a heritage preservation project on the main arterial boulevard of the neighborhood, Muʿiz Street. The project entailed the conservation of all monuments and visible façades of buildings (private and public) to create a harmonized

Figure 5.1. Muʿiz Street after implementation of a heritage preservation project. Source: author, December 2010.

historical look (see figure 5.1). As part of their effort to beautify the street's façades, they were installing carved wooden latticework, or *mashrabiyya*, windows instead of the chaotic variety of window styles that previously adorned building façades. The ministry was demanding that Umm Ayman allow the team to remove the aluminum windows and install *mashrabiyya*, at no cost to her, as part of that harmonizing effort.

Umm Ayman was not convinced that the ministry's engineers needed to remove her aluminum windows and install *mashrabiyya* to make the street more beautiful. Not only would the *mashrabiya* block cool air from entering the apartment, but it would also be much more difficult to clean than her aluminum panes. Umm Ayman decided to put up a fight. For three years, and until I met the project's site leader in 2011, the ministry's team had not been able to amicably convince Umm Ayman of installing *mashrabiyya* on her windows. The ministry's next step would have been to involve the governor and local municipality, who would then issue decrees demanding that she allow the workers to install the *mashrabiyya*.[6]

For Umm Ayman, an aluminum window embodied far more than a simple view to the outside world. When closed, her tinted windows allowed Umm

Ayman to look out onto her neighborhood and likely keep surveillance over her neighbors, undetected, in the comfort of her home attire. When open, they allowed in cool air while the attached screen kept insects out. Importantly, few people in the neighborhood had aluminum windows, and they signaled wealth and status. Umm Ayman's windows were valued not just because of functionality but also the social power it allowed her to exercise as she kept an undetected eye on the neighborhood and signaled wealth to her neighbors. While the *mashrabiyya* would allow her to keep a vigilant eye undetected, it neither afforded her the comforts of the aluminum windows nor the signal of wealth that aluminum evoked, since it would be known that the state had installed the *mashrabiyya*. As heritage preservation and its accompanying tourism becomes increasingly embraced as a redistributive practice, residents of low-income communities will have to negotiate and often accept the increasing power of the value placed on historical accuracy and the aesthetic beauty of their built environments that flattens other ways they may value the visible and invisible contours of their lived spaces. The Ministry of Culture's project in Gamaliyya was not by any means a redistributive project. It was fixated on heritage preservation and attracting tourism to Historic Cairo and uninterested in intervening in real estate markets, either upward or downward. I bring it into this conversation, however, because it further showcases the practices (alongside those discussed in chapter 3) emboldened as tourism and heritage preservation become increasingly embraced as redistributive.

Moushira, one of the project directors, explained the HCO's plan as one aiming to transform the area into an "open-air museum." One of the main projects that the team undertook was the relocation of the neighborhood's lemon and onion market to the city's periphery. The team's fixation on managing tourists' senses, and especially their sight, came to life when Moushira explained,

> First of all, imagine you're entering the street from this entrance and it smells like onions and smells like garlic. Of course it's very unappealing [*mesh thareefa*] that you start your journey with this visual image or with this smell. Moreover, the peel of the onions and the garlic cloves used to fly all over the street and ruining it. So it created a lot of damage and an uncivilized image. They would spread their goods outside and sit on the sidewalk so the image is not attractive to any visiting tourist. Because of that it left a bad imprint [*bassma*] at the beginning of the street, at the beginning of the journey from Bab El-Fotouh.[7]

The centrality of visual appeal to the ministry's plans for the neighborhood became even starker during her discussion of their efforts to harmonize Muʿiz Street's façades according to one architectural style. When I asked if they worked on all buildings in the street, she replied: "Yes, we renovate the old and the new buildings. Like on your left you can see a new building and on your right you can see several old buildings."[8] Sure enough, the old and new buildings had very similar façades, with identical wooden *mashrabiyya* work regardless of whether or not such latticework adorned the original building. In this case, the primacy of the street's visual harmony overrode even the logic of historical accuracy. While this takes the fixation on visual aesthetics to an extreme in a way that defies a redistributive project's need for historical accuracy (as discussed in chapter 3), it does demonstrate the ways in which visual aesthetics could become hegemonic with an increasing embrace of heritage preservation aimed at attracting a tourist's gaze as a redistributive practice and public good.

Such hegemony of visual aesthetics and historical worth redraws public/private boundaries in several ways. Most directly, it redraws the control owners have over their private property. In Gamaliyya, the Ministry of Culture chipped away at the control private owners had over two facets of their property. With harmonization so crucial to the project, the ministry was decreeing that private owners would lose control over the design of their building façades, including features such as Umm Ayman's aluminum windows, colorfully painted exteriors, neon signage, or metal gates. Just how draconian these measures were came to light as Moushira explained the role the policing state had in enforcing these new boundaries:

> The governorate or the local municipality help us . . . if, for instance, there are people whose building façades are in violation [of our plan] . . . when we finish our work, we require that people build in accordance with the façade and lighting patterns that we did. We renovate façades, place storefront signs, modify street lighting and lighting for individual stores so that the lighting does not cause a glare for the tourist.[9]

Suddenly, ownership regimes lost their meaning in governing the control owners had over their property. Whether or not they owned their building, private owners had relinquished their control over the exterior of their building to the state.

When it came to assigning responsibility to the state for providing urban services, however, that relationship turned on its head. Private property boundaries became sacrosanct. The ministry invested millions in infrastructural updating, but that infrastructure was deliberately designed to service monuments and not neighborhood residents. The project upgraded the entire water, sewage, and electrical grid beneath the neighborhood but only connected the new infrastructure to pipes servicing the street or monuments and had a rule against connecting it to private residential or commercial buildings. In other words, the HCO dug up the rotting infrastructure from beneath the neighborhood, often keeping street guts open for two years at a time, but deliberately decided not to use that opportunity to fix pipes that connected to private buildings. By design, citizens' working and living spaces were not directly serviced by the state's project.

In addition, any indirect benefits citizens may have reaped were framed as serendipitous by-products rather than any rights citizens may have to state-provided services. During my fieldwork, I spent hours listening to conservation consultants, the project directors, and engineers explain the technical reasons behind fixing that infrastructure, deeming it essential for the health of the neighborhood's historical fabric and monuments. They explained the importance of building new aqueducts to decrease water levels and preserve monuments from water damage, the necessity of removing layers of asphalt to dig up monument entrances that had been buried under years of superficial street repairs, and even the importance of fixing electricity networks to support the new spotlights lighting monuments by night in the neighborhood. Completely absent from these conversations, however, was any mention of the daily needs of neighborhood residents. The benefits they may have been reaping from this massive state investment were usually mentioned as a positive externality of the project rather than as a deliberate decision to service the citizens' needs. Moushira made this clearest when she explained: "It is very possible that they hate the project. They see millions of Egyptian pounds being spent on the street that they believe should be theirs.... I explain to them that they should in fact protect the monuments because the monuments are the reason why they are getting these services."[10] The monuments were being serviced because of the public good they were providing, but urban services were not a guaranteed public good to be expected by citizens. As such, private boundaries became especially important in delineating where the state's responsibility stopped. Moushira explained that even if they could service private residences, they did not, because "if you enter into one house, all the rest will say, 'Me too!' and they may even break their own sewage systems so that you would have to enter and fix them."[11] In the provision of services to its citizens, boundaries between what is public and private became more rigid and sacred than ever. Public monuments were entitled to services, but citizens were not. The state's priorities had been written into stone.

DARB EL-AHMAR

The design of Darb El-Ahmar's visual topography was a central feature of the AKTC's project and was mainly shaped by the linkage between Azhar Park and the neighborhood. One of the first logics that the AKTC used to decide how it would allocate home restoration grants was a home's visibility from the park. Although the ability of a building's residents to coordinate as a community eventually became the main determinant of grant allocation, the first phase of the project, through which ten buildings were restored with the AKTC covering 90 rather than 70 percent of costs, focused exclusively on restoring buildings that were visible from the park or were visible on the neighborhood's main thoroughfare, Darb Shoghlan.

The AKTC had several explanations for that focus. First, Samy explained that this choice fulfilled the AKTC's pro-poor mission since these houses were the poorest in the neighborhood after having bordered a landfill for centuries. Second, as discussed in chapter 4, restoring this façade was especially important for protecting the area from a predatory state that would be gazing at the neighborhood (and its apparent debilitation) from the park. Third, the façade would also attract visitors from the park. When he explained the linkage between the park and the neighborhood, Samy zeroed in on buildings within park visitors' line of sight and along their path into the neighborhood, saying, "This is the area bordering the park, and thus any interface between the park and Darb El-Ahmar occurred along this strip.... It was important that we identify at the very least the spots or places that would serve as an entrance to the neighborhood and begin to develop them."[12] Starting with buildings that were visible from the park and on the neighborhood's main thoroughfare would attract visitors into the neighborhood and spur economic revival from the project's earliest phases. Fourth, restoring visible buildings would gain neighborhood residents' trust in the project early on. Samy explained that residents only trusted results they could see, and so the project focused on restoring houses that would be visible on the main thoroughfare to convince residents that their houses would be restored and returned to them if they agreed to vacate their houses for a year or so to allow for restorations to take place.[13] Similarly, Elif from the European Union's (EU) project in Fener-Balat explained to me that one of the metrics that the EU used to allocate restoration funds was "location of the house, so that it would create visibility at the beginning for the first phase."[14] Again, Elif emphasized the importance of restoring highly visible homes first to gain people's trust while they were marketing the project to residents. Managing the visual topography of the neighborhood would secure it against a predatory state, build the neighborhood's trust in the project, and spur economic revival from its visitors. The visitors' gaze from the park was leaving an unmistakable imprint on the neighborhood's built topography.

Visitors' lines of sight and movements had an even starker impact on urban services. The AKTC created planned tourist routes that would take the tourist from one exit of the park to another entrance or walk them out of Darb El-Ahmar to Gamaliyya neighborhood through one of the city gates, Bab Zuweila. As the AKTC planner Mounir explained to me, the only public infrastructural work that the AKTC completed in Darb El-Ahmar occurred along those "tourist routes." The streets on tourist routes were cleaned, provided with new sewage systems and lighting fixtures, and adorned with visually appealing brick.[15] Interestingly, the provision of services along tourist routes stands in tension with a logic of communal provision of services that would detract from the neighborhood's attractiveness to gentrifiers (as discussed in chapter 4). The tourist's gaze demarcated the boundaries between a public (of sorts) provision of urban services and a communal responsibility for the commons.

Visual Topographies and the Accessibility of Space: An Expanded, Gazing Public

As they worked to attract tourists to rehabilitated neighborhoods, the AKTC and EU profoundly transformed the accessibility and sociability of shared spaces.[16] Marketing the visual appeal of the built environment entails an expansion of the parameters of the gaze of strangers upward and deeper into the neighborhood. It operates on the assumption that what is visible is public and fair game for gazing, photographing outsiders. Delving into the everyday rhythms of neighborhood streets and their gendered dynamics, I investigate here the blind spots of such an assumption, how it violates the dynamics of daily livelihood, and ultimately redraws the once-negotiated parameters of the public for urban dwellers.

Our Streets

The street may be assumed to be the space that is most acceptable for the stranger's presence, gaze, or even photography—a navigational space where passersby are naturally expected to see whatever activity is practiced in that "public" space. In reality, not all streets in Istanbul and Cairo are simply navigational. Streets are home to a variety of everyday activities that are practiced alongside, and sometimes override, their navigational uses. Geographically enclosed streets such as side streets, dead-ends, and alleyways are particularly amenable to such activities. As I passed through such streets, I would find women sitting on the steps of their homes in small clusters chatting, cooking, cleaning rugs on their doorsteps, and watching their children play on the street. Men would also spend long hours on the streets, either clustered on seats at the corners with their eyes on several intersecting streets or if there was a coffee shop, men would overflow from the coffee shop onto the street. Along with spending most of her time on her dead-end street in Gamaliyya socializing with her friends, Habiba also made her living on the street. She used to wipe down and clean parked cars. Habiba lamented that with the recent pedestrianization of the street, cars didn't park there anymore and she had to search for a new source of income away from her home.[17]

During meal and recreational times, the street became a place for even more elaborate social interactions. Halime Hanım, who had lived in Tarlabaşı, Istanbul (the neighborhood undergoing mass evacuations to make way for Çalık's upgrading project discussed in chapter 2) for more than forty years before the evacuations, described how during the first twenty years or so, she had lived in a building removed from the main thoroughfare, lower down the hill, on a narrow side street. She remembered that the street was central to her life with her Roma neighbors at the time. They regularly had *mangal*, or barbecues, on the street and ate together. Moreover, both men and women would watch television together on their shared TV set in front of the building. When Halime moved in the 1990s to her newly owned apartment in Tarlabaşı on the main thoroughfare, her socializing with her now mostly Kurdish neighbors changed from the street to the home and the park.[18] It was the physical dimension of the street, not the fact that it was visible or invisible, that governed where Halime would share meals with her neighbors. Similarly, Nurgul Hanım in Sulukule, the predominantly Roma neighborhood of Istanbul discussed in chapter 2, was fixated on her parents' street as the center

Visible Publics 195

of *komşuluk*, or neighborliness.[19] Most vivid for her was dining with neighbors on the street. They would cook dinner together as neighbors inside or outside their homes. They would then set up small tables outside, and the neighbors would eat together almost every night. This was especially true during Ramadan. Moreover, the street was the space for celebrations, whether they were wedding processions or *sünnet* (circumcision) celebrations.[20] Such celebrations also filled the streets of other neighborhoods in Istanbul and Cairo. Workshop-dominated Darb El-Ahmar was particularly festive on Sundays, the weekly workshop holiday. Thus, the streets were home to many fluid activities that are central to repeated and prolonged social interactions governed by negotiated social protocols.

Gendered Asymmetries

The constant inflow of tourists, students, and so on is bound to have multiple ramifications on the social dynamics of a neighborhood. Such ramifications are not experienced symmetrically by urban dwellers, however. The expansion of the gaze upward and deeper into neighborhoods will affect different groups divided along gender, class, property ownership, commercial activity, religion, and so on asymmetrically. I address other transitional asymmetries elsewhere in the book, but in this section, I focus on gendered asymmetries as one of the starkest differentiations resulting from the expansion of the gaze in Istanbul and Cairo.

Scholarship on Muslim-majority countries has predominantly translated the religious beliefs and cultural practices of Muslim communities into a rigid division of public and private spaces along gendered lines: the public is a male-dominated sphere, and the private is a female-dominated sphere (e.g., see Mernissi 1987; Hessini 1994). Such categorization and depiction is problematic on multiple levels. First of all, on a theoretical and normative level, the public/private dichotomy generally relegates female activities to private concerns that do not merit recognition as political and matters of social justice (see Benhabib 1992; Fraser 1992). Moreover, such scholarship operates on the assumption that the public/private dichotomy operates on the boundaries of what is visible and invisible, which does not acknowledge the fluidity of activities across these boundaries in the urban Middle East. I join scholarship that asserts that the notion that women, religious or not, do not have a presence in "public" or shared spaces in Middle Eastern cities is simply inaccurate (e.g., see Ghannam 2002; Ismail 2006; Reynolds 2012). Rather than relying on preordained assumptions of how such public/private boundaries operate, I argue here that the relationships between men and women in shared spaces are bound by a history of shared practices that develop soft and negotiated boundaries and gender protocols. It is the threatening of these soft and negotiated boundaries by the constant inflow of gazing, roaming, and photographing outsiders that leads to dramatic gendered asymmetries in the use of shared spaces in restored neighborhoods.

Women are visible on the streets of Cairo and Istanbul. They chat, sell trinkets from their small shops, peddle vegetables and fruits, cook, watch their children play, clean their rugs, watch TV, and share meals with their neighbors on the street. Moreover, when these streets are adjacent to their homes, women often appear in clothes they would mainly wear indoors and are generally more comfortable in their demeanor. Many of these activities are done on streets shared with neighborhood men, but this sharing is managed through carefully negotiated protocols. Most important to these protocols is the management of the gaze that defined the soft and negotiated boundaries of male-female relations. According to Islamic religious edicts, men and women should lower their gaze (*ghadd el bassar*) when interacting and communicating with members of the opposite sex. While levels of religiosity vary in these neighborhoods, a lowered or respectful gaze has developed into an important protocol for managing male-female relations. The lowered gaze operates according to a logic that is in direct opposition to the logic of the expanded gaze.

The expanding gaze of tourists is not only moving deeper into neighborhoods but is also expanding upward to visible purviews of the home. Balconies, *cumbas* (protruding windows popular in historical Turkish homes, pronounced *jumba*), and clotheslines have now become the object of the tourist's gaze and photography. The history and architectural styles of these visible aspects of the home have become the centerpieces of guided tours. Unabashed guidance of the gaze upward, however, assumes that what is visible is "public" and fair game to the stranger's eye. On the other hand, both men and women in Cairo and Istanbul treat these protruding purviews as extensions of the home that are valuable connectors to their social worlds outdoors. The balconies are especially important for women. They communicate with one another, sharing stories, gossip, advice, and even utensils, on a regular basis. Balconies and *cumbas* are also important connections to the street. In particular, women buy their groceries through the baskets they drop from their balconies and windows, in which their orders are placed. Trusting in the protocols of the lowered gaze, most women appear in clothes they would wear at home. Male passersby or grocers and bakers filling their baskets are expected to communicate with a respectful gaze and not stare at women in the balconies.

These soft and negotiated boundaries are at the heart of managing male-female relationships in shared and visible spaces. The expansion of the outside visitor's gaze deeper and upward violates these protocols, bringing rigidity to these boundaries and asymmetrically violating the comfort women have in establishing their social universe in these shared and visible spaces. As we stuffed grape leaves in the kitchen of a women's association in Fener, Istanbul (the site of the EU's rehabilitation project), I discussed the place of women in shared spaces with six women who lived in the neighborhood (encountered in chapter 2). During the conversation, Ayşe Hanım expressed her discomfort in spending time in the park on the banks of the Golden Horn, where strange Turkish men would stare at her and her friends every time she sat there. Instead, the women expressed comfort in spending time in the courtyard of the mosque at the top of the hill in Çukurbostan and the tea garden up on the Molla Aşkı hill. The location of these spaces up the hill and deeper into the community provided reassurance that they would be around a community, male or female, that respected the shared protocols of soft and negotiated gender boundaries. Melek Hanım finally summed up such places of comfort as what she termed *"belirli mekanlar,"* or well-known places, and the rest of the group agreed: "Yes, *belirli mekanlar!*"[21] As outsiders increasingly ascend higher up the hill and deeper into the neighborhood, such *belirli mekanlar* governed by well-known and shared gender protocols will disappear, limiting the presence of these women in their neighborhood's shared spaces. The withdrawal of women from these shared spaces will of course directly limit their daily exposure to wide social networks, commercial encounters, the circulation of news, and so on. It is important to realize, however, that this is not a unidirectional story. For Heba and Umm Amira in Gamaliyya, Cairo, the presence of outsiders had its benefits alongside its nuisances. As discussed previously, tourists made Umm Amira feel safer. For Heba, the increasing presence of strangers in the neighborhood, she hoped, would increase levels of anonymity. Heba found the dense and overseeing nature of her alley's network suffocating for a young woman like herself seeking independence and greater mobility in the city.[22] What is clear then is that the influx of an outside audience of tourists and students will result in dramatic shifts for how women occupy shared spaces and navigate their city.

What also becomes clear from this mapping of women's navigation of shared spaces is that urban dwellers, and especially women, have always worked to remake shared and "public" space into *particular* spaces bound by known and shared protocols accessed by knowable city dwellers. They innovatively mobilized the city's topography of narrow alleyways, hilltops, balconies, and protruding windows to create spaces of sociability, network-building, and political engagement in an arena mirroring that of the "public sphere" that is marked by particularism and the management of access essential for that sociability and political engagement. In other words, it was the particularism of space, or *belirli mekanlar*, and not its "publicness" that guaranteed a space's accessibility to city dwellers, demonstrating the exclusivity that "public" spaces can and do produce, as Fraser (1992) and Benhabib (1992) argue. The move toward fostering particularistic local community as a mode of channeling redistribution through market logics, as seen in chapter 4, then intersects with this preexisting particularism through which dwellers, and especially women, navigate the city in several politically productive ways. The rest of the chapter interrogates this intersection and the impact of fostering particularism as redistributive practice on the city's accessibility and patterns of public goods provision.

Spatial Particularism and Public/Private Boundaries

Wust El-Balad's Architectural Gems

A pedestrian's first encounter with Wust El-Balad is usually an overwhelming one. With a topography marked by large boulevards radiating from several roundabouts that are arterial to Cairo's traffic patterns, Wust El-Balad's boulevards have turned into chaotic traffic dens difficult to navigate by car, let alone on foot. The large boulevards are not the only navigable pathways through Wust El-Balad, however. One of the neighborhood's best-kept secrets is an intricate web of interconnected passageways that covers the neighborhood. One could theoretically walk across the entirety of Wust El-Balad through these walkways. As such, they have developed into what most closely resemble alleyways in more enclosed neighborhoods. The passageways are the most likely places to find all the amenities and stores that cater to permanent residents. Here one would find the tailor, the ironing service, the small kitchenette selling homemade food to local residents and workers, and, most importantly, the local *qahwa* (coffee shop). The walkways closest to Wust El-Balad's commercial areas such as Tala'at Harb Street become extensions of the commercial scene, with many vendors and small stores squeezed into the alley providing a more enclosed commercial space. Thus, the passageway operates as a space of motion and navigation as well as economic exchange and repeated social interactions. They are by no means an exclusive space to a particular social group, but they develop a familiarity and protocol of their own. Most passersby are "regulars" to the passageway, expected to at least know and greet those around them if not engage them in longer conversations.

To the Ismailia Consortium, who are developing luxury real estate in Wust El-Balad, these walkways are architectural gems. Without them, their project would fall apart. The passageways present the perfect spaces to cultivate the "community of strangers" that guarantees the exclusivity and security that the consortium sought to engender in the midst of the city's messiness (see chapter 4). The semi-enclosed yet open nature of the passageways provides a space that naturally fosters the particularism inherent to the commercial and cultural spaces meant to produce a "community of strangers" without the need to erect visible barriers that detract from Wust El-Balad's seeming messiness.

The topography of the space was not its only virtue, however. Over and above their spatial particularism, the passageways are zoned as *private* spaces. As one of the planners from the I2UD planning consultancy working with Ismailia Consortium explained to me, the walkways are zoned as privately owned by the owners of buildings overlooking each walkway.[23] Although these passageways remain mostly open and navigable to all city dwellers (I was able to walk through most of them unhindered), historically, building owners coordinated to close off the walkways with large iron gates during episodes of havoc and insecurity. Although those passageways were owned by building owners, residents long expected the state to service them and provide necessary lighting, water and sewage infrastructure, and sanitation services along the walkways, as they did any other "street." The Ismailia Consortium relished the opportunity to flip that expectation on its head. As Karim Shafei, the consortium's CEO, and the I2UD planner both explained to me, the consortium bought buildings in Wust El-Balad in clusters so that they would own the entirety of buildings overlooking a given passageway and have legal control over not only the commercial activity but also the infrastructural works taking place there. Controlling the walkways' infrastructure would allow the consortium to service the walkways at the standards that their luxury clientele would expect without having to deal with the limits of state or residents' budgets. Such control would also allow them to manage the visible contours of streets, including signage and lighting, to cultivate the particularistic commercial and cultural environment they had planned for Wust El-Balad. In an era where protagonists are actively working to manipulate real estate markets, they relish the opportunity to channel responsibility for servicing the "commons" away from the state and into their control as they work to foster particularism in the city.

In normalizing a shift of responsibility for urban services away from the state, these protagonists are not simply "privatizing public space," as is often lamented in the literature on neoliberal cities. Instead, they are capitalizing on long-negotiated and carefully crafted particular yet accessible spaces in the city to foster the communal particularism essential for manipulating market value upward. In doing so, they are slowly but surely transforming those protocols into a shared set of tastes and expectations that exclude the very people who had initially crafted these particularistic spaces, producing a radical shift in the composition (especially along class lines) of the dwellers navigating shared spaces in the city. Slowly, this shift would bring wealthier residents out from secured malls, sports or country clubs, and gated compounds to the seemingly open and messy spaces of the city while erecting soft boundaries against the mostly low-income dwellers who had so carefully crafted these particularistic spaces. Such a transformation is far more insidious than what scholars refer to as a "privatization of public space" since it is far more difficult to see, and resist, the soft boundaries of exclusivity that preserve many elements of the particularistic spaces upon which these projects capitalize. It also highlights the irrelevance of juxtaposing public to private spaces as absolutes when the struggle for the city is actually being waged in the realm of the particularistic semi-private/semi-public.

Rooftops

Protagonists working to corner markets downward are mobilizing particularistic spaces just as actively as those working to corner them upward. Rooftops are just as central to the urban imaginaries and experiences of Wust El-Balad's residents as they were to Haga Samia and Umm Hassan from chapter 4. The Model Citizens project, undertaken by the Dutch artists Elke Uitentuis and Wouter Osterholt in residency at the Townhouse Gallery in 2008–2009 (introduced in chapter 1), illustrated the many ways in which rooftops shape and mediate residents' experiences of Wust El-Balad. As part of the project, Uitentuis and Osterholt created a scaled maquette that mirrored the reality of

Antikhana alleyway (within the parameters of the Ismailia Consortium's project), and they interviewed one hundred dwellers of Antikhana about changes they hoped to see in their neighborhood. They then produced a new imaginary maquette based on those collated visions.[24] Rooftops featured heavily as spaces residents would transform. For example, citizen #6 (as identified by the artists) wanted "to create a pergola on the roof of the Lipton Coffeeshop. He hope[d] it [would] become an intellectual communal space, where people [could] socialize, draw, hold workshops, etc. He would like to build a staircase leading to the roof that does not interfere with the present coffee shop." Citizen #7 "lives in an apartment on the rooftop of the Townhouse building. He loves art and is dreaming of transforming the outdoor area on the rooftop into an independent art space for exhibitions, theater performances and concerts." Similarly, citizen #10 wanted "to clean the coffeeshop rooftop. He would like this space to be used as a social club. The social club would charge a monthly membership fee and would include a ping-pong table, a television set, games for children and youth, as well as artistic activities. The social club will provide the neighborhood families with a safe space for socialization and recreational activities." Twenty-nine of the forty-seven residents interviewed by the artists hoped to transform and re-use neighborhood rooftops.[25] Although not all the suggestions were as creative as the ones quoted above, the reimagining of Antikhana showed just how central rooftops are to Cairenes in daily life.

The rooftop lends itself to fostering "open" particularistic spaces even more easily than Wust El-Balad's walkways, since its location on top of buildings accessible through controllable staircases produces opportunities for hosting activities to a knowable public. This particularism also produces flexibility with the space; it could be imagined as a theater by one person or a social club by another because of the ability to control that space in ways that are difficult to do for open streets without state support. That particularism also opens up opportunities for the creation of income-based boundaries, as suggested by citizen #10, who suggested a monthly membership fee for access to the rooftop, signaling a movement from a low-income community toward privatized rooftops exclusive to restaurant clients and the like in other neighborhoods in Cairo. As the AKTC and other protagonists embraced the rooftop as a coveted social space for cultivating particularistic community, they also worked to strengthen and prioritize the rooftop as a communal space, with its penchant for forced particularism, over other shared spaces where such particularism is more negotiated in its boundedness.

Visibility and Particularism at Work in the Tarlabaşı Garden

In the spring of 2012, as Tarlabaşı was being evacuated for Çalık Holding's renewal project, a group of activists that brought together a mostly professional group of urban planners, architects, artists, and filmmakers, worked to reclaim the neighborhood's spaces for its residents by creating a neighborhood *bahçe*, or garden, right on the edge of the renewal zone being evacuated. They aimed to create a space that was particularly inviting to neighborhood residents, one that would encourage them to stay in the neighborhood and resist its takeover in the face of a heavy-handed state. The visual topographies and particularism of the space of the *bahçe* became as central to these activists' project as it had been for other actors working to manipulate markets encountered in this chapter. I relate an excerpt from my field notes as I shadowed the urban activists in Tarlabaşı to unpack the communal dynamics their tactics produced.

I met with the urban activists on a Saturday afternoon on one of Tarlabaşı's main thoroughfares, on the boundaries of Çalık Holding's renewal project. We were going to start planning the *bahçe* the activists hoped to create. The day before, we had met and decided that the garden should be a green space resembling a park, where neighborhood children would play, take classes, and attend movie screenings. This Saturday, we were to see the place that the activists had rented for the park and start planning it.

As we started our journey, we took several turns and entered a small side street on our way to the park. As we entered the side street, I saw a familiar scene. The entire street was lined with clusters of women seated together, chatting and preparing food on the steps of their buildings, and a group of young men were huddled at the other end of the street. I knew from my own research that this alleyway was dominated by a Kurdish community.

We then surprisingly stopped at a makeshift gate covered by two large blankets, and our leader pushed it aside and entered. This was where we were going to build the park. The space where two demolished small buildings used to stand in the past stood empty. It was long rather than wide and had two levels of elevation. The ground was nothing but dirt, but a tree had grown, creating some shade. Two old chairs stood at the arched windows on the other end of the space.

We took a few minutes to survey the space, and the activists started throwing around ideas for the park's design. They started making drawings. A planner suggested that greenery should be planted on the sides and a soft surface should be installed in the middle where the children would play. Someone then suggested painting one of the walls white to act as a screen where movies could be projected. The discussions were slightly interrupted when five to six men from the community entered the space. Two of the men were older while the rest I recognized as the young men who were huddled at the other end of the street. They entered quietly and started listening to the plans and ideas floating around. The activists then turned to look at the makeshift wall and gate enclosing the space. They saw that the stones constituting a freestanding wall were unconnected to the walls of the buildings on either side of the space. Not only were these stones unnecessary, exclaimed an activist, but they also presented a safety hazard. The activists quickly and unanimously concurred that the wall and gate must go. They were designing the *bahçe* to be an open public space, thus it would need to be inviting and visible to everyone in the community.

The young men listening to this discussion lost no time interjecting. "The wall and covered gate must stay," they pronounced. I had just learned that these young men were the ones renting the place to the activists, and they had veto power over what was to be done with the park. The young owners then proceeded to explain how they used this space and what they wished to preserve from its current design, attempting to make a convincing argument for the wall. One of the young men pointed to the windows of the building overlooking the park and explained that they drop electrical wires from these windows to connect them to their TV and PlayStation. They met here most evenings of the summer to play video games. They also spent a lot of time in the chairs by the arched windows, smoking and talking into the night. The young men then made it clear that they would continue using this space in the evenings after the children had gone home and would like to keep the privacy provided by the wall and gate.

The activists then retorted that they saw no reason why removing the gate and wall would have any effect on the young men's ability to meet in the evenings. They promised that they would keep the chairs and electrical cords but maintained that it would be absolutely essential that they remove the wall so that the park would be inviting to children and seen as safe by their parents. It would be defying the idea of building a public park, the activists argued, if it was not visible, easily reachable, and open. One of the young men then felt the need to make his case very explicit: "We use recreational drugs in this space, if you know what I mean, and we'd like to make sure it remains an unassuming place that would hide our activities and not arouse police suspicion." It then became clear what was at stake for the young men. As the stakes started to dawn on them, the activists started to think of more creative solutions to this impasse. One of the activists then suggested that they paint the walls from the outside. They could use stencils and colorful designs that would still be inviting. The young owner then retorted that even this creative solution is problematic. A colorful wall would attract the attention of the police as much as it would the children. More importantly, the young owner questioned the activists' concern. He argued that the park does not have to be visible and open for the children to come. Since all the children and parents in the area knew each other, he was sure that the location of the park and the opportunities it provided would spread through word of mouth. He did not see any reason to think it would be any less accessible with this wall. The meeting ended with the unspoken agreement that the wall would not be torn down or painted. After all, owners had the veto.[26]

As they negotiated the fate of the *bahçe*'s makeshift gates and walls, the activists were forced to grapple with the reality that the "community" that they had come to empower was not an identifiable whole. Moreover, the idealized visible and open "public" space was not all-inclusive after all. A belief in the visibility and openness of public space as necessarily accessible assumes that the community coincides with the legal and a shared set of norms, most likely desired by neighborhood parents, that would withstand state and societal surveillance. That visible notion of community had no room for the young men's transgressions and privacy, however. Assumptions that equate visibility and openness of a space with its accessibility to a public, even a bounded and particular public like Tarlabaşı's residents, assumes that a shared set of norms governs this particularistic community as a unified whole. More importantly, at stake in contesting these assumptions for the young men were not only differing paradigms of what and who composes that community but more urgently being possibly exposed to coercive state machinery, reshaping state-society relations in Tarlabaşı. As nonstate actors increasingly work to safeguard affordable housing by encouraging marginalized populations threatened with displacement to invest in their neighborhoods through mobilizing particularistic spaces such as a *bahçe* for community residents in the depths of Tarlabaşı, the assumptions they make about the workings of public space redraw communal and state-society dynamics.

Conclusion

STRUGGLES OVER THE PLANNING and design of the city's built environment are rampant in contemporary Istanbul and Cairo. Urban protagonists are dedicating considerable funds and years of their lives contesting the design of electrical wiring, rooftops, paint colors, clotheslines, bathrooms, balconies, and many other private, intimate, and invisible city crevices. Zeynep and Hikmet defended their home's "historically inauthentic" second bathroom against European Union (EU) plans to demolish it as part of a heritage-focused home restoration program on Istanbul's Golden Horn, and they ultimately rejected the EU's grant (chapter 3). Umm Ayman thwarted the Egyptian Ministry of Culture's efforts to standardize street façades in Historic Cairo in order to protect her home's aluminum windows from the ministry's plans to replace them with wooden *mashrabiyya* (chapter 5). The Ismailia Consortium planned its transformation project in Wust El-Balad around buying buildings with private ownership rights to Wust El-Balad's network of passageways to avoid conflict with the state as it upgraded infrastructure for its luxury clientele (chapters 4 and 5). Urban activists clashed with the owners of a plot they were turning into a neighborhood garden in Tarlabaşı in Istanbul, when the owners demanded that the activists not demolish the dangerous makeshift walls surrounding their plot in case they needed to retreat to the plot for recreational drug use shielded from police eyes (chapter 5). The Denizli family suffered the loss of status and artistic beauty in their Fener home in Istanbul as they hid long-lost murals with a thick layer of paint to protect their home's sanctity from the zeal of heritage conservationists (chapter 3). Aga Khan architects and planners risked prison time as they brokered informal agreements with building owners in Darb El-Ahmar in Cairo to ensure that they didn't report their buildings as "collapsed," nullifying rent-controlled contracts while the Agha Kahn Trust for Culture (AKTC) demolished and restored them, though not always succeeding, as seen with Umm Mustafa's travails (chapter 1). In turn, Elif risked her job as an architect with the EU's team in Istanbul when she went against her employers' wishes and invested in designing more durable clotheslines across Fener's buildings, valuing them as spaces of sociality, despite her bosses deeming them ugly and antithetical to a heritage-focused project (chapter 3).

How do we make sense of all the energy and resources dedicated to conflicts over the design of the city's built environment? How do we explain the *location* of these conflicts around intimate, private, and invisible city crevices? I've argued that the effervescence of conflict around the city's design at that intimate and private scale is not accidental nor simply a continuation of age-old struggles over the city. It is produced by a systemic neoliberal *displacement* of political struggles (especially class-based redistributive struggles) away from traditional political arenas and onto more subtle, seemingly apolitical arenas such as urban planning and architectural design. Despite the foreclosure of many traditional spaces for political struggles over redistribution with the neoliberalization of the economy, these struggles didn't simply disappear or retreat to an ineffectual margin. They mutated and rematerialized in new and unfamiliar guises, including in a fierce battle over intricate designs of the city's built environment.

In relation to property markets, the battle for housing continues to rage in Istanbul and Cairo and has not been fully decided in favor of rampant dispossessive capital accumulation. When confronted with a shrinking space for familiar welfare state policies such as rent controls or housing subsidies, urban protagonists got creative and worked with now-dominant market rationales to realize a diverse array of redistributive agendas. They redistributed access to housing by manipulating the inner workings of markets in a way that would secure affordable housing or corner real estate markets to intensify profits.

Crucial to the workings of any market is the process of *valuing* commodities exchanged on that market. Urban protagonists manipulated market dynamics by transforming how housing came to be *valued* by particular groups on an open property market, what I term *particularistic value*, and they turned to the careful design of the urban built-environment to engineer a wholesale shift in that "market value." As demonstrated throughout the book, they designed urban built-environments that would preserve heritage, engineer "community," or transform disaster risk to shift how particular groups came to value a neighborhood's urban fabric. Fostering such particularistic value around a neighborhood's property then tilted markets in ways that restricted access to the neighborhood's housing in favor of low-income residents or high-end clientele. The battle for housing was unfolding from *within* the rationales of market dynamics as a struggle over how the value of homes is being defined, claimed, and experienced. The political struggle over housing had not disappeared with the dismantling of traditional redistributive arenas. It is alive and well but is being *displaced* to the subtle, quiet machinations of careful urban design rather than manifesting as loud and overt class-based struggles over the city's resources.

The displacement of class politics onto the subtle machinations of urban design has produced a number of conundrums. First, burdening the design of intricate spaces such as water pumps, rooftops, clotheslines, and electrical wiring with the work of shifting property value often comes at the expense of its immediate functionality. Time and again, homes restored in line with a social justice agenda were riddled with inconveniences for their supposed beneficiaries. Residents had to share water pumps or expose their electrical wiring outside of their walls or lose the beautiful, century-old murals that had adorned their walls. These immediate losses pushed residents who could afford it to reject fully subsidized home restorations but left many others with baffling inconveniences that would stay with them in their newly restored homes for many years to come.

Muddling a social justice agenda by channeling it through the rationale of the market not only inconvenienced its main beneficiaries but also spread a lot of confusion and ambiguity around the actual politics behind these urban interventions. When the Aga Khan Foundation deployed urban design to engineer "community," many of the technical decisions they made left residents who were not privy to their underlying vision utterly confused. It was unclear how the foundation was choosing the buildings it would restore or why they demanded people to divide building shares unequally or why they insisted that rooftops be shared rather than individually owned spaces. The ambiguity around these decisions bred suspicion of the organization and the circulation of damaging rumors about it rather than acknowledgment of the social justice agenda motivating a lot (if not all) of its work in the neighborhood. Similar dynamics manifested in Fener, Istanbul, when the Habitat coalition formed an unlikely alliance with a heritage-obsessed United Nations Educational, Scientific and Cultural Organization (UNESCO) and EU, creating endless stipulations and contradictions for residents that few could understand. Again, suspicion and even more damaging rumors circulated about the Fener-Balat project that significantly undermined its reach to the city's low-income residents. As residents and, at times, experts themselves confronted and challenged these ambiguities and contradictions, they not only stalled the projects on a practical level but also *repoliticized* them, making visible the politics (including class or identity-based politics) masked by the subtle work of channeling redistribution through market rationales. Repoliticization materialized, though, as conflict around the same intricate urban crevices that had been burdened with performing redistributive work. The systemic neoliberal displacement of political struggle away from overt political arenas shifted the locus of layered political strife onto the city's most intimate, private, and invisible spaces. Locating political strife within intimate crevices leaves urban dwellers with festering struggles that are much more difficult to negotiate and recuperate as a polity.

Further Reflections

A Built Citizenship

The neoliberal displacement of political struggles onto unfamiliar subtle machinations such as urban design has had several wider political reverberations. I focus here on two. First, it transforms how urban dwellers experience *citizenship* in cities like Istanbul and Cairo. It is remarkable how present the specter of the urban built-environment was in the recent mass protests that erupted in both locations. Istanbul's Gezi protests of 2013, which brought almost three million people to the streets, were all about urban conflict. The protests erupted over an urban dispute, when the police violently dispersed urban activists defending redevelopment of the central Gezi Park adjacent to Taksim Square into a glorified shopping mall. While the protesters expressed a number of grievances, organizing around urban and environmental issues remained central to the protests. Neighborhood councils threatened by the state's redevelopment schemes organized several marches during Gezi, and protests regularly featured slogans such as "Biz bir kentsel dönüşüm projesi değiliz!" ("We are not an urban transformation project") which was spray-painted on a building adjacent to Taksim Square (figure C.1).[1]

In Cairo, too, the city's built environment captured protesters' political imagination during the 2011 uprisings. The built environment forcefully entered the conversation when on February 2, 2012, a political cartoon (figure C.2)

Figure C.1. Graffiti that reads, "We are not an urban transformation project" found in the neighborhood of Cihangir, adjacent to Taksim Square, during the Gezi Protests. Source: Avital Livny, June 2013.

Figure C.2. Cartoon by Egyptian Satirist Ala'a G produced and circulated on February 2, 2012. The upper slogan translates to "Pretend you're a building!" The lower slogan translates to "Urgent: The army moves to protect buildings in Port Said." Source: Rezo (@Rezo), "Pretend you're a building #Bey2ollak," Twitter, January 27, 2013, 5:46 p.m., https://twitter.com/Rezo/status/295585581328683008.

entitled "*'E'mel nafsak mabna*" ("Pretend You're a Building"), by the Egyptian satirist Ala'a G, started circulating on Facebook. The cartoon depicted five men assembled in the image of a house standing alongside a brick-and-mortar house guarded by an army officer. The cartoon's caption read, "Urgent: The army moves to protect buildings (*monsha'at*) in Port Said." The cartoon was released the day after over seventy football fans were trampled to death in Port Said's stadium under the unflinching watch of state security forces in one of the most shocking and horrific episodes in Egypt's post-2011 revolutionary moment. The army (the country's transitional ruler at the time) reportedly surrounded and secured buildings rather than victims. The cartoon distilled the regime's violence down to its prioritization of buildings over people, even in the country's most confrontational, hopeful, and fragile of times. The cartoonist was not alone in making this critique. In fact, the cartoon brought to life a hashtag that had lived on Twitter for a few months before the Port Said incident, when people started circulating the following message: "The army has pledged to protect Egyptians' assets . . . not Egyptians . . . if you are attacked #**pretend_you're_a_building**" (boldface in original).[2] The hashtag originated on Twitter in December 2011 during one of the violent episodes that erupted between the army and protesters, where several people lost their lives at the hands of officers. In the midst of the violence, one of the institutes housing the country's scientific archives, L'Institut D'Egypte (founded by Napoleon in 1798), caught on fire. In response to the fire, the army released a video declaration where it pledged to secure the country's public buildings and assets while continuing to target, maim, and kill protesters outside those buildings. The hashtag had struck such a nerve with protesters that it continued to resonate with Egyptians during one of the most horrifically violent moments of the uprisings after the Port Said massacre. While the Tahrir Square uprisings did not erupt over urban issues like the Gezi protests had, the specter of the city and its buildings still hovered forcefully in how protesters understood their citizenship and relationship to the state.

During both the Gezi and Tahrir uprisings, protesters came to the street with a wide array of grievances. Even when protests were about the city, there were many layers to grievances. In Istanbul in particular, urban activists were protesting the ruthless, extractive machine turning the city into exploitable development for the ruling regime and its corporate cronies. While exploitative development violently dispossessed city dwellers in both Istanbul and Cairo, as shown in chapters 1 and 2, and demanding an end to it is urgent, this is not the only way that the city's specter haunted protesters' imagination. Slogans like "We are not an urban transformation project" and "Pretend you're a building" resonated on a deeper level with how protesters were experiencing their citizenship in Istanbul and Cairo. When neoliberalism shifted the locus of politics onto subtle, quiet machinations such as urban planning and design, Egyptians and Turks came to experience the city as mediating their citizenship. When (contested) designs of the built environment became crucial to how political projects were enacted in a neoliberal moment, it was *as if* the city's buildings had gained their own *personhood*. Even getting access to socially motivated housing grants (like the AKTC's or EU's) elevated the protection of a building's intricate design over residents' immediate needs.

Neoliberalism had generated such primacy for newly politicized arenas such as the city's built environment that it was only through negotiating its primacy and growing personhood that Egyptians and Turks could negotiate and claim their own citizenship.

Populism and Neoliberalism

Alongside inspiring eruptions of mass protest in which Egyptians and Turks have both demonstrated astute awareness of the mediated nature of citizenship under neoliberalism, the last decade has also witnessed the rise of a remarkably emboldened populism in both countries. Leaders of both countries, Presidents Abdel Fattah El-Sisi in Egypt and Recep Tayyip Erdoğan (especially in the aftermath of the attempted coup of 2016) in Turkey, have embraced fearmongering populist politics to justify despotic rule (varying in its ruthlessness in relation to the ruling regimes that were already in place of course).[3] Egypt and Turkey have not been alone. In the past decade, populism has been on the rise around the globe, exemplified with the ascendance of Narendra Modi in India, Jair Bolsonaro in Brazil, Donald Trump in the United States, Vladimir Putin in Russia, and the far right all over Europe, among others. By now, scholars and pundits are well aware that the rise of fearmongering populism is not accidental to one charismatic leader here or a country's specific history with xenophobia there, but is a widely spreading phenomenon. To explain its ubiquity, many have turned to tides of immigration (often singling out Middle Eastern conflict as its source) or instability in the aftermath of uprisings (including the color revolutions, the Arab Spring, and Occupy movement). While there is no doubt that a confluence of events and forces shaped the rise of populism, I want to draw out a strong linkage between populism and neoliberalism.

The displacement of political struggle (especially but not exclusively class politics) onto unfamiliar sites such as contestations over the city's intimate, private, and invisible crevices creates the festering, fractured, conspiratorial political climate upon which populism thrives. Dislocating a political battle as crucial as the battle for housing onto contestations over the intricate architectural designs of the built environment transforms them into confusing, obscured, fragmented microbattles that are difficult to see as shared struggles and impossible to harness and negotiate overtly as a polity. It is no accident that conspiracy theories were one of the main ways that residents challenged urban interventions that obscured their political projects in both Istanbul and Cairo. Such conspiratorial thinking is a product of neoliberal political displacement and is reverberating far and wide beyond the battle for housing. In other words, we should be seeing the populist despotism that erodes the rule of law (and protections of property rights) that many have argued as crucial to free-market economics not as antithetical to neoliberalism but as a direct extension of it. The neoliberal displacement of the political is creating the populism that many have erroneously dubbed postneoliberal. We are living with the political ramifications of a neoliberal shift, and it is only through a careful tracing of the location of the political under neoliberalism can we see these connections and perhaps more productively address the roots of populism's ascendance.

Notes

INTRODUCTION

1 See chapter 1 for a tracing of why Darb El-Ahmar's urban fabric remained unmaintained and decaying during most of the twentieth century.
2 Anonymous, pers. comm., Darb El-Ahmar, Cairo, November 2011.
3 AKTC personnel, pers. comm., Cairo, December 2011.
4 I follow scholarship that illuminates the political work underlying scientific/technical expertise (e.g., Latour 1993; Mitchell 2002) in unmasking that sociopolitical work.
5 I use the term *redistributive politics* to denote the *contest* over the distribution of a society's resources. As such, resources could be redistributed downward (say, to secure affordable housing) or upward (to the benefit of the elite). Studying contests around redistribution that vie to corner resources both upward and downward together show shared dynamics at work in both directions of the struggle that are otherwise difficult to unmask.
6 I read Istanbul and Cairo as experiencing processes shared with many neoliberalizing postcolonial cities in the non-West within and outside the Middle East as part of an epistemological and political project to de-exceptionalize the region and its cities (joining, for example, Hazbun 2008; Kanna 2011; Menoret 2014). For further discussion of the genealogies exceptionalizing Middle Eastern cities and their politics, see El-Kazaz and Mazur (2017).
7 It is important to note here that in reading the work of nonprofit organizations such as the Aga Khan Foundation or the developmental arm of the EU as part of urban coalitions that are actively contesting a dispossessive class politics, I am reading these organizations quite differently from how they've been read in a critical literature on the "development industry." While incisive literature on the nonprofit sector in a neoliberal era (e.g., Ferguson

1994; Elyachar 2005; Muehlebach 2012; Atia 2013; Fennell 2015; Zencirci 2015), whether studying development aid agencies, private charities, or religious organizations, has shown the powerful ways through which the sector perpetuates neoliberal dispossession, I find that this work has assumed an unfounded linearity to that politics. Rather than assume that these actors are all aligned to linearly empower the same dispossessive project, I open up my study to the possibilities that the nonprofit sector may be involved in a wide array of political projects (that, in some cases, truly embrace social justice agendas) to see what can be learned about neoliberalism if they are not read exclusively as actors that linearly enable neoliberal dispossession. In chapters 3 and 4 I focus on several examples of the nonlinear political work produced by what I term "self-reflexive experts."

8 There is a long history to how "value" has been understood and interrogated in scholarship (e.g., Graebber 2001; Elyachar 2005). What I focus on in the book is how the flexibility and malleability of value to urban dwellers is renegotiated and abstracted as it becomes urgent to render that value calculable on open markets with neoliberalization.

9 For an intricate unpacking of this process of "valuation," see Çalışkan and Callon (2010, 3–8).

10 Burdening urban built-environments with the responsibility to perform sociopolitical work is not new by any means. This book is inspired in its focus on the design of the urban built-environment by a rich scholarship that has interrogated the ways in which the careful design of built environments has been expected to shoulder the burden of sociopolitical engineering in modern times (e.g., Mitchell 1988; Holston 1989; Lefebvre 1991; Kotkin 1997; Scott 1998; Blau 1999; Bozdoğan 2001; Ghannam 2002; Weizman 2007; Crane 2017). Most of this scholarship focuses on explicit colonial and postcolonial state modernizing projects, where spatial design mirrors the state's explicit modernizing/socializing designs in other arenas. Notably, the literature on globalizing and neoliberalizing cities (e.g., Harvey 1989; Zukin 1996; Keyder 1999; Sassen 2001; Caldeira 2008; Ghertner 2015) has mostly moved away from studying such spatial societal engineering, reading global-capital flows as organically "commodifying" the city's built environment, and with few exceptions (e.g., Murphy 2013; Fennell 2015) assuming that societal engineering through careful design is on the wane. What I show in this book is that indeed the burden on a carefully designed built environment to perform political work has intensified as more traditional political channels have closed off, and both state and nonstate actors are expecting carefully designed urban spaces to perform more sociopolitical work than ever.

11 While heavily influenced by this literature, my methodology departs from it in two respects. First, a focus on spatial tactics often entails a romanticization of urban dwellers as unproblematically resisting top-down projects, leaving little room for interrogating the not-so-romantic politics in which

urban dwellers are often implicated and the ways in which they are embedded within networks of dispossessive as well as resistant politics in the city. Instead, in tracing spatial tactics, I am also careful to follow the example of the few scholars who also map out the divisive politics (along religious, class, ethnic, and other divides) that urban dwellers engage in as they shape how the political manifests through the city's spaces (e.g., Caldeira 2000; Ismail 2006; Mills 2010).

Second, most of this literature reproduces a division between top-down expertise and bottom-up subaltern politics. Throughout this book urban dwellers as well as experts seamlessly cross that line and complicate a top-down/bottom-up narrative unfolding in the city. Tracing how urban dwellers negotiate neoliberal logics and embed themselves in struggles over redistribution, this book shows the ways in which urban dwellers are often not romantic, are embedded in divisive politics, and are savvy in their understanding and deployment of market logics as they seamlessly cross our imagined boundaries between the "top-down" and "bottom-up."

12 One of the most piercing critiques of assemblage urbanism is that tracing assemblages ignores or downplays the impact of power differentials (or structures) as it focuses on tracing the contingency of human-nonhuman agency. This critique is eloquently articulated by Brenner et al. (2011, 233): "The descriptive focus associated with ontological variants of assemblage urbanism leaves unaddressed important explanatory questions regarding the broader (global, national and regional) structural contexts within which actants are situated and operate — including formations of capital accumulation and investment/disinvestment; historically entrenched, large-scale configurations of uneven spatial development, territorial polarization and geopolitical hegemony." Although Bennett (2005) and others are careful to point out that there exist power differentials among coherent "entities" and more fleeting "forces," I agree with Brenner et al. (2011) that such theorizing often falters when applied to empirical analysis. To that end the book mobilizes multisited ethnography and comparative juxtaposition to help unmask these power differentials and systemic pressures across different contexts while maintaining a commitment to tracing the agency of assemblages. For an illustration of this methodology in practice, see an analysis of how rumor campaigns materialize differently across Darb El-Ahmar and Fener-Balat in chapter 4.

CHAPTER ONE. CAIRO

1 The conversion rate used is from 2011: US$1 = 6.2 Egyptian pounds.
2 Law no. 49, §31 (1977).
3 AKTC personnel, pers. comm., Cairo, October 2011.
4 Although miasmatists had been airing such fears on and off over the centuries, the deployment of statistical and cartographic tools in the nineteenth

century went a long way to empower their campaign. For more details on their movement, see Fahmy (2018, ch. 3). For example, they deployed the statistic that Cairo's growth rate was barely 90 percent over the nineteenth century in spite of mounting rural-urban migration while the rest of Egypt's had leapt to 130 percent (Abu-Lughod 1971, 119).

5 For details of the Khedive's plans, see Abu-Lughod (1971), ch. 7. For a critical analysis of the "modern" ideas, and especially about the aesthetics of order, that shaped this planned redevelopment of the city, see Mitchell (1988, 63–69). For a historicization of the Khedive's plans into longer trajectories of city planning that date back to Mehmed Ali, see Fahmy (2018, ch. 3).

6 A similar infrastructural dynamic materialized in Istanbul with the construction of Tarlabaşı Boulevard.

7 Umm Hassan appears again in chapter 4, in the discussion of rooftops.

8 Anonymous, pers. comm., Gamaliyya, Cairo, September 2011.

9 One narration claimed that the shop was abandoned by its owner with the Greek exodus from Cairo with no heirs to claim it, and another narration claimed that it was sold to Mohamed Lipton by the Greek man's heirs.

10 Elke Uitentuis and Wouter Osterholt, "Collective Memory," 2009, sound piece, *Model Citizens* exhibit, Townhouse Gallery, Cairo, 32:52, http://www.wouterosterholt.com/model-citizens/collective-memory (author's translation).

11 Elke Uitentuis and Wouter Osterholt, "Collective Memory," 2009, sound piece, *Model Citizens* exhibit, Townhouse Gallery, Cairo, 34:01, http://www.wouterosterholt.com/model-citizens/collective-memory (author's translation).

12 Elke Uitentuis and Wouter Osterholt, "Collective Memory," 2009, sound piece, *Model Citizens* exhibit, Townhouse Gallery, Cairo, 34:32, http://www.wouterosterholt.com/model-citizens/collective-memory (author's translation).

13 Elke Uitentuis and Wouter Osterholt, "Collective Memory," 2009, sound piece, *Model Citizens* exhibit, Townhouse Gallery, Cairo, 36:13, http://www.wouterosterholt.com/model-citizens/collective-memory (author's translation).

14 Elke Uitentuis and Wouter Osterholt, "Collective Memory," 2009, sound piece, *Model Citizens* exhibit, Townhouse Gallery, Cairo, 31:38, http://www.wouterosterholt.com/model-citizens/collective-memory (author's translation).

15 For examples and analysis of the literary depiction of the Cairo Fire as "suicide," see Reynolds (2012, 194–97).

16 For a discussion of the politics of similar architectural hybridity in French colonial Morocco, see Wright (1991).

17 For an incisive tracing of the complexity of these meaning-making practices, see how Reynolds (2012) analyzes sartorial mixing, circuits of capital and

goods, popular-culture media, and anti-colonial boycotts to complicate any binary understandings of foreign and local or of Wust El-Balad as a distinctly "foreign" or colonial district disconnected from the rest of the city.

18 Of the state's 5,744 units in (mostly downtown) Cairo, 3,978 are rented through rent control contracts today. "The Real Estate Portfolio of Misr Real Estate Asset Management Company until 9/2021," Misr Real Estate Asset Management Company, accessed October 10, 2021, http://www.misrrea.com/Pages/513/mafatha2.html.
19 See, for example, El Kadi and ElKerdany (2006).
20 Anonymous, pers. comm., Wust El-Balad, Cairo, December 2011.
21 Elke Uitentuis and Wouter Osterholt, "Collective Memory," 2009, sound piece, *Model Citizens* exhibit, Townhouse Gallery, Cairo, 0:52, http://www.wouterosterholt.com/model-citizens/collective-memory (author's translation).
22 Elke Uitentuis and Wouter Osterholt, "Collective Memory," 2009, sound piece, *Model Citizens* exhibit, Townhouse Gallery, Cairo, 1:39, http://www.wouterosterholt.com/model-citizens/collective-memory (author's translation).
23 Elke Uitentuis and Wouter Osterholt, "Collective Memory," 2009, sound piece, *Model Citizens* exhibit, Townhouse Gallery, Cairo, 1:24, http://www.wouterosterholt.com/model-citizens/collective-memory (author's translation).
24 There are many accounts of Estoril's history in the press that put it side by side with other Wust El-Balad establishments such as Café Riche and Groppi. See, for example, John Harris, "Estoril: A Downtown Gem That Stands the Test of Time," *Egypt Independent*, April 26, 2011, https://egyptindependent.com/estoril-downtown-gem-stands-test-time/.
25 See Waterbury (1983) for further details on Sadat's Infitah policies.
26 Karim Shafei, pers. comm., Wust El-Balad, Cairo, July 2011.
27 Karim Shafei, pers. comm., Wust El-Balad, Cairo, July 2011.
28 Karim Shafei, pers. comm., Wust El-Balad, Cairo, July 2011.
29 Karim Shafei, pers. comm., Wust El-Balad, Cairo, July 2011.
30 AKTC personnel, pers. comm., Cairo, October 2011.
31 AKTC personnel, pers. comm., Cairo, October 2011.
32 Gift booklet created for Aga Khan's visit to Azhar Park and Darb El-Ahmar, dated March 25, 2005. Copy of booklet shared with author from AKTC's private archive October 2011.
33 These numbers come from a survey conducted by local consultants for UNESCO. One of the consultants gave me access to the raw survey data in November 2011.
34 See Elyachar's (2005) insightful work on the relationship between neoliberalization and informality in Cairo, and especially her analysis of the dispossessive nature of projects working to formalize the informal sector's "dead capital" (De Soto 1989).

35 HCO personnel, pers. comm., Cairo, September 2011.
36 HCO personnel, pers. comm., Cairo, September 2011.
37 See chapter 5 for more detail on the HCO's project and its workings in Gamaliyya.
38 For further information on these conglomerates, histories, and political connections, see Mitchell (2002, ch. 9); Roll (2013); and Adly (2020, ch. 5).
39 The bridge's construction actually started under Nasser in 1969 but took almost thirty years to be completed and was not inaugurated until 1996. Omnia Ossama, "Closer Look at Cairo's Enchanted Bridges," *Egypt Today*, December 3, 2017, https://www.egypttoday.com/Article/6/35168/Closer-look-at-Cairo's-enchanted-bridges.
40 "Mubarak Inaugurates Time-Saving Azhar Tunnels," *Al-Bawaba*, October 29, 2001, https://www.albawaba.com/news/mubarak-inaugurates-time-saving-azhar-tunnels.
41 For info on the state's efforts to clear the vendors, see Jared Malsin, "Cairo Street Traders Squeezed Out in Push to Make City 'Revolution Free,'" *Guardian*, September 5, 2015, https://www.theguardian.com/world/2015/sep/05/cairo-street-traders-squeezed-out-city-revolution-free.
42 Anonymous, pers. comm., Gamaliyya, Cairo, November 2011.
43 See Sims (2015) for a comprehensive study on Cairo's "desert cities."
44 For further insightful literature on the violence of property rights regimes, see Sartori (2014); and Bhandar (2018).

CHAPTER TWO. ISTANBUL

1 Although Kemal Bey referred to the process as "buying," oftentimes property owners referred to buildings that they occupied in the aftermath of non-Muslim exodus from the city and then retroactively gained rights to (as explained later) as benignly bought rather than occupied. It is unclear whether he bought or occupied the building in 1973.
2 Anonymous, pers. comm., Fener, Istanbul, May 2012.
3 Internal report prepared by Çalık Holding on May 5, 2012. The author was given access to the report by Çalık's team on July 4, 2012.
4 For more information on Atatürk's étatism, see Keyder (1987, chs. 4 and 5).
5 For more information on the importance of regionalism to Turkey's modernization, and especially the highway as facilitator of that project, see Adalet (2018).
6 Anonymous, group pers. comm., Fener, Istanbul, June 2012.
7 Anonymous, group pers. comm., Fener, Istanbul, May 2012.
8 See Bali (2005) for further discussion of these taxes.
9 For discussion of the riots and their place in Istanbul's collective memory, see Mills (2010, ch. 1).
10 Anonymous, pers. comm., Tarlabaşı, Istanbul, June–July 2012.

11 For detailed analysis of that transition, see Keyder (1987).
12 Outside the scope of this study, there are several theories as to why the Islamically oriented industrialists were the largest beneficiaries of Özal's policies, and these studies debate the ways in which their identity as Islamically oriented may have contributed. See, for example, Yavuz (2003); Buğra and Savaşkan (2014); and Livny (2020).
13 They formalized that distinct identity in 1990 with the formation of MÜSIAD (Müstakil Sanayici ve İşadamları Derneği, or the Independent Industrialists' and Businessmen's Association), which was independent from the chamber of commerce associated with an old economic elite, TÜSIAD (Türk Sanayicileri ve İş İnsanları Derneği, or the Turkish Industrialists' and Businessmen's Association).
14 For maps of those conglomerates and evidence of that expansion, see home page, Networks of Dispossession, accessed May 8, 2019, http://mulksuzlestirme.org/.
15 Home page, Networks of Dispossession.
16 It is important to note here that Islamic revivalism is a large and varied sphere in Turkey, but two of the main wings supported by this corporate-capitalist class were the movements that eventually morphed into the AKP and the Gülenist movement. Most members of the MÜSIAD chamber of commerce were aligned with the movement behind the AKP, and the TUKSON chamber of commerce was more closely aligned with the Gülenists. For the first two decades of the rise of this corporate-capitalist class, they worked in tandem in spite of their varied orientations toward Islamic revival. This unity began to fray in the early 2010s and was dealt a final blow with the attempted coup of 2016.
17 Egypt did have a narrow capitalist class fueling an Islamically oriented opposition, but that class remained in the opposition and out of favor with the state, save for the brief period of the Muslim Brotherhood's rule in 2012–13, and could not rely on state strategies for gaining access to these markets. For more on the workings of the corporate-capitalist class behind the Muslim Brothers in Egypt, see, for example, Atia (2013).
18 For more information on the assault of informal housing and activism around the project in Maltepe specifically, see Kuyucu and Ünsal (2010).
19 Ali Dağlar, "Sulukule Projesi Iptal" [Annulment of Sulukule Project], *Hurriyet Gündem*, June 13, 2012, http://www.hurriyet.com.tr/gundem/20748277.asp.
20 For more information on the activism and legal battles around the project, see Kuyucu and Ünsal (2010).
21 Fatma Aksu, "Fener-Balata'a da iptal" [Annulment in Fener Balat Too], *Hurriyet Gündem*, June 21, 2012, https://www.hurriyet.com.tr/gundem/fener-balat-a-da-iptal-20807607.
22 For such an analysis of the temporalities shaping politics around the Tarlabaşı project, see Arıcan (2020).

23 It is important to note that the risks that the AKP took were not foolproof and eventually shook their electoral dominance, as for example the AKP was electorally defeated in Istanbul as the mayorship was transferred to the opposition CHP party, with the election of Ekrem Imamoğlu in 2019. One of the first things that the mayor has done since his election is launch an investigation into the corrupt relations between the AKP and the construction industry. For an account of the mayor's press release on the problematic urban and infrastructural works launched in Istanbul under the AKP, see Carlotta Gall, "Istanbul's New Mayor Outlines Gross Mismanagement Under Erdogan's Allies," *New York Times*, December 23, 2019, https://www.nytimes.com/2019/12/23/world/middleeast/istanbul-mayor-erdogan.html.

24 This video is posted on the municipality's website. See Fatih Municipality, accessed January 19, 2018, http://www.fatih.bel.tr/icerik/6868/sulukule-kentsel-yenileme-projesi/.

25 "Sulukule'nin Tarihçesi" [Sulukule's History], *Mimarizm*, February 5, 2008, http://www.mimarizm.com/makale/sulukule-nin-tarihcesi_113458.

26 Amberin Zaman, "Foreign Journal," *Washington Post*, October 25, 1999, https://www.washingtonpost.com/archive/politics/1999/10/25/foreign-journal/9e74b536-b1be-4433-82a0-1429f43f3435/?utm_term=.90fc032add03.

27 Although ANAP combined neoliberal secular and religiously conservative members, Tantan affirmed his commitment to a conservative agenda when he founded Yurt Partisi (Homeland Party) in 2002, espousing a decidedly nationalist, religiously conservative platform.

28 "Sulukule'nin Tarihçesi."

29 Gülden Aydın, "Devletin polisi homoseksüelden dayak yiyor mu dedirtecektim" [Could I let people say that the state's police officers were beaten by a homosexual], *Hurriyet*, January 1, 2005, http://www.hurriyet.com.tr/devletin-polisi-homoseksuelden-dayak-yiyor-mu-dedirtecektim-292556.

30 Fatih Municipality personnel, pers. comm., Istanbul, May 2012.

31 For an interview with Pündük, see Fazila Matt, "An Urban-Renewal Plan for Istanbul Has Been Destroying Entire Neighbourhoods and Expelling Residents to the City's Periphery," *Osservatorio Balcani e Caucaso Transeuropa*, February 9, 2009, https://www.balcanicaucaso.org/eng/Areas/Turkey/The-New-Istanbul-46827.

32 Anonymous, pers. comm., Beyoğlu, Istanbul, June 2012.

33 Internal report prepared by Çalık Holding on May 25, 2012. The author was given access to the report by Çalık's team on July 4, 2012.

34 Recording techniques probably changed over time so the increase may also reflect better reporting and not just an increased number of incidents.

35 For more detailed analysis of the replanning and "regularization" of Istanbul's urban fabric in the nineteenth century in tandem with the fires, see Çelik (1986, ch. 3).

36 See "Istanbul Population 2022," World Population Review, accessed June 25, 2021, https://worldpopulationreview.com/world-cities/istanbul-population.
37 Ethnographic notes from personal attendance, Urban Transformation Conference, organized by Istanbul's Friends Society, Eyup, Istanbul, June 10, 2012.
38 Elizabeth Angell was the first to alert me to the way the government was co-opting the language and tactics of this movement.
39 By "healthy" I mean markets that are selling property in these city centers at prices that are seen as reasonable (aka high) in relation to their lucrative location in globalizing metropolises, rather than continuing to host affordable housing as they have for decades.

CHAPTER THREE. HERITAGE

1 Anonymous, pers. comm., Fener, Istanbul, May 2012.
2 UNESCO, "Convention Concerning the Protection of the World Cultural and Natural Heritage," World Heritage Convention, accessed March 27, 2013, http://whc.unesco.org/en/conventiontext/.
3 See United Nations, "Outcomes on Human Settlements," General Assembly 25th Special Session, June 6–8, 2001, http://www.un.org/en/development/devagenda/habitat.shtml.
4 United Nations, "Report of the United Nations Conference on Human Settlements (Habitat II)," June 3–14, 1996, Istanbul, Turkey, https://undocs.org/A/CONF.165/14.
5 The survey's results were released in 1998 as a book-length report published in French and Turkish titled "Rehabilitation of the Balat and Fener Districts (Historic Peninsula of Istanbul): Diagnosis and Proposal for Renovation."
6 Even though the municipality initially agreed to be a fully contributing partner and provide €7 million to the project, the municipality later reneged on that commitment. With numerous changes in municipality leadership, the project stalled. When finally implemented in 2003, the municipality argued that it had already invested over €7 million in infrastructure changes in the neighborhood over the past decade and would only contribute manpower thereafter.
7 World Heritage Committee, "Mission Report: Historic Areas of Istanbul (Turkey) 356," UNESCO, May 8–13, 2008, http://whc.unesco.org/document/100746.
8 See the Fatih Municipality website, accessed August 27, 2019, http://www.fatih.bel.tr/icerik/1156/fener-balat-semtlerinin-rehabilitasyon-projesi/.
9 For the full text, see "National Cultural Heritage Laws," UNESCO, accessed December 6, 2017, http://whc.unesco.org/en/statesparties/tr/laws/.
10 EU personnel, pers. comm., Istanbul, May 2012.
11 Anonymous, pers. comm., Fener, Istanbul, June 2012.
12 Anonymous, pers. comm., Fener, Istanbul, May 2012.
13 EU personnel, pers. comm., Istanbul, July 2012.

14 EU personnel, pers. comm., Istanbul, May 2012.
15 EU personnel, pers. comm., Istanbul, May 2012, emphasis added.
16 UNESCO had sponsored the pilot survey for the rehabilitation project before the EU had agreed to fund it, and so many of the residents confused the EU and UNESCO as implementers of the project.
17 Anonymous, pers. comm., Fener, June 2012.
18 Anonymous, pers. comm., Cairo, August 2011.
19 Anonymous, pers. comm., Gamaliyya, Cairo, January 2012.
20 AKTC personnel, pers. comm., Cairo, December 2011.
21 EU personnel, pers. comm., Istanbul, July 2012.
22 I use the term *self-reflexive expert* to denote experts who are particularly well attuned to neighborhood residents and the potential vagaries of urban planning. They are often trained in and are in conversation with critical urban studies, and complicate the way experts are often positioned in opposition to residents within that literature. Particularly stark examples of such experts in this book are Elif and Samy (chapter 4).
23 EU personnel, pers. comm., Istanbul, May 2012.
24 EU personnel, pers. comm., Istanbul, May 2012.
25 EU personnel, pers. comm., Istanbul, May 2012.
26 EU personnel, pers. comm., Istanbul, May 2012.
27 EU personnel, pers. comm., Istanbul, May 2012.
28 EU personnel, pers. comm., Istanbul, May 2012.
29 Anonymous, pers. comm., Fener, Istanbul, May 2012.
30 Anonymous, pers. comm., Tarlabaşı, Istanbul, June 2012.
31 Anonymous, pers. comm., Tarlabaşı, Istanbul, June 2012.
32 See Ismail (2006) for detailed discussions of informal arbitration in Cairo's popular neighborhoods.
33 The violence of the anti-minority riots and forced deportations of Greek residents after the Greek/Turkish Cyprus crisis of 1964 forced most non-Muslim residents to flee Istanbul in the 1950s and 1960s and leave their property behind, as explained in chapter 2. It is unclear whether Murat Bey legally attained the store or occupied it illegally after its owner fled the city.
34 Anonymous, pers. comm., Tarlabaşı, Istanbul, June 2012.
35 Anonymous, pers. comm., Tarlabaşı, Istanbul, June 2012.
36 Anonymous, pers. comm., Tarlabaşı, Istanbul, June 2012.

CHAPTER FOUR. COMMUNITY

Portions of chapter 4 appeared in "Building 'Community' and Markets in Contemporary Cairo," *Comparative Studies in Society and History* 60, no. 2 (2018): 476–505.

1 AKTC personnel, pers. comm., Cairo, December 2011. The AKTC's partners were the Egyptian-Swiss Development Fund and the Egyptian government's

Social Development Fund. To read more about the state's Social Development Fund and another urban project they sponsored, see Julia Elyachar's 2005 account of the making of "Madinet el-Hirafiyeen" on the outskirts of Cairo in the mid-1990s.

2 Anonymous, pers. comm., Darb El-Ahmar, Cairo, December 2011.
3 AKTC personnel, pers. comm., Cairo, December 2011.
4 AKTC personnel, pers. comm., Cairo, December 2011.
5 See, for example, Muehlebach (2012) and Atia (2013) for versions of this argument.
6 The consortium is named Ismailia after the name downtown Cairo was given in Khedival times and is not related to the Ismaili sect of Shi'ism or to the Aga Khan as royalty to an Ismaili sect. The proximity in names is by sheer coincidence.
7 Karim Shafei, pers. comm., Cairo, July 2011. This interview was conducted in English and so usage of the word *community* here is entirely as the interviewee used it.
8 As it does so, the book does not claim to measure the overall impact of those interventions on communal strength.
9 For more details on the creation of Azhar Park, see "Al-Azhar Park in Cairo and the Revitalisation of Darb Al-Ahmar," AKDN, August 6, 2012, https://www.akdn.org/publication/al-azhar-park-cairo-and-revitalisation-darb-al-ahmar.
10 According to a survey conducted in 2003, 68 percent of Darb El-Ahmar's residents lived in rent-controlled housing at the time. See Van der Tas (2004).
11 AKTC personnel, pers. comm., December 2011.
12 AKTC personnel, pers. comm., December 2011.
13 Comparative note: The AKTC team's commitment to communal cohesion is reminiscent of many of Elif's (from the EU team) commitments to cohesion among Fener-Balat's residents in Istanbul. This raises the question of why the Habitat coalition chose to deploy heritage preservation while the AKTC focused on engineering community as modalities for safeguarding affordable housing. Of course, these decisions are layered and shaped by many factors, but it is important to consider that the degree of legal security tenants have will likely shape how these practices are chosen. While engineering "community" may come with less rigidity in how homes are restored compared with a heritage preservation project committed to historical accuracy, it does not bring with it any legal regimes such as the ones that heritage preservation affords for helping secure tenants in their homes (for at least the first half decade), as discussed in the previous chapter. In Cairo, the AKTC's team could rely on rent controls to provide that basic level of tenant security (however complicated, as seen in chapter 1) whereas the Habitat coalition could not lean on any such guarantees and rights for tenants in Istanbul.
14 AKTC personnel, pers. comm., December 2011, emphasis added. Samy switched out of using Arabic during the interview to use the English term *community* both times in this passage.

15 See chapter 1 of Ghannam (2002) for a detailed and insightful account of how "rule by aesthetics" intersected with modernizing reforms to produce and legitimize relocation.
16 Anonymous, pers. group comm., Darb El Ahmar, Cairo, December 2011.
17 Anonymous, pers. comm., Darb El Ahmar, Cairo, December 2011.
18 AKTC personnel, pers. comm., December 2011.
19 AKTC personnel, pers. comm., December 2011.
20 Anonymous, pers. group comm., Darb El Ahmar, Cairo, December 2011.
21 Elke Uitentuis and Wouter Osterholt, "Collective Memory," 2009, sound piece, *Model Citizens* exhibit, Townhouse Gallery, Cairo, 54:46, http://www.wouterosterholt.com/model-citizens/collective-memory (author's translation).
22 Elke Uitentuis and Wouter Osterholt, "Collective Memory," 2009, sound piece, *Model Citizens* exhibit, Townhouse Gallery, Cairo, 55:15, http://www.wouterosterholt.com/model-citizens/collective-memory (author's translation).
23 Elke Uitentuis and Wouter Osterholt, "Collective Memory," 2009, sound piece, *Model Citizens* exhibit, Townhouse Gallery, Cairo, 55:27, http://www.wouterosterholt.com/model-citizens/collective-memory (author's translation).
24 Elke Uitentuis and Wouter Osterholt, "Collective Memory," 2009, sound piece, *Model Citizens* exhibit, Townhouse Gallery, Cairo, 1:00:59, http://www.wouterosterholt.com/model-citizens/collective-memory (author's translation).
25 Comparing how the rumor campaigns materialized and repoliticized the projects along different dimensions in Darb El-Ahmar and Fener-Balat also methodologically addresses one of the most piercing critiques of assemblage urbanism: that assemblage urbanism ignores or downplays the impact of power differentials (or structures) as it focuses on tracing the contingency of human-nonhuman agency (see, for example, Brenner et al. 2011). Comparison that is attuned to bottom-up human-environment interactions can help capture how both contingency and systemic forces interact.
26 While a central piece in explaining the divergence of the political projects that the rumors evoked in each neighborhood, other factors no doubt played a role. For one thing, it is likely that the EU's framing of the project in Fener-Balat around heritage preservation contributed to the repoliticization of the project along identity-based lines in ways that engineering community would not. In that vein, there are many ways mobilizing heritage or community or disaster prevention as redistributive practices will shape the substance and nature of the repoliticization that unsettles these projects. Since the book is focused on mapping out how these practices are entangled with market-making and similarities in the redistributive work performed through what seem to be these disparate fields, in order to say something larger about redistributive politics under neoliberalism, it does not produce a comprehensive chronicling

of such comparisons, but that is an interesting layer of the analysis worth investigating further.

27 Anonymous, pers. comm., Gamaliyya neighborhood, September 2011.
28 Anonymous, pers. comm., Darb El-Ahmar neighborhood, November 2011.
29 AKTC personnel, pers. comm., December 2011.
30 AKTC personnel, pers. comm., October 2011.
31 AKTC personnel, pers. comm., October 2011.
32 AKTC personnel, pers. comm., October 2011.
33 AKTC personnel, pers. comm., December 2011.
34 AKTC personnel, pers. comm., December 2011.
35 AKTC personnel, pers. comm., December 2011.
36 AKTC personnel, pers. comm., October 2011.
37 AKTC personnel, pers. comm., October 2011.
38 AKTC personnel, pers. comm., December 2011.
39 AKTC personnel, pers. comm., October 2011.
40 Anonymous, pers. comm., Darb El-Ahmar, November 2011.
41 See work by Ghannam (2002) and Ismail (2006) that expands on the importance of such information gathering and dispute resolution on wielding political and economic power in local neighborhood settings in Cairo.
42 For more information on Cairo's suburban development, see Sims (2015).
43 "'Al-Ismailia Lelestethmar Al-'Aqari' Tatalaqa 'Ourodhan Leshera' 200 'Aqar Fe Manteqat Wust El-Balad" [Al-Ismailia for real estate investment receives 200 sales offers in Wust El-Balad], *Shorouk News*, June 22, 2014, http://www.shorouknews.com/mobile/news/view.aspx?cdate=22062014&id=a73a1fc4-19c6-4be1-9f02-d1c40b4b9675.
44 Karim Shafei, pers. comm., Cairo, July 2011.
45 See chapter 1 for more on Wust El-Balad's history with out-migration.
46 Karim Shafei, pers. comm., Cairo, July 2011.
47 Karim Shafei, pers. comm., Cairo, July 2011.
48 Karim Shafei, pers. comm., Cairo, July 2011.
49 Town House Gallery personnel, pers. comm., Cairo, August 2011.
50 For more details, see home page, Downtown Contemporary Arts Festival, accessed December 30, 2022, http://d-caf.org.
51 See "About," Downtown Contemporary Arts Festival, accessed April 26, 2016, http://d-caf.org/about/.
52 See, for example, Ahmed Nagy, "Hal Yataḥawal 'Wust El-Balad' Fel Qahira Kama Taḥawal Wassat Madinat Beirut?" [Will Wust El-Balad in Cairo transform as did Beirut's downtown?], *Raseef 22*, April 7, 2015, http://raseef22.com/culture/2015/04/07/will-cairo-downtown-transform-like-beirut-downtown/.
53 Karim Shafei, pers. comm., Cairo, July 2011.
54 Putnam's ideas drew on a long lineage (see Joseph 2002, 11–13, for discussion of lineage), but the timing of his work is especially notable as it coincides with

the fall of the Berlin Wall and abandonment of the welfare-state model across the developed world.

CHAPTER FIVE. VISIBLE PUBLICS

1 AKTC personnel, pers. comm., December 2011.
2 See "Where We Work," Aga Khan Development Network, accessed January 1, 2023, https://www.the.akdn/en/where-we-work.
3 There are exceptions to that rule, including work by Murphy (2013) and Fennell (2015).
4 Anonymous, pers. comm., Gamaliyya, Cairo, September 2011.
5 Ghannam (2002) similarly describes the importance of aluminum windows to residents of a mass housing project on Cairo's periphery.
6 As narrated by HCO personnel, pers. comm., September 2011.
7 HCO personnel, pers. comm., September 2011.
8 HCO personnel, pers. comm., September 2011.
9 HCO personnel, pers. comm., September 2011.
10 HCO personnel, pers. comm., September 2011.
11 HCO personnel, pers. comm., September 2011.
12 AKTC personnel, pers. comm., December 2011.
13 AKTC personnel, pers. comm., December 2011.
14 EU personnel, pers. comm., May 2012.
15 AKTC personnel, pers. comm., October 2011.
16 Comparative note: Fener-Balat in Istanbul also saw an influx of tourists to the neighborhood that coincided with the EU's heritage preservation project there. During fieldwork from 2011 to 2012, I regularly saw walking tours and university arts and architecture class visits, among other tourist activities. Moreover, the neighborhood was used as a backdrop for a number of TV and movie sets (including a James Bond movie) during that time. The presence of tourists and outsiders was a by-product of the project that the EU team was aware of and discussed during our interviews, bringing up many of the tensions discussed in the chapter. Planning the neighborhood's rehabilitation around tourist needs (in a way similar to the AKTC routes) was not as pronounced in their plans, however. The main physical building designed around tourist needs was the local park that the EU started restoring as a public space but then handed over to a private café. In a way, heritage preservation is often seen as more tourism-oriented in its ethos than engineering community would be, but the EU did less work to directly service tourists than the AKTC. Perhaps the EU team saw less of a need to service tourism with a project already dedicated to heritage, but it's also possible that they were more ambivalent about the impact of tourism on the neighborhood.
17 Anonymous, pers. comm., Gamaliyya, Cairo, October 2011.
18 Anonymous, pers. comm., Tarlabaşı, Istanbul, July 2012.

19 See Mills (2010) for importance of streets to urban memory in Istanbul.
20 Anonymous, pers. comm., Sulukule, Istanbul, July 2012.
21 Anonymous, group pers. comm., Fener, Istanbul, June 14, 2012.
22 Anonymous, pers. comm., Gamaliyya, Cairo, August 2011.
23 I2UD personnel, pers. comm., Boston, United States, April 2015.
24 For full information on the project, see Elke Uitentuis and Wouter Osterholt, *Model Citizens* exhibit, Townhouse Gallery, Cairo, accessed May 5, 2016, http://www.wouterosterholt.com/model-citizens/model-citizens.
25 Elke Uitentuis and Wouter Osterholt, "*Model Citizens*: Interviews/Pictures of Phase One," author acquired copy of this booklet for research use from the artists.
26 Participant observation notes, Tarlabaşı, Istanbul, June 2012.

CONCLUSION

1 For more analysis of urban activism during the Gezi protests, see El-Kazaz (2013).
2 See, for example, Shohada' 25 Yanayar (@shaheed_25jan), "El geish aqsam 'ala hemayat momtalakat el masreyeen mesh el masreyeen . . . fe halet el hogom 'aleik 'e'mel nafsak mabna" [The army swore to defend Egyptians' assets not Egyptians. . . . [I]f you are attacked, pretend you are a building], Twitter, December 18, 2011, 1:39 p.m., https://twitter.com/shaheed_25jan/status/148396941594738688.
3 In the urban arena, this despotism has in fact accelerated the many dispossessive patterns of property transfer and infrastructural development that I discussed in chapters 1 and 2, encroaching on the space for alternative political projects even more aggressively. Rather than see this as a failure of neoliberalism or an indication that we are in a postneoliberal moment, it is essential that we see how neoliberalism produces the political climate that perpetuates such despotism. Tracing what happens in the 1990s and 2000s, as I do in this book, is crucial to understanding how populist despotism gained such potency in Egypt and Turkey.

References

Abdelmonem, Mohamed Gamal. 2015. *The Architecture of Home in Cairo: Socio-Spatial Practice of the Hawari's Everyday Life*. New York: Routledge.

Abu-Lughod, Janet L. 1971. *Cairo: 1001 Years of the City Victorious*. Princeton, NJ: Princeton University Press.

Adalet, Begüm. 2018. *Hotels and Highways: The Construction of Modernization Theory in Cold War Turkey*. Stanford, CA: Stanford University Press.

Adly, Amr. 2020. *Cleft Capitalism: The Social Origins of Failed Market-Making in Egypt*. Stanford, CA: Stanford University Press.

Aga Khan Trust for Culture. 2005. *Cairo: Urban Regeneration in the Darb El-Ahmar District—A Framework for Investment*. Rome: Artemide Edizioni Press.

Akcan, Esra. 2012. *Architecture in Translation: Germany, Turkey, and the Modern House*. Durham, NC: Duke University Press.

Allais, Lucia. 2018. *Designs of Destruction: The Making of Monuments in the Twentieth Century*. Chicago: University of Chicago Press.

Altınsay Özgüner, Burçin. 2009. "Fener-Balat Districts Rehabilitation Programme: Revitalizing Buildings and Keeping the Locals Comfortably 'At Home': Is It Viable?" Proceedings of the International IAPS-CSBE and Housing Network, Istanbul, October 12–16.

Anderson, Benedict. 1983. *Imagined Communities: Reflections on the Origin and Spread of Nationalism*. New York: Verso.

Angell, Elizabeth. 2014. "Assembling Disaster: Earthquakes and Urban Politics in Istanbul." *City: Analysis of Urban Trends, Culture, Theory, Policy, Action* 18, no. 6: 667–78.

Arıcan, Alize. 2020. "Behind the Scaffolding: Manipulations of Time, Delays and Power in Tarlabaşı, Istanbul." *City and Society* 32, no. 3 (December): 482–507.

Atia, Mona. 2013. *Building a House in Heaven: Pious Neoliberalism and Islamic Charity in Egypt*. Minneapolis: University of Minnesota Press.

Augé, Marc. 1995. *Non-Lieux*. New York: Verso.
Bali, Rıfat N. 2005. *The "Varlık Vergisi" Affair: A Study of Its Legacy with Selected Documents*. Istanbul: Isis Press.
Barak, On. 2013. *On Time: Technology and Temporality in Modern Egypt*. Berkeley: University of California Press.
Barnes, Jessica. 2014. *Cultivating the Nile: The Everyday Politics of Water in Egypt*. Durham, NC: Duke University Press.
Bartu, Ayfer. 1999. "Who Owns the Old Quarters? Rewriting Histories in a Global Era." In *Istanbul: Between the Global and the Local*, edited by Çağlar Keyder, 31–46. Rowman and Littlefield.
Bayat, Asef. 1997. *Street Politics: Poor People's Movements in Iran*. New York: Columbia University Press.
Benhabib, Seyla. 1992. "Models of Public Space: Hannah Arendt, the Liberal Tradition and Jurgen Habermas." In *Habermas and the Public Sphere*, edited by Craig Calhoun, 73–98. Cambridge, MA: MIT Press, 1992.
Benjamin, Walter. 1968. *Illuminations: Essays and Reflections*, edited by Hannah Arendt. New York: Harcourt Brace.
Benjamin, Walter. 1999. *The Arcades Project*. Translated by Howard Eilan and Kevin McLaughlin. Cambridge, MA: Belknap Press of Harvard University Press.
Bennett, Jane. 2001. *The Enchantment of Modern Life: Attachments, Crossings and Ethics*. Princeton, NJ: Princeton University Press.
Bennett, Jane. 2004. "The Force of Things: Steps toward an Ecology of Matter." *Political Theory* 32, no. 13: 347–72.
Bennett, Jane. 2005. "The Agency of Assemblages and the North American Blackout." *Public Culture* 17, no. 3: 445–65.
Bezmez, Dikmen. 2008. "The Politics of Urban Waterfront Regeneration: The Case of Haliç (the Golden Horn), Istanbul." *International Journal of Urban and Regional Research* 32, no. 4 (December): 815–40.
Bhandar, Brenna. 2018. *Colonial Lives of Property: Law, Land and Racial Regimes of Ownership*. Durham, NC: Duke University Press.
Blau, Eve. 1999. *The Architecture of Red Vienna 1919–1934*. Cambridge, MA: MIT Press.
Boyer, M. Christine. 1996. *The City of Collective Memory: Its Historical Imagery and Architectural Entertainments*. Cambridge, MA: MIT Press.
Bozdoğan, Sibel. 2001. *Modernism and Nation Building: Turkish Architectural Culture in the Early Republic*. Seattle: University of Washington Press.
Brennan, Teresa. 2004. *The Transmission of Affect*. Ithaca, NY: Cornell University Press.
Brenner, Neil, David J. Madden, and David Wachsmuth. 2011. "Assemblage Urbanism and the Challenges of Critical Urban Theory." *City: Analysis of Urban Trends, Culture, Theory, Policy, Action* 15, no. 2: 225–40.
Brenner, Neil, and Nik Theodore. 2002. "Cities and the Geographies of 'Actually Existing Neoliberalism.'" *Antipode* 34, no. 3 (July 1): 349–79.
Brown, Wendy. 2015. *Undoing the Demos: Neoliberalism's Stealth Revolution*. New York: Zone Books.

Buğra, Ayşe, and Osman Savaşkan. 2014. *New Capitalism in Turkey: The Relationship between Politics, Religion and Business*. Cheltenham, UK: Edward Elgar Publishing.

Caldeira, Teresa P. R. 2000. *City of Walls: Crime, Segregation and Citizenship in São Paulo*. Berkeley: University of California Press.

Caldeira, Teresa P. R. 2008. "From Modernism to Neoliberalism in São Paulo: Reconfiguring the City and Its Citizens." In *Other Cities, Other Worlds*, edited by Andreas Huyssen, 51–78. Durham, NC: Duke University Press.

Çalışkan, Koray, and Michel Callon. 2010. "Economization, Part 2: A Research Programme for the Study of Markets." *Economy and Society* 39, no. 1 (February): 1–32.

Çelik, Zeynep. 1986. *The Remaking of Istanbul: Portrait of an Ottoman City in the Nineteenth Century*. Berkeley: University of California Press.

Crane, Sheila. 2017. "Housing as Battleground: Targeting the City in the Battles of Algiers." *City and Society* 29 (April): 187–212.

De Certeau, Michel. 1984. *The Practice of Everyday Life*. Translated by Steven Randall. Berkeley: University of California Press.

Denis, Eric. 2006. "Cairo as Neo-Liberal Capital? From Walled City to Gated Communities." In *Cairo Cosmopolitan: Politics, Culture, and Urban Space in the New Globalized Middle East*, edited by Diane Singerman and Paul Amar, 47–72. Cairo: American University in Cairo Press.

Derrida, Jacques. 1998. *Archive Fever: A Freudian Impression*. Chicago: University of Chicago Press.

De Soto, Hernando. 1989. *The Other Path: The Invisible Revolution in the Third World*. New York: Harper Collins and Row.

De Soto, Hernando. 2007. *The Mystery of Capital: Why Capitalism Triumphs in the West and Fails Everywhere Else*. New York: Basic Books.

El Araby, Mostafa Morsi. 2003. "The Role of the State in Managing Urban Land Supply and Prices in Egypt." *Habitat International* 27, no. 3 (September 1): 429–58.

El Kadi, Galila, and Dalila Elkerdany. 2006. "Belle Époque Cairo: The Politics of Refurbishing the Downtown Business District." In *Cairo Cosmopolitan: Politics, Culture, and Urban Space in the New Globalized Middle East*, edited by Diane Singerman and Paul Amar, 345–74. Cairo: American University in Cairo Press.

El-Kazaz, Sarah. 2013. "It Is About the Park: A Struggle for Turkey's Cities." In *JADMAG 1.4: "Resistance Everywhere." The Gezi Protests and Dissident Visions of Turkey*, edited by Anthony Alessandrini, Nazan Üstündağ, and Emrah Yildiz, 65–67. Washington, DC: Tadween Publishing.

El-Kazaz, Sarah, and Kevin Mazur. 2017. "Introduction to Special Section: The Un-Exceptional Middle Eastern City." *City and Society* 29, no. 1 (April): 148–61.

El-Shakry, Omnia. 2006. "Cairo as Capital of Socialist Revolution?" In *Cairo Cosmopolitan: Politics, Culture, and Urban Space in the New Globalized Middle East*, edited by Diane Singerman and Paul Amar, 73–98. Cairo: American University in Cairo Press, 2006.

Eldem, Edhem, Daniel Goffman, and Bruce Masters. 1999. *The Ottoman City between East and West*. Cambridge: Cambridge University Press.

Elyachar, Julia. 2005. *Markets of Dispossession: NGOs, Economic Development, and the State in Cairo*. Durham, NC: Duke University Press.

Evin, Ahmet, ed. 1985. *The Expanding Metropolis: Coping with the Urban Growth of Cairo*. Singapore: Concept Media/Aga Khan Award for Architecture.

Fahmy, Khaled. 2018. *In Quest of Justice: Islamic Law and Forensic Medicine in Modern Egypt*. Berkeley: University of California Press.

Fennell, Catherine. 2015. *Last Project Standing: Civics and Sympathy in Post-Welfare Chicago*. Minneapolis: University of Minnesota Press.

Ferguson, James. 1994. *The Anti-Politics Machine: "Development," Depoliticization and Bureaucratic Power in Lesotho*. Minneapolis: University of Minnesota Press.

Foggo, Hacer. 2007. "The Sulukule Affair: Roma against Expropriation." *Roma Rights Quarterly*, no. 4: 41–47.

Foucault, Michel. 1977. *Discipline and Punish: The Birth of the Prison*. New York: Vintage Books.

Foucault, Michel. 1991. "Governmentality." In *The Foucault Effect: Studies in Governmentality*, edited by Graham Bruchell, Colin Gordon, and Peter Miller, 87–104. Chicago: University of Chicago Press.

Fraser, Nancy. 1992. "Rethinking the Public Sphere: A Contribution to the Critique of Actually Existing Democracy." In *Habermas and the Public Sphere*, edited by Craig Calhoun, 109–42. Cambridge, MA: MIT Press.

Ghannam, Farha. 2002. *Remaking the Modern: Space, Relocation, and the Politics of Identity in a Global Cairo*. Berkeley: University of California Press.

Ghertner, Asher. 2015. *Rule by Aesthetics: World-Class City Making in Delhi*. Oxford: Oxford University Press.

Graebber, David. 2001. *Toward an Anthropological Theory of Value: The False Coin of Our Dreams*. New York: Palgrave.

Gül, Murat. 2009. *The Emergence of Modern Istanbul: Transformation and Modernisation of a City*. New York: I. B. Tauris.

Harvey, David. 1989. "From Managerialism to Entrepreneurialism: The Transformation in Urban Governance in Late Capitalism." *Geografiska Annaler: Series B, Human Geography* 71, no. 1 (April 1): 3–17.

Harvey, David. 2005. *A Brief History of Neoliberalism*. Oxford: Oxford University Press.

Hazbun, Waleed. 2008. *Beaches, Ruins, Resorts: The Politics of Tourism in the Arab World*. Minneapolis: University of Minnesota Press.

Hessini, Leila. 1994. "Wearing the Hijab in Contemporary Morocco: Choice and Identity." In *Reconstructing Gender in the Middle East*, edited by Fatima Muge Gocek and Shiva Balaghi, 40–56. New York: Columbia University Press.

Holland, Alisha C. 2017. *Forbearance as Redistribution*. Cambridge: Cambridge University Press.

Holston, James. 1989. *The Modernist City: An Anthropological Critique of Brasilia*. Chicago: University of Chicago Press.

Huyssen, Andreas. 2003. *Present Pasts: Urban Palimpsests and the Politics of Memory*. Stanford, CA: Stanford University Press.
Ismail, Salwa. 2006. *Political Life in Cairo's New Quarters: Encountering the Everyday State*. Minneapolis: University of Minnesota Press.
Ismail, Shehab. 2017. "Engineering Metropolis: Contagion, Capital, and the Making of British Colonial Cairo, 1882–1922." PhD diss., Columbia University.
Işın, Engin. 2010. "The Soul of a City: Hüzun, Keyif, Longing." In *Orienting Istanbul: Cultural Capital of Europe?*, edited by Deniz Göktürk, Levent Soysal, and Ipek Tureli, 35–49. New York: Routledge.
Jacobs, Jane. 1961. *The Death and Life of Great American Cities*. New York: Vintage Books.
Jamal, Amaney A. 2007. *Barriers to Democracy: The Other Side of Social Capital in Palestine and the Arab World*. Princton, NJ: Princeton University Press.
Joseph, Miranda. 2002. *Against the Romance of Community*. Minneapolis: University of Minnesota Press.
Kanna, Ahmed. 2011. *Dubai, the City as Corporation*. Minneapolis: University of Minnesota Press.
Keyder, Çağlar. 1987. *State and Class in Turkey: A Study in Capitalist Development*. New York: Verso.
Keyder, Çağlar. 1999. *Istanbul: Between the Global and the Local*. New York: Rowman and Littlefield.
Kotkin, Stephen. 1997. *Magnetic Mountain: Stalinism as Civilization*. Berkeley: University of California Press.
Kuyucu, Tuna, and Özlem Ünsal. 2010. "'Urban Transformation' as State-Led Property Transfer: An Analysis of Two Cases of Urban Renewal in Istanbul." *Urban Studies* 47, no. 7 (June 1): 1479–99.
Latour, Bruno. 1993. *The Pasteurization of France*. Translated by Alan Sheridan and John Law. Cambridge, MA: Harvard University Press.
Lefebvre, Henri. 1991. *The Production of Space*. Translated by Donald Nicholson-Smith. Oxford: Blackwell.
Li, Tania Murray. 2007. *The Will to Improve: Governmentality, Development, and the Practice of Politics*. Durham, NC: Duke University Press.
Livny, Avital. 2020. *Trust and the Islamic Advantage: Religious-Based Movements in Turkey and the Muslim World*. Cambridge: Cambridge University Press.
McCall, Betsy Birn. 1988. "The Effects of Rent Control in Egypt: Part I." *Arab Law Quarterly* 3, no. 2 (May): 151–66.
Menoret, Pascal. 2014. *Joyriding in Riyadh: Oil, Urbanism, and Road Revolt*. Cambridge: Cambridge University Press.
Mernissi, Fatima. 1987. *Beyond the Veil: Male-Female Dynamics in Modern Muslim Society*. Bloomington: Indiana University Press.
Meyer, Gunter. 1987. "Employment in Small-Scale Manufacturing in Cairo: A Socio-Economic Survey." *Bulletin (British Society for Middle Eastern Studies)* 14, no. 2: 136–46.

Mills, Amy. 2010. *Streets of Memory: Landscape, Tolerance, and National Identity in Istanbul.* Athens: University of Georgia Press.
Mirowski, Philip, and Dieter Plehwe, eds. 2009. *The Road from Mont Pelèrin: The Making of the Neo-Liberal Thought Collective.* Cambridge, MA: Harvard University Press.
Mitchell, Timothy. 1988. *Colonising Egypt.* Berkeley: University of California Press.
Mitchell, Timothy. 2002. *Rule of Experts: Egypt, Techno-Politics, Modernity.* Berkeley: University of California Press.
Muehlebach, Andrea. 2012. *The Moral Neoliberal: Welfare and Citizenship in Italy.* Chicago: University of Chicago Press.
Murphy, Keith M. 2013. "A Cultural Geometry: Designing Political Things in Sweden." *American Ethnologist* 40, no. 1 (February): 118–31.
Navaro-Yashin, Yael. 2012. *The Make-Believe Space: Affective Geography in a Postwar Polity.* Durham, NC: Duke University Press.
Nora, Pierre. 1996. *Realms of Memory: Conflicts and Divisions.* New York: Columbia University Press.
Ong, Aihwa. 2006. *Neoliberalism as Exception: Mutations in Citizenship and Sovereignty.* Durham, NC: Duke University Press.
Osman, Suleiman, 2011. *The Invention of Brownstone Brooklyn: Gentrification and the Search for Authenticity in Postwar New York.* Oxford: Oxford University Press.
Pamuk, Orhan. 2006. *Istanbul: Memories and the City.* New York: Vintage Books.
Putnam, Robert D. 1993. *Making Democracy Work: Civic Traditions in Modern Italy.* Princeton, NJ: Princeton University Press.
Putnam, Robert D. 2000. *Bowling Alone.* New York: Simon and Schuster.
Reynolds, Nancy. 2012. *A City Consumed: Urban Commerce, the Cairo Fire, and the Politics of Decolonization in Egypt.* Stanford, CA: Stanford University Press.
Robins, Kevin, and Asu Aksoy. 1995. "Istanbul Rising: Returning the Repressed to Urban Culture." *European Urban and Regional Studies* 2, no. 3 (July 1): 223–35.
Robinson, Andrew. 2013. *Earthquake: Nature and Culture.* London: Reaktion Books.
Roll, Stephan. 2013. *Egypt's Business Elite after Mubarak: A Powerful Player between Generals and Brotherhood.* Berlin: Stiftung Wissenschaft und Politik German Institute for International and Security Affairs.
Rose, Nikolas. 1996. "Governing 'Advanced' Democracies." In *Foucault and Political Reason: Liberalism, Neo-Liberalism, and Rationalities of Government*, edited by Andrew Barry, Thomas Osborne, and Nikolas Rose, 37–64. London: UCL Press.
Sabancıoğlu, Müsemma. 2003. "Jacques Pervititch and His Insurance Maps of Istanbul." *Dubrovnik Annals* 7:89–98.
Said, Edward. 1978. *Orientalism.* New York: Vintage Books.
Sand, Jordan. 2013. *Tokyo Vernacular: Common Spaces, Local Histories, Found Objects.* Berkeley: University of California Press.
Sartori, Andrew. 2014. *Liberalism in Empire: An Alternative History.* Berkeley: University of California Press.

Sassen, Saskia. 2001. *The Global City: New York, London, Tokyo*. 2nd ed. Princeton, NJ: Princeton University Press.

Scott, James C. 1998. *Seeing like a State: How Certain Schemes to Improve the Human Condition Have Failed*. New Haven, CT: Yale University Press.

Searle, Llerena Guiu. 2016. *Landscapes of Accumulation: Real Estate and the Neoliberal Imagination in Contemporary India*. Chicago: University of Chicago.

Shehayeb, Dina. 2011. "Backtracking to Sustainable Urban Development and Working with Local Communities: The al-Darb al-Ahmar Project in Islamic Cairo." *Égypte/Monde arabe* 8:109–29.

Shehayeb, Dina, and Mohamed Abdel Hafiz. 2006. "Tradition, Change, and Participatory Design: Re-Designing Tablita Market in Historic Cairo." *Open House International* 31, no. 4 (December): 67–76.

Shehayeb, Dina, and Yaldiz Eid. 2007. "Neighbourhood Design and Community Building: A Model of Social Interaction." In *The Appropriate Home: Can We Design "Appropriate" Residential Environments?*, edited by Dina Shehayeb, H. Turgut Yildiz, and Peter Kellett. Proceedings of the First HBNRC and IAPS-CSBE Network Joint Symposium, Cairo.

Shehayeb, Dina, and Mohamed El-Mikawi. 2003. "Improving Quality of Life through Sustainable Rehabilitation of Low Income Housing in Historic Cairo." Arab Regional Conference, Cairo, December 15–18.

Simone, Abdou Maliq. 2008. "The Last Shall Be First: African Urbanities and the Larger Urban World." In *Other Cities, Other Worlds*, edited by Andreas Huyssen, 99–120. Durham, NC: Duke University Press.

Sims, David. 2010. *Understanding Cairo: The Logic of a City Out of Control*. Cairo: American University in Cairo Press.

Sims, David. 2015. *Egypt's Desert Dreams: Development or Disaster?* Cairo: American University in Cairo Press.

Singerman, Diane. 1995. *Avenues of Participation: Family, Politics, and Networks in Urban Quarters of Cairo*. Princeton, NJ: Princeton University Press.

Slobodian, Quinn. 2018. *Globalists: The End of Empire and the Birth of Neoliberalism*. Cambridge, MA: Harvard University Press.

Uslaner, Eric M. 2002. *The Moral Foundations of Trust*. Cambridge: Cambridge University Press.

Van der Tas, Jurjen. 2004. "Preliminary Results of a Socio-Economic Survey in al-Darb al-Ahmar." In *Cairo: Revitalizing a Historic Metropolis*, edited by Stefano Bianco and Philip Jodidio. Turin: Umberto Allemandi and C. for Aga Khan Trust for Culture.

Vitalis, Robert. 1995. *When Capitalists Collide: Business Conflict and the End of Empire in Egypt*. Berkeley: University of California Press.

Vitalis, Robert, and Steven Heydemann. 2000. "War, Keynesianism, and Colonialism: Explaining State-Market Relations in the Postwar Middle East." In *War, Institutions, and Social Change in the Middle East*, edited by Steven Heydemann, 100–145. Berkeley: University of California Press.

Waterbury, John. 1983. *The Egypt of Nasser and Sadat: The Political Economy of Two Regimes*. Princeton, NJ: Princeton University Press.

Weizman, Eyal. 2007. *Hollow Land: Israel's Architecture of Occupation*. New York: Verso.

Wright, Gwendolyn. 1991. *The Politics of Design in French Colonial Urbanism*. Chicago: University of Chicago Press.

Yavuz, M. Hakan. 2003. *Islamic Political Identity in Turkey*. Oxford: Oxford University Press.

Zencirci, Gizem. 2015. "Illusory Debates." *Asian Journal of Social Science* 43, nos. 1–2 (January 1): 125–50.

Zukin, Sharon. 1996. *The Cultures of Cities*. New York: Wiley.

Zukin, Sharon. 2009. *Naked City: The Death and Life of Authentic Urban Places*. Oxford: Oxford University Press.

Index

Page locators in italics indicate figures.

Abanumay, Sulaiman, family of, 172
Abu-Lughod, Janet L., 28
accumulation, 5–8, 219n12; and construction industry, 85; "by dispossession," 6, 8, 86, 101–3, 208; and "indigenous" social capital, 181; and market distortion, 182
aesthetics, 3; coded politics, 124–25; and nostalgia, 141–42; prioritization by heritage industry, 110–11, 133, 135, 138, 160–61; "rule by," 158, 186; sartorial, 81–82, 124; of security, 175, 178; and "urban crisis," notions of, 102; visible, 159, 171, 185–87, 191, 207; and vulnerability to predatory state, 158–59, 193–94
affective experiences, 13–15, 73–75, 80–83, 190, 209; spatial-affective-material transformation, 14–15, 23–24, 37, 55, 62–64, 70, 102–3
affordable housing, 7, 79; and "community," 149–50, 155, 159–60, 163, 169, 185, 187–88, 227n13; and heritage preservation, 2–3, 10, 15, 109–10, 115–18, 138; targeted for dispossession, 87–88, 91, 103, 172–73, 177; valuing of, 68–69, 101–2
Aga Khan, 50, 153, 161–62, 185
Aga Khan Foundation, 1–2, 15, 22, 49, 153, 217n7; field trips for children, 160–61

Aga Khan Trust for Culture (AKTC), 22–23, 62, 207–9, 226n1, 227n13; and collaborative community, 148–50, 155–58, 166–69, 179, 181; and contradictions of "community" as object of intervention 167–69; and designing community, 166–67; and independence from predatory state, 158–59, 193–94; and invested community, 153–72, 179; and logics of redistributive funding, 156–57; rumors about, 161–65; and visual topography, 193–94. *See also* Darb El-Ahmar neighborhood (Cairo)
Akcan, Esra, 74
Ala'a G, 212
Allais, Lucia, 113
ANAP (Motherland Party) (Turkey), 90
Anatolia, 71, 76, 85–86, 97, 129
Anatolian Tigers, 85–86
Anderson, Benedict, 112, 151–52
Angell, Elizabeth, 99
Ankara (Turkey), 71–72
Antikhana alleyway, 30, 40–41, 164, 201–2; red palace of, 164
Arab Contractors (Osman Ahmed Osman and Co.), 59
"Architectural Transformations in the Islamic World" workshops, 153

archive, memory as, 112
archiving, and communal power, 138–45; barbershop mirror fixtures, *139*, 139–41; hardware store drawers, 141–44, *142*
Armenian Genocide, 72, 122
Aslam Square (Darb El-Ahmar), 169–70
assemblage urbanism, 12, 219n12, 228n25
Association of Foreign Insurance Companies Operating in Turkey, 95
Aswan Dam, 26
Atatürk, Mustafa Kemal, 71–74, 80
automobile-based infrastructure: Cairo, 14, 24, 28, 51, 57–61; Istanbul, 76–77, 92
Ayyubids, 24
Azhar Park (Cairo), 1, *18*, 61, *159*, 166; AKTC transformation of, 153–55, *154*; Ayyubid Wall, 162; as cultural space, 176; gallery, 50–52, 184; gift booklet, 50, 221n32; and rumors, 159–62; and visible publics, 183–85, 187, 193; and vulnerability of affordable housing, 158–59

Bab Zuweila (Fatimid gate, Cairo), 26, 28, 51, 194
Baehler Society, 35
Bank Misr (Egypt), 35, 36, 37
Bayraktar, Erdoğan, 100
Beit El-Kharazaty (home, Gamaliyya), 29, 166
belirli mekanlar (well-known places), 198–99
Benhabib, Seyla, 199
Benjamin, Walter, 112
Bennett, Jane, 13
Bico, Cem, 13–14
Bosporus Strait, 7, 74–75
Bowling Alone (Putnam), 180
Brennan, Teresa, 13
Brenner, Neil, 219n12
Britain: colonial rule in Egypt, 27, 32, 34–35, 42–44; insurance industry in Istanbul, 94–95; monopolistic contracts awarded to "foreign" companies, 34–35; and World War II, 42–44
Brooklyn, New York, 114
Bulaq neighborhood (Cairo), 158

Cairo, 2–3, 6–7, *18*; automobile-based infrastructure, 14, 24, 28, 51, 57–61; Azhar Boulevard, 28, 51, 58; Azhar Tunnel, 58, 59–60; Bab Zuweila (Fatimid gate), 26, 28, 51, 194; Bulaq neighborhood, 158; Citadel, 162, 164; core complex, 14, 24–28, 49; cultural scene, 63; and cultural work, 173–77; "desert cities," 62; exodus and rootedness in, 28–32; fire and riots (1952), 14, 32, *33*, 37, 220n5; "foreign" capital in, 33–35; Garden City neighborhood, 35; Ibrahim Pasha's palace, 35; industrial and infrastructural sensoria, 50–52, 55–56; industrialization, 14, 24, 52–57; industrialization, mapping in time and space, 52–55; industrial workshops, 51, 53–55, 57, 62; infrastructural work, 27–28; infrastructural work given to "foreign" companies, 34–35; Isma'iliyya neighborhood, 27; Khalij canal, 25, 26; mass housing projects, 29, 31, 168; medieval city, 25–26; mid-1800s public health campaign, 25; migrants, and World War II, 43; migrants, rural, 6, 29–31, 62, 219–20n4; migrants, non-Muslim, 33–34, 40–41; minarets, 1, *5*, 24, 49, 166, 184; modernization projects, nineteenth century, 27–28; Mu'iz Street, 26, 51, 61, 188–91, *189*; Nile River, *18*, 24–27, 158; in nineteenth century, 24; nineteenth-century water delivery system, 25–26; population surge, 28; property owner–tenant struggles, 22, 24, 50; property regime transformation, 21–23, 44, 62–64; Ring Road, *18*, 158; seasonal canals, lakes, and ponds, 24–25; industrial towns on periphery of, 52–53; 6th of October Bridge, 58, 59–60; spatial-affective-material transformations, 14, 23–24, 37, 55, 62–64; street vendors, 55, 60; and subterranean topography, 163–65; suburban enclaves, 172; Tahrir Square, 60, *212*, 212–13; Tawfiqiyya neighborhood, 27; and "urban crisis," notions of, 55–56, 61, 62; water delivery system, mid-1860s, 27; water ecologies and remaking of, 26–28; water ecologies of, 14, 23, 24–28;

Zamalek, *18*, *35*, *63*. See also Azhar Park (Cairo); Darb El-Ahmar neighborhood (Cairo); earthquake, Cairo (1992); Egypt; Gamaliyya neighborhood (Cairo); luxury clientele, Cairo; rent control, Cairo; rent control laws, Egypt; Wust El-Balad (downtown Cairo)

Caldeira, Teresa, *175*, *178*

Çalık Holding, *9*, *93*, *138*, *141*, *144*, *195*, *203*

Çalışkan, Koray, *9*

Callon, Michel, *9*

capitalists: conglomerates, *59*, *62*, *86*; corporate-capitalist class, *5–6*, *8*; corporate-capitalist class, Turkey, *85–86*; large-scale, *58–59*; new capitalist class, Egypt, *23*, *86*. See also colonial-capitalist entanglement, Egypt

care, discourse of, *129–30*, *146–47*

Çelik, Zeynep, *93*

Cicurel (department store), *36*, *37*

citizenship, *210–14*, *211*, *212*

class: commercial, *54*, *81*; and shifting property landscapes, *24*, *31–32*; intraclass politics, Istanbul, *81*; isolation of socioeconomic classes, *175*; and judgments of worthiness, *125–31*; merchant class, Istanbul, *70–72*; *nas nedheefa* (clean, or civilized), *174–75*

class, Egypt: and cosmopolitanism, *37–41*; dissipating wealth of, *46–47*; landlords, disorganization of, *21–23*, *43–44*, *46–47*; new capitalist, *23*, *86*; and nostalgia, *39*; oligopolistic conglomerates, *59*, *62*, *86*; oligopolistic local/"Egyptian" capitalists, *35*, *37–38*, *43*; World War II's effect on, *44*. See also colonial-capitalist entanglement, Egypt

class, Istanbul: affect, class, identity politics and globalization, *80–83*; merchant class, *70–72*; working class, *79–80*, *102*

class politics: of conservation, *125–31*; displacement of, *9–10*, *209*; on level of urban design, *2*, *8–10*, *122–25*, *208–10*; repoliticization of, *15*, *125*, *210*. See also identity politics

coalitions, urban, *7*, *9–10*, *109–11*; Habitat coalition, *115–19*, *132*, *145*, *209–10*, *227n13*

Cold War politics, *113*

colonial-capitalist entanglement, Egypt, *5*, *14*, *23*, *32–41*, *62*; postcolonial class and cosmopolitan entanglements, *37–41*; "foreign" capital in Cairo, *33–35*; oligarchic multisectoral, familial groups, *35*, *37–38*, *43*; and World War II, *42–44*; and Wust El-Balad, *36–37*. See also capitalists; class, Egypt

colonialism, *5*; anticolonialism, *35*; British, in Egypt, *32–38*

commercial class, *54*, *81*

community: and difference, *152*, *182*; Greek, Istanbul, *72*, *78*, *119–22*, *142*, *226n33*; and hierarchy, *144*, *169–71*; Kurdish, Tarlabaşı, *82*, *88*, *140*; neoliberal configuration of, *150–51*; new hierarchy, *171–72*; power dynamics of, *152–53*; Roma, Sulukule, *88*, *89*, *195–96*; social capital, *168–69*, *180–81*

"community," engineered, *148–82*, *218n10*; and affordable housing, *149–50*, *155*, *159–60*, *163*, *169*, *185*, *187–88*, *227n13*; AKTC and contradictions of, *167–69*; independence from predatory state, *158–59*; collaborative, *2*, *148–50*, *155–58*, *166–69*, *179*, *181*; and stemming gentrification, *150*, *159*; invested community concept, *153–72*, *179*; and particularistic value, *150*, *152*, *172*; political reorganization around, *150–51*; redistributive funding logics, *156–57*; and contingent service provision, *150*, *159*; and politics of technical practices, *2*, *149*, *153*, *166–67*, *209*; and valuing of property, *2–3*, *7–9*, *150*, *152*, *172*; and visible aesthetics, *186–87*

community of strangers, *150–52*, *172–79*; and interconnected passageways, *200–201*; as spatial modality, *177*, *179*

conservation, class politics of, *125–31*, *146*

construction industry, *23*, *59*, *85*, *224n23*

consumption, and particularistic value, *181–82*

corporate-capitalist class, *5–6*, *8*, *85–86*

corporate-capitalist developers, 3, 11, 15; Cairo, 45-46, 61-63; subtle manipulation, Egypt, 63-64; and Turkey's Renewal and Preservation Law no. 5366 (2005), 66, 100; violent expropriation by in Turkey, 15, 63, 86-87, 93, 99-100, 143. *See also* dispossession; neoliberalism

cosmopolitanism: Cairo, 23, 37-41, 178-79; Istanbul, 82-83, 121, 125, 143, 146-47; and nostalgia, 39-41, 82-83, 143

crevices, intimate and private, 2, 207-10, 214; displacement of politics onto, 8, 10-11, 111, 122-25, 147, 149-50, 208-10; everyday uses of streets, 195-96; and heritage preservation, 108-9, 111, 122-25, 147; politics manifested in, 10-11, 149; violation of everyday dynamics, 194-96, 198

critical political economy, 6

cumba (protruding window), 65, 94, 197

Dalan, Bedrettin, 77, 83-84

Darb El-Ahmar neighborhood (Cairo), 4, 5, 11, 18; and 1992 earthquake, 1-2, 21-22, 46-49, 48; primacy of, 26-27; Aslam Square, 169-70; Azhar Park gallery, 50-52, 184; demolition decrees, 49; garbage dump, 1, 153-54, 183; industrial workshops, 51; number of buildings restored, 2, 133, 148, 156; particularistic community in, 152; pathway for women, 170-71; public/private boundaries, 193-94; streets, 28; subdivided homes, 28-29; Tablita Market, 169; visual topographies and public/private boundaries, 193-94. *See also* Aga Khan Trust for Culture (AKTC); Cairo

"dead capital," 55, 181, 221n34

De Amicis, Edmondo, 93

debt economy, 90

decolonization, Egypt, 32-33, 38

deindustrialization, Istanbul, 84-85, 88, 97, 115, 138

Demokrat Partisi (Democrat Party, DP) (Turkey), 76, 80, 83, 95-96

Denis, Eric, 175, 178

depoliticization, 9-10, 15, 123, 147; double performance of, 10

deregulation of property markets, 2, 101, 103, 119, 179

design, class politics of, 2, 8-10, 122-25, 208-10

despotism, 214-15, 231n3

developmental organizations, 1; displacement of welfare state responsibilities onto citizens, 149-50, 179-81, 208; Fatih Municipality, 90, 116-17, 134-35, 145-46, 225n6, 225n8; Habitat coalition, 115-19, 132, 209-10, 227n13; Mass Housing Authority (TOKİ), 66, 87-88, 91, 121; *See also* Aga Khan Foundation; Aga Khan Trust for Culture (AKTC); European Union (EU) rehabilitation program

development industry, 55, 100-101, 149, 217-18n7. *See also* heritage industry

Disaster Law (*Afet Yasası*) (Turkey), 68, 70, 100

disaster prevention, 8-9, 228n26; mismanagement, 14, 47-50. *See also* earthquake, Cairo (1992); earthquake, Istanbul, (1999 Marmara Earthquake)

displacement, neoliberal: of identity politics, 111, 123-25, 147; onto intimate and private crevices, 8, 10-11, 111, 122-25, 147, 149-50, 208-10; of politics away from traditional arenas, 3, 7-11, 123-24, 208-10, 213; suspicion as product of, 214-15, 231n3. *See also* neoliberalism

dispossession, 23, 24; accumulation by, 6, 8, 86, 101-3, 208; affordable housing targeted for, 87-88, 91, 103, 172-73, 177; and British colonialism in Egypt, 34, 37-38; and "development industry," 217-18n7; entanglements used to normalize, 101; social capital, valorization of, 180-81; violence of, Egypt, 11-12, 14-15, 23, 27-28, 60, 64, 213; violence of, Istanbul, 12, 15, 63, 68, 80-81, 84, 86-93, 99-100, 143. *See also* corporate-capitalist developers; neoliberalism

earthquake, Cairo (1992), 7, 21-24, 99; and Azhar Park, 153-55; and attracting heritage industry, 23, 55-56, 62; mismanagement of, 14, 47-50, 62, 63

244   Index

earthquake, Istanbul, (1999 Marmara Earthquake), 7, 70, 97–100, 102

Egypt: anticolonialism, 35; Bank Misr, 35, 36, 37; bread riots (1977), 45, 158; British control of, 27, 32, 34–35, 42–44; capital, "Egyptian" vs. "local," 32–33; colonial-capitalist entanglement, 23, 32–41; cotton production, 27, 33, 42; coup of 1952, 38; decolonization, 32–33, 38; dynastic rule, 27; Free Officers, 38, 44–45; Import-Substitution-Industrialization (ISI), 52–54; *Infitah* (open-door policies), 45, 54–55, 57, 158; inheritance, 41–42, 45–47, 154, 173; Ismailia (canal town), 32; Israel, war with (1967), 53–54; Mixed Courts, 34; Muslim Brotherhood, 223n17; nationalism, 32, 35, 38–39, 52, 63, 173–75, 178; new capitalist class, 23, 86; populism, 41, 44–46; Port Said massacre, 212–13; postcolonial rule, 38, 53; postindependence regime, 32–33; privatization, 54, 58–59; protectionism, 35, 52, 54; revolution (2011), 60, 210–13, *212*; state as major property owner, 38, 62, 221n18; tourism, 16, 56–57, 61, 161. *See also* Cairo; class, Egypt; colonial-capitalist entanglement, Egypt; earthquake, Cairo (1992); rent control laws, Egypt

"Egyptianization," 3, 29, 35, 39, 173–75; of industry, 52

electioneering dynamics, Istanbul, 14–15, 78–79, 87, 121

El-Shakry, Omnia, 53

Elyachar, Julia, 180–81

'emarat Wust El-Balad (buildings of downtown Cairo), 36–38, 47, 63, 173–76, *174*

"emergency nationalization" (*acil kamulaştırma*) (Turkey), 66–68, 67, *68*, 88, 100

engineering. *See* "community," engineered

environmental landscapes, 145; as totality, 10, 15, 112–13; transformation from monumental to environmental, 9–10, 15

environmentally-attuned ethnography, 12–14

"environmental turn," 113, 115, 125, 145, 147, 188

Erdoğan, Recep Tayyip, 76–77, 84, 93, 213

Estoril (restaurant, Cairo), 41, 221n24

European Capital of Culture 2010, Istanbul as, 121, 125, 146, 147

European Union (EU) rehabilitation program, 15, 66, 72, 117–19, *118*, 207, 217n7, 230n16; companies working for, 136; conflicts within team, 132–34; classed politics of care for historical landscapes, 125–31, 146; contract, *118*, 121; documentary film, 138; fixation on historical accuracy, 107–9, 127–28; rumors and repoliticization, 119–22, 165; self-reflexive experts, 131–37; and visible public spaces, 193–94

exceptionalization, of Middle East as region, 217n6

"The Expanding Metropolis: Coping with the Urban Growth of Cairo" conference, 153

experts, 99–100, 153, 217n4, 218–19n11; self-reflexive, 131–37, 218n7, 226n22

extra-market redistributive mechanisms, 3, 88, 109, 116

"eyes on the street," 175–76, 178

Ezz, Ahmed, 59

Ezz Steel, 59

Fatih Municipality, 90, 116–17, 134–35, 145–46, 225n6, 225n8

Fatimids, 24–25

Fener and Balat Neighborhood Rehabilitation Program, 117. *See also* European Union (EU) rehabilitation program

Fener-Balat neighborhood (Istanbul), 11, 15, 17, 66, 67, 72, 88, 230n16; abandonment of properties, 96–97; carpet cleaning, clotheslines, and social bonds, 132–33, *134*, 208; Conservation Board regulations, 111, 131–33; heritage as redistribution, 115–19; migrants to, 79; rumor campaigns in, 119–22, 228n25, 228n26; wooden construction, 94, 96–97, *98*. *See also* Istanbul

fire: and Cairo, 14, 32, *33*, 37, 220n15; and Istanbul, 65, 70, 73, 89, 93–97, *98*, 108

Fraser, Nancy, 199

"free markets," 4–5, 39, 54, 103

Index   245

Free Officers, 38, 44-45
Fustat Garden (Cairo), 155

Gamaliyya neighborhood (Cairo), 11, *18*; and 1992 earthquake, 47; and its primacy, 26-27; Beit El-Kharazaty (home), 29, 166; Fatimid gates, 26-27; industrial workshops, 51, 62; public/private boundaries, 188-93; streets, 27-28, 58; visual topographies and public/private boundaries, 188-93; *wekala* buildings, 53-55. *See also* Cairo
gaze: expanded, of public, 194-99; and gendered asymmetries, 196-97
gentrification, 150, 159, 172, 177, 188; regulation against, 117, 119
geopolitics: of World War I, 14, 70-73; of World War II, 14, 41, 42-44, 113
Gezi Park (Istanbul), *17*, 210, *211*
Ghertner, Asher, 158, 186
"global cities," 78, 83-84, 91-92, 101; and memory, 114-15; and visual topographies, 186-87
Global South, 5-7, 146
Golden Horn (Istanbul), 3, 17, 65-66, 72, 91; as cultural epicenter, 84; and Habitat coalition, 115-19, 132, 145, 209-10, 227n13; smells of, 76-77, 84. *See also* Istanbul
grassroots movements, 113-14, 127; hijacking of, 3, 86, 100, 102-3
Greek community, Istanbul, 72, 78, 119-22, 142, 226n33
Greek Orthodox Patriarchate, 116, 119, 122
Gül, Murat, 71

Habitat coalition, 115-19, 132, 145, 209-10, 227n13
Hague, The, 1
Harvey, David, 186
"hauntings," 75, 120-25, 145, 165
Hausmann, Georges-Eugène, 27, 93
"healthy" property markets, 64, 103, 225n39
Helwan (industrial town, periphery of Cairo), 52
heritage, 3, 10, 107-47; affordable housing as, 109-10; and markets, environmental perspective, 111-15; as redistribution, 15, 115-19, 185; and tourism, 114-15, 187; "universal heritage of mankind," 113; visible spaces, 16, 115
heritage industry, 3, 23, 55-57, 62, 107-9, 110, 122, 135, 145, 187. *See also* development industry; European Union (EU) rehabilitation program; United Nations Educational, Scientific and Cultural Organization (UNESCO)
heritage preservation: aesthetics prioritized, 110-11, 133, 135, 138, 160-61; and affordable housing, 2-3, 10, 15, 109-10, 115-18, 138; brokers, 136-38; environmental landscapes, heritage as, 9-10, 15, 110, 145; "environmental turn," 113, 115, 125, 145, 147, 188; fixation on historical accuracy, 107-9; gentrification, regulation against, 117, 119; and identity politics, 9-10, 15, 109, 119-22; and "informality," 55-57; intimate and private crevices, 108-9, 111, 122-25, 147; Ministry of Culture project, Cairo, 56, 188-93, 207; from monumental to environmental practice, 9-10, 15, 113, 115, 125, 145, 147, 188; monuments, focus on, 56-57, 61, 109-10, 192; "my homeism," 114; pedestrianization, 61, 195; repoliticization of, 111, 123-25, 145-47; and self-reflexive experts, 131-37; social justice discourse, 116-17, 119, 122, 129, 135, 145, 196, 209, 218n7; of social spaces, 132-36, *139*, 139-41, 208; and technical practices, 10, 110, 122, 125, 145; and urban crisis discourse, 15, 55-56, 61, 62. *See also* European Union (EU) rehabilitation program
Heydemann, Steven, 42-44
hierarchy, 144, 169-71; new communal, 171-72; visible, 144
Hisar, Abdülhak Şinasi, 74-75
Historic Cairo Organization (HCO), 188-93
history, acceleration of, 112
housing rehabilitation: mass housing blocks, 29, 31, 168; as political tool, 2-3
Huysen, Andreas, 111, 114
hüzün (melancholy), 14, 70, 73-75, 80-81

identity politics: and coded paint colors, 124-25; displacement of, 111, 123-25, 147;

on eve of globalization, Istanbul, 80–83; and heritage preservation, 9–10, 15, 109; and memory, 119–22; and redistribution, 109–11; religion-based identity groups, 123; repoliticization of, 15, 125, 210; resistance to heritage preservation projects, 119–22. *See also* class politics

Idris, Yusuf, 32

Imagined Communities (Anderson), 151–52

Imami Ismaili Shi'ite sect of Muslims, 153

Imamoğlu, Ekrem, 224n23

Import-Substitution-Industrialization (ISI), 52–54, 83, 85

indebtedness, cycles of, 180–81

industrialization: Cairo, 14, 24, 52–57; deindustrialization, Istanbul, 84–85, 88, 97, 115, 138; and fallacies of "informality" studies, 55–57; Import-Substitution-Industrialization (ISI), 52–54, 83, 85; Istanbul, 14, 69, 70, 96

industrial workshops (Cairo), 51, 53–55, 57, 62

Infitah (open-door policies), 45, 54–55, 57, 158

"informality," 55–57, 180–81

inheritance, 41–42, 45–47, 154, 173

insurance industry, 94–95

iptal karar decrees (Turkey), 87–88, 100

Işın, Engin, 80–81

Ismailia (canal town), 32

Ismailia Consortium, 15, 39, 47, 63–64, 150, 172–79, 207, 227n6; community, understanding of, 151–52; culture, community, and exclusion, 175–77; funding of, 172; and interconnected passageways, 200–201. *See also* luxury clientele, Cairo; Wust El-Balad (downtown/Historic Cairo)

Israel, 53–54

Istanbul, 3, 6–7, *17*; affect, class, and identity politics on the eve of globalization, 80–83; affordable housing, 79; anti-minority violence, 14, 70, 72, 78, 96, 116, 142, 143, 226n33; automobile-based infrastructure, 76–77, 92; Başıbüyük neighborhood, 87; brick housing, 65–66; British insurance industry in, 94–95; criminalization of informal housing, 86–87; *cumba* windows, 65, 94; deindustrialization of, 84–85, 88, 97, 115, 138; demographic decline, 71–73; earthquakes, 7, 97–100, 102; electioneering dynamics, 14–15, 78–79, 87, 121; as European Capital of Culture 2010, 121, 125, 146, 147; European Union rehabilitation project, 66, 72; exodus, 14, 70, 72, 78, 95–96, 226n33; fires, 65, 70, 73, 89, 93–7, *98*, 108; Galata neighborhood, 73; Gezi protests, 210, *211*, 213; as global hub, 14, 70, 83–86, 91–92, 101; Greek community, 72, 78, 119–22, 142, 226n33; historical epochs, 70; "historical zones," 95; holistic infrastructural programs, 14, 70, 188; industrial and infrastructural sensoria, 70, 76–78; industrialization, 14, 69, 70, 96; infrastructures of "crisis" in Tarlabaşı, 91–93; *Istanbullus*, 80–81; Istiklal Boulevard, 73, 84; Karagumruk neighborhood, 91; *kargir* building materials, 94, 99; Kurdish migrants to, 82, 88, 140; Kuzguncuk neighborhood, 82; legal battles, 87, 96; linear narrative of, 80–81; literary writing about, 73–74; *manzara* (view), 69, 77; mapping project, nineteenth century, 95; merchant class, 70–72; migrants, job loss by, 84–85; migrants, property ownership by, 65–66, 69–70, 84–85, 102, 222n1; migration to, 69–70, 79–84, 96, 99, 124, 140; and modernization, 74, 76; neighborhood associations, 66–68; nineteenth-century redesign projects, 93–94; non-Muslim residents, 71–73, 78–79, 81–82, 96, 116–17, 120, 123–24, 143–44, 147, 226n33; pedestrianization, 84, 92; Pera district, 73, 81, 94; peripheralization, 70–73, 79, 95; population increase, 97; protectionism, 83; as regional-industrial and global hub, 76–83; as regional industrial hub, 14, 70, 96; "renewal zones," 66–68, *67*, 69, 87–89, 91, 139, 203; sartorial aesthetics, 81–82; as seat of Ottoman Empire, 70–71; *şehrin keyfi* (enjoyment of the city), 80–81; as space of *hüzün* (melancholy), 14, 70, 73–75; spatial-affective-material transformations, 70, 102; Taksim Square, 210, *211*; Tarlabaşı Boulevard, 84, 91–92; Taşoluk

Istanbul (continued)
  neighborhood, 91; tourism, 83–84, 92, 109, 230n16; "urban crisis," notions of, 70, 89–93, 102; wooden houses, 73, 93–96, 98, 99, 108, 141; working class, 79–80, 102. *See also* Fener-Balat neighborhood (Istanbul); Golden Horn (Istanbul); heritage preservation; Sulukule neighborhood (Istanbul); Tarlabaşı neighborhood (Istanbul); Turkey
İstanbul Ansiklopedisi (Koçu), 74
Istanbul: Memories and the City (Pamuk), 73–74
Istanbul Planning Agency, 95

Jacobs, Jane, 151, 152, 175, 178
Joseph, Miranda, 151, 152, 181–82
Justice and Development Party (Adalet ve Kalkınma Partisi, AKP, Turkey), 68, 70, 77, 86, 88–90, 102, 223n16, 224n23

kebeer (neighborhood head), 170
Khalij (canal, Cairo), 25, 26
Khedive Ismail, 27, 220n5
Koçu, Reşat Ekrem, 74
komşuluk (neighborliness), 195–96
Kurdish community (Tarlabaşı), 82, 88, 140

Law on the Conservation of Cultural and Natural Property (Turkey, 1983), 117
League of Nations, 113
L'Institut D'Egypte, 213
loans, and informal economy, 180–81
local, the, 34, 37, 151–52
longue-durée processes, 70, 88–89, 100
luxury clientele, Cairo, 3, 15, 27, 45, 63, 150, 152, 188, 207; as community of strangers, 150–52, 172–79, 200–201; culture, community, and exclusion, 175–77; visible public spaces cleared for, 183–85. *See also* Ismailia Consortium; visible public spaces; Wust El-Balad (downtown/Historic Cairo)

Mahfouz, Naguib, 32, 37
Mahur Beste (Tanpınar), 74

Making Democracy Work (Putnam), 180
Mamluk, 164
Mansour Group, 59
manzara (view), 69, 77
"marketization," 9, 88, 186
market-making, neoliberal, 7, 11–12, 23, 73, 101, 130, 187, 228n26
markets: and commodity exchange, 7, 208; distortion of, 103, 182; efficiency of, 180–82; environmental perspective on heritage, 111–15; "free," 4–5, 39, 54, 103; operating from within, 3–4, 6, 209; redistributive, 4–8. *See also* property markets
Markets of Dispossession (Elyachar), 180–81
market value, 7, 41, 63, 111, 116, 145, 179, 187, 201, 208–9
mashrabiyya (wooden latticework), 189, 189–91, 207
Mass Housing Authority (TOKİ) (Turkey), 66, 87–88, 91, 121
meaning-making, 7, 13, 37, 39, 73, 75, 220–21n17
Mehmed Ali, 27, 164
melancholy (*hüzün*), 14, 70, 73–75, 80–81
memory, 109–16, 122; as archival, 112; and "hauntings," 75, 120–25, 145, 165; and identity politics, 119–22; modernity, psychological responses to, 111–12, 115; nostalgia, 39–41; "real memory," 112; without border, 111, 114
Menderes, Adnan, 76, 77, 83, 84
miasmatic school of medicine, 25, 219–20n4
Middle East Supply Center, 42, 43
Mills, Amy, 82
Ministry of Culture (Egypt), 56, 188–93, 207
Mitchell, Timothy, 59, 64, 153
Model Citizens project, 30, 40, 164, 201–2
modernity, psychological response to, 111–12, 115
Mohamed Mahmoud Sons Group, 59
monumental, the, 9–10, 56–57, 61, 109–10; turn to the "vernacular," 114–15
morality, politics of, 70, 89–91, 102
Mubarak, Ali, 27–28
Mubarak, Gamal, 59, 163

Mubarak, Hosni, 46, 58–59, 163
Mubarak, Susan, 159
Muehlebach, Andrea, 180
MÜSIAD (Müstakil Sanayici ve İşadamları Derneği), 86, 223n13, 223n16
Muslim Brotherhood, 223n17

nas nedheefa, 174–75
Nasser, Gamal Abdel, 38, 39, 41, 44, 52, 55, 63; neglect of transit infrastructure, 57
National Democratic Party (NDP) (Egypt), 59
nationalism, Egypt, 32, 35, 52, 63; assault on local Egyptian capital, 38–39; cultural revival, 173–75, 178
nationalism, Turkey, 15
natural disasters, 7; (un)natural disasters, 47–50, 93–101
Navaro-Yashin, Yael, 12–13, 75, 125, 228n25
neoliberalism, 3, 217n6; "actually existing," 12; and "as if" personhood of built environment, 213–14; community, configuration of, 150–51; as corporate-capitalist project, 5–6, 8; and despotism, 214–15, 231n3; dismantling of welfare state, 5, 145, 149–50, 179–81, 229n54; entanglements used to normalize dispossession, 101; equated with depoliticization, 9–10; "free markets," 4–5, 39, 54, 103; grassroots movements, hijacking of, 3, 86, 100, 102–3; market-making, 7, 11–12, 14, 23, 73, 101, 130, 187, 228n26; populism linked with, 214–15, 231n3; and property markets in Istanbul, 85–86; redistribution displaced by, 5, 7–11, 208; redistribution operating from within, 3–4, 6, 209. *See also* corporate-capitalist developers; displacement, neoliberal; dispossession
Networks of Dispossession project, 86
New Deal, 114
new urbanism, 175, 178–79
Nile River, *18*, 24–27, 158; Aswan Dam, 26
non-human, political agency of, 12–13, 219n12, 228n25
Nora, Pierre, 112
nostalgia, 39–41, 82–83, 143, 174

oil embargo (1973), 54
Olaylar (anti-Greek and minority riots) (Istanbul), 14, 70, 72, 78, 96, 116, 142, 143, 226n33
Orascom Construction PLC, 59
Osman, Suleiman, 114
Osterholt, Wouter, 30, 40, 164, 201–2
Ottoman Empire, and World War I, 14, 70–71, 73

Pamuk, Orhan, 73–74, 80–81
Paris, France, 93
particularistic value, 3, 8, 110, 208–9; and consumption, 181–82; and engineered "community," 150, 152, 172; spatial, 199–201; and Tarlabaşı garden, 203–5, 207; and visible aesthetics, 186, 199. *See also* value; valuing of property
pedestrianization, 61, 84, 92, 195
personhood, of built environment, 213–14
Pervititch, Jacques, 95
politics: displacement of away from traditional arenas, 3, 7–11, 123–24, 208–10, 213; #pretend_you're_a_building hashtag, *212*, 213; "We are not an urban transformation project" slogan, 210, *211*, 213; where to locate neoliberal, 4, 6, 9, 210. *See also* class politics; depoliticization; geopolitics; identity politics; repoliticization
populism: Egypt, 41, 44–46; neoliberalism linked with, 214–15, 231n3; Turkey, 125
#pretend_you're_a_building hashtag, *212*, 213, 231n2
print capitalism, 151–52
privatization, 54, 58–59; of public space, 201
property markets, 6; deregulation of, 2, 101, 103, 119, 179; "freely traded," 3; "healthy," 64, 103, 225n39; for luxury clientele, 172–79; market-making, 7, 11–12, 14, 23, 73, 101, 130, 187, 228n26; and particularistic community, 150, 152; retroactive deeds, 79, 87, 121, 124; and rising corporate-capitalist class, 85–86; and World War II, 43. *See also* Cairo; Istanbul; market-making, neoliberal
property regimes, 11–12; Cairo, 21–23, 44, 64; Istanbul, 68, 81, 87

protectionism, 35, 52, 54, 83
public good, 70, 180–81, 191–93, 199. *See also* welfare state, neoliberal dismantling of
public/private boundaries, 16, 185–88; Darb El-Ahmar, 193–94; Gamaliyya, 188–93; and gender, 196–99; semi-private/semi-public, 201. *See also* visible public spaces
public spaces. *See* visible public spaces
Putnam, Robert, 180–82, 229n54

real estate: boom, 54, 69, 142; brokers, 66; speculation, 6, 62–63, 84–85, 119, 122, 172. *See also* construction industry; corporate-capitalist developers; Ismailia Consortium; luxury clientele, Cairo
real estate markets. *See* property markets
redistribution: displaced by neoliberalism, 5, 7–11, 208; funding logics, 156–57; heritage as, 15, 115–19, 185; and identity politics, 109–11; operating from within neoliberalism, 3–4, 6, 209; rent control as, 43; skewed efforts, 110–11; state-led efforts, 5, 6; and tourism, 187–94
redistributive markets, 4–8, 15
redistributive mechanisms: extra-market, 3, 88, 109, 116
redistributive politics, 4–9, 15, 182, 217n5
redistributive practices: engineered "community" as, 15–16; heritage as pro-poor practice, 15, 193
relationality, 12–13, 141, 144, 151–52, 181–82; of strangers, 152
Renewal and Preservation Law no. 5366 (2005) (Turkey), 66, 87, 100
rent control, Cairo, 14; and 1952 earthquake, 23–24, 41–42, 153–55; building collapse, 21–22, 47–50, *48*; building collapse and contract annulment, 21–22, 49, 63, 154; and geopolitics of World War II, 41, 42–44; lived realities of, 46–47; opportunity costs for landlords, 22; and populism, 41, 44–46; state ownership of *'emarat Wust El-Balad* buildings, 38. *See also* Cairo; rent control laws, Egypt
rent control laws, Egypt: 1941 emergency decree, 41, 43–44; 1947, 21, 41, 43–44; 1996,

11–12, 14, 21–22, 38, 63–64, 101, 172–73; contracts signed before and after 1944, 44–45, 51; *el 'eigar el gedeed* (new rental system), 22, 23, 62; gradual reversal of, 21–23, 41; "key money," 45, 173; as opportunity for luxury developers, 172–73, 182; violence of, 11–12, 14, 213; *'eigar el qadeem* (old rental system), 22, 23. *See also* rent control, Cairo
repoliticization, 9–11; of class-based and identity-based conflicts, 15, 125, 210; of heritage projects, 111, 123–25, 145–47; and rumors, 119–22, 159–65, 228n25, 228n26
Reynolds, Nancy, 37
risk cartographies, 94–95
Roma community (Sulukule), 88, 89, 195–96
rooftops, 4, 5, 89, 102, 201–2; as communal spaces, 166–67
Rose, Nikolas, 150–51
rumors, 147, 219n12, 228n25, 228n26; and repoliticization, 119–22, 159–65, 228n25, 228n26; repoliticization and stolen treasures, 159–62; and subterranean topography, 163–65
rural-urban migration, 6, 220n4; Cairo, 29–31, 43, 62; Istanbul, 69–70, 79–84, 96, 99, 124

Sadat, Anwar, 45–46, 54, 57, 58, 62, 158
Said Pasha Halim, 164
Sand, Jordan, 113, 114–15
saradeeb (tunnels), 163–64
sartorial aesthetics, 81–83
Sawiris, Samih, 172
Searle, Llerena Guiu, 102–3
secularism, 112
securitization, 177–79; aesthetics of security, 175, 178; "eyes on the street," 175–76, 178. *See also* surveillance
self-reflexive experts, 131–37, 218n7, 226n22
sensoria, industrial and infrastructural, Cairo, 50–52; and heritage industry, 55–57; transport infrastructures and construction industry, 57–61
sensoria, industrial and infrastructural, Istanbul, 70, 76–78
service provision, 150, 159, 200–201

250   Index

Shafei, Karim, 39, 46, 151, 152, 173–75, 200
Shubra al-Khayma (industrial town, periphery of Cairo), 52
Sims, David, 45, 52–53, 158
El-Sisi, Abdel Fattah, 214
social capital, 168–69, 180–81
social justice agenda, 116–17, 129, 145, 196, 218n7; compromising of, 119, 122, 135, 209–10
social media, *212*, 212–13, 231n2
social spaces, and heritage preservation, 132–36, *139*, 139–41, 208
solidarity, 180
Soto, Hernando de, 181
spatial-affective-material transformations, 14–15, 103; Cairo, 14, 23–24, 37, 55, 62–64; Istanbul, 70, 102. *See also* affective experiences
spatial tactics, 181, 218–19n11
storytelling, dying art of, 112
structural adjustment programs, 7, 23, 55
subterranean topography, 163–65
Suez Canal, 33, 38
Sulukule neighborhood (Istanbul), 11, 15, *17*, 66, *69*, 87; entertainment industry, 89–91; morality and "urban crisis," 70, 89–91, 102; Roma community, 88, 89, 195–96; violent expropriation in, 89–93. *See also* Istanbul
"super-modernity," 112
surveillance, 178–79, 186, 190, 205. *See also* securitization
suspicion, 11, 117, 119–22, 136, 160, 163, 204–5; as product of neoliberal displacement, 214–15, 231n3; rumors about AKTC project 159–65; rumors about EU project, 119–22, 209–10

Tablita Market, 169
tactics, 12, 16, 103, 159, 203; spatial, 181, 218–19n11
Tanpınar, Ahmet Hamdi, 74
Tantan, Saadettin, 90, 224n27
Tarlabaşı neighborhood (Istanbul), 11, 15, *17*, 66, *67*, *68*, 72, 88; commercial activity in, 141–43, *142*; infrastructures of "crisis" in, 91–93; migrants to, 79, 140; particularistic value and garden design, 203–5, 207; sartorial aesthetics, 81–83; urban archiving and communal power in, 138–45; violent expropriation in, 15, 81, 86–87. *See also* Istanbul
technical practices, 110, 209; and engineered "community," 2, 149, 153, 166–67, 209; and heritage preservation, 10, 110, 122, 125, 145; and redistribution, 8; and repoliticization 10, 111, 123, 125, 145–46
terrain, urban, 6
Tokyo, Japan, 114
top-down/bottom-up practices, 113, 218–19n11, 228n25
tourism: Egypt, 16, 56–57, 61, 161; as engine of "economic revival," 187; gentrifying effects of, 188; and heritage, 114–15, 187; Istanbul, 83–84, 92, 109, 230n16; and redistribution, 187–94; and urban services, 194
Townhouse Gallery (Wust El-Balad), 30, 176, 201
Treaty of Lausanne, 72
trust, 168–69, 178–82, 194
TUKSON chamber of commerce (Turkey), 86, 223n16
Tura (industrial town, periphery of Cairo), 52
Turkey, 3; Anatolia, 71, 76, 85–86, 97, 129; Ankara, capital relocated to, 71; attempted coup (2016), 214; Beyoğlu district, 90; construction industry, 86–87; coup of 1980, 83, 85; Democrat Party, 76, 80, 83, 95–96; Disaster Law (*Afet Yasası*), 68, 70, 88, 100; "emergency nationalization" (*acil kamulaştırma*), 66–68, *67*, *68*, 88, 100; étatism (state-led economic development), 71–72; European Union (EU), accession to, 145; executive arm, 87–88; *gecekondu* (night housing), 87; grassroots environmental movement appropriated by, 3; Import-Substitution-Industrialization (ISI), 83, 85; inflation crisis (2001), 88; *iptal karar* decrees, 87–88, 100; Islamic revivalism, 85, 86, 223n16;

Index   251

Turkey (continued)
isolationism, 71; law no. 5237, 86–87; Law on the Conservation of Cultural and Natural Property (1983), 117; longue-durée processes, 70, 88–89, 100; Mass Housing Authority (TOKİ), 66, 87–88, 91, 121; nationalism, 15; nationalization of properties, 66–68, 67, 68, 78; Ottoman defeat, World War I, 14, 70; Renewal and Preservation Law no. 5366 (2005), 66, 70, 87, 100; Republican era, 71–72, 76, 89, 95–96; ruling regime, 15; rural-urban migration, 78; state ownership of property, 66–68, 71–72; violent expropriation in, 12, 15, 63, 68, 80–81, 84, 86–93, 99–100, 143. *See also* Istanbul; Justice and Development Party (Adalet ve Kalkınma Partisi, AKP, Turkey)
TÜSIAD (Türk Sanayicileri ve İş İnsanları Derneği), 86, 223n13

Uitentuis, Elke, 30, 40, 164, 201–2
Ulusoy, Süleyman (Hortum), 89–90
United Nations Educational, Scientific and Cultural Organization (UNESCO), 15, 113, 115–17, 209; survey of industrial work in Cairo's core, 51–52; World Heritage Report, 117
urban activists, Istanbul, 3, 10, 15
urban built-environments, 3, 7–8, 218n10
"urban crisis," notions of, 15; Cairo, 55–56, 61, 62; Istanbul, 70, 89–93, 102
urbanism: assemblage, 12–13, 219n12, 228n25; new, 175, 178

value: abstract, 181–82, 218n8; asymmetrical experience of, 31–32; market value, 7, 41, 63, 111, 116, 145, 179, 187, 201, 208–9; particularistic, 3, 8, 110, 150, 152, 181–82, 186, 208–9
"value creation," 110
valuing of property, 167; affordable housing, 68–69, 109–10; comparison of Cairo and Istanbul, 15, 31, 68–69, 101–2; and engineering of "community," 2–3, 7–9, 150, 152, 172; in generalized sense, 56–57, 181–82, 218n8; and hereditary practices, 47, 154; and *hüzün* (melancholy), 73; as limitless, 84–85, 101–2; and memory, 112; and mismanagement, 49–50; urban design-cultural-environmental practices, 9–10. *See also* heritage preservation; particularistic value
violence: anti-minority, Istanbul, 14, 70, 72, 78, 96, 116, 142, 143, 226n33; Istanbul, 68; of property dispossession, Egypt, 11–12, 14–15, 23, 27–28, 60, 64, 213; of property dispossession, Istanbul, 12, 15, 63, 68, 80–81, 84, 86–93, 99–100, 143; reasons for state turn to, 68–69
visible aesthetics, 159, 171, 183–87; harmonization vs. historical accuracy, 191, 207; and societal engineering, 186–87
visible public spaces, 16, 115, 183–205; accessibility and sociability of shared spaces, 194–99, 201; Azhar Park, 183–85, 187, 193; *belirli mekanlar* (well-known places), 198–99; gendered asymmetries, 196–99; lines of sight, 185; *mashrabiyya* (wooden latticework) project, *189*, 189–91, 207; and state-making, 186, 187; and urban services, 194; visible aesthetics and societal engineering, 186–87. *See also* luxury clientele, Cairo; public/private boundaries
Vitalis, Robert, 35, 42–44

wage liberalization, 54
water ecologies, Cairo, 14, 23, 24–28
wekala buildings, 53–55
Welfare Party (Turkey), 84
welfare state, neoliberal dismantling of, 5, 145, 149–50, 179–81, 229n54. *See also* public good
women, and gendered asymmetries, 196–99
wooden construction: *cumba* (protruding window), 65, 94, 197; Istanbul, 73, 93–96, 98, 99, 108, 141; *mashrabiyya* (wooden latticework) project, *189*, 189–91, 207
World Heritage Convention (UNESCO), 113
World Heritage Report (UNESCO), 117
World War I, 14, 70–73; Ottoman defeat, 14, 70–71, 73; population exchanges, 72

World War II, 14; and environmental turn, 113; and rent control in Cairo, 41, 42–44; shipping capacity, 42, 44

Wust El-Balad (downtown Cairo), 11, 15, *18*; Antikhana alleyway, 30, 40–41, 164, 201–2; automobile congestion, 59–60; broad concept of community in, 151; commercial areas, 27, 36–37, 150, 173, 175–78, 199–200; *'emarat Wust El-Balad* (buildings of downtown Cairo), 36–38, 47, 63, 173–76, *174*; and entangled capital, 36–37; fire and riots (1952), 14, 32, *33*; interconnected passageways as architectural gems, 199–201; Ismailia Consortium projects in, 150; lived realities of rent control, 46–47; Model Citizens project, 30, 40; "Mohamed Lipton" coffee shop, 29–31, 202; particularistic community in, 152; Townhouse Gallery, 30, 176, 201. *See also* Ismailia Consortium; luxury clientele, Cairo

Yurt Partisi (Homeland Party) (Turkey), 224n27

Zamalek (Cairo), 35, 63